NAVIGATING CLIMATE CHANGE POLICY

THE
EDGE

Books on Environmental Science, Law, and Policy

Other books in this series

Conservation of Shared Environments: Learning from the United States and Mexico, edited by Laura López-Hoffman, Emily D. McGovern, Robert G. Varady, and Karl W. Flessa

Series editors

Marc Miller, Vice Dean and Ralph W. Bilby Professor of Law at the University of Arizona

Barbara Morehouse, associate research scientist at the Institute of the Environment at the University of Arizona

Jonathan Overpeck, codirector of the Institute of the Environment at the University of Arizona

Development editor

Emily McGovern, research analyst and editorial associate at the Udall Center for Studies in Public Policy at the University of Arizona

Program coordinator

Betsy Woodhouse, deputy director of the Institute of the Environment at the University of Arizona

NAVIGATING
CLIMATE CHANGE POLICY
The Opportunities of Federalism

Edited by Edella C. Schlager, Kirsten H. Engel, and Sally Rider

with a foreword by Fran Pavley

The University of Arizona Press Tucson

The University of Arizona Press
© 2011 The Arizona Board of Regents
All rights reserved

www.uapress.arizona.edu

Library of Congress Cataloging-in-Publication Data
Navigating climate change policy : the opportunities of federalism / edited by Edella
C. Schlager, Kirsten H. Engel, and Sally Rider ; with a foreword by Fran Pavley
        p. cm. — (The edge: environmental science, law, and policy)
    Includes bibliographical references and index.
    ISBN 978-0-8165-3000-7 (pbk. : alk. paper) 1. Climatic changes—Government
policy—United States. 2. Environmental policy—United States. 3. Environmental
law—United States. 4. Federal government—United States. 5. United States—Politics
and government. I. Schlager, Edella, 1960– II. Engel, Kirsten. III. Rider, Sally, 1957–
    QC903.2.U6N39 2011
    363.738'745610973—dc22

                                                                    2011014241

Manufactured in the United States of America on acid-free, archival-quality paper
containing a minimum of 30 percent postconsumer waste and processed chlorine free.

Tree image © CLoopAll/Crestock

16   15   14   13   12   11   6   5   4   3   2   1

Board of Advisors

Edge Partners at the University of Arizona

Institute of the Environment (www.environment.arizona.edu)

James E. Rogers College of Law (www.law.arizona.edu)

Biosphere 2 and the Biosphere 2 Institute (www.b2science.org)

Udall Center for Studies in Public Policy (www.udallcenter.arizona.edu)

University of Arizona Press (www.uapress.arizona.edu)

Support for *Navigating Climate Change Policy*
(University of Arizona entities)

Institute of the Environment

James E. Rogers College of Law

University of Arizona Law Review

School of Government and Public Policy

Biosphere 2 and the Biosphere 2 Institute

William H. Rehnquist Center on the Constitutional
    Structures of Government

*For Congresswoman Gabrielle Giffords and
Judge John M. Roll*

Congresswoman Gabrielle Giffords is one of the most thoughtful leaders in the federal government regarding the impacts and policy dimensions of climate change. She has been a leader in promoting the transformation of American energy systems, with a particular emphasis on the solar opportunities in Arizona and the Southwest. As a former Arizona state legislator and a current member of Congress, she understands the interplay of critical policy matters among federal, state, and local governments.

We also dedicate this book to Gabby's friend and colleague Judge John M. Roll. Judge Roll was a distinguished chief judge of the US District Court for the District of Arizona. His career embodied service as a prosecutor in both the state and federal systems, and in those roles, and as a chief judge and jurist he often wrestled with issues of the interaction of federal and state laws. A thoughtful and decent person, he embodied the American ideal of the rule of law.

Contents

Foreword

A book examining climate policies at the subnational level is a welcome addition to the evolving climate-change discussion. In recent years, most of the focus of this discussion as it pertains to policy has been on what action to take at the federal/national level. But for a decade, most of the real action and progress toward finding practical ways to reduce greenhouse-gas emissions have been taking place at the state and local levels.

We saw this in California in 2002, with the adoption of tailpipe emission standards that have now become national standards. We saw it beginning in 2005, with Seattle Mayor Greg Nickels's initiation of the US Conference of Mayors Climate Protection Agreement, which as of spring 2011 includes 1,047 city mayors who have vowed to reduce carbon emissions in their cities below 1990 levels, in line with the Kyoto Protocol. We saw it with the adoption of the Regional Greenhouse Gas Initiative, an agreement among seven northeastern states to reduce their utility emissions, including a trading scheme. There are many more examples of regional, state, and local actions to reduce emissions, increase energy efficiency, promote low-carbon alternatives, reduce vehicle miles traveled, and otherwise adopt cost-effective ways to reduce carbon dioxide and equivalent emissions. And with its Assembly Bill 32, passed and signed into law in 2006, California became the first state in the nation to impose a statutory cap on greenhouse-gas emissions.

Some may say that climate policy is a global problem requiring global solutions. We need to encourage the innovation and experimentation that are taking place at the subnational level. Many of the programs being pioneered to achieve the goals of Assembly Bill 32 and other state or local programs could be used as national models. The fact is that in reducing climate pollution emissions we need to rethink how we produce and consume energy, and this will require our best efforts at all levels.

Fran Pavley
California State Senator

NAVIGATING CLIMATE CHANGE POLICY

Introduction

Climate change is a global problem that demands global solutions, but while national governments have been fighting over emission targets, subnational governments like California have been adopting their own targets, laws, and policies. And the truth is, the world's national governments cannot make the progress that is needed on global climate change alone, they need the help of cities, states, provinces and regions in enacting real climate solutions.
—Former California governor Arnold Schwarzenegger,
   December 15, 2009, Copenhagen

This volume challenges the notion that, because climate change is inherently a global problem, only efforts to craft global policies can lead to a solution. This assumption about the policy response to climate change is rooted in the science of climate change. Climate change is the phenomenon of increasing mean global temperature caused by human-generated greenhouse gases emitted into Earth's atmosphere. Because greenhouse gases produced anywhere around the planet mix into the atmosphere, climate change does have an obvious global dimension. But as California's former governor Arnold Schwarzenegger pointed out to the 2009 United Nations Climate Change Conference, attending to the international dimensions of climate change should not blind us to the local causes and impacts of climate change, as well as recent developments in environmental policy among governments, from cities to international agreements.

This volume explores why national governments and international agreements, if they are to be successful in addressing the causes and impacts of climate change, require the active participation and engagement of governments at multiple levels. US state and local governments, singly and collectively, have adopted and implemented climate-change policies for the last fifteen years. They have done so through policies designed to reduce greenhouse-gas emissions and to encourage local economies, governments, and individual behaviors to address climate impacts. And they have done so during a time when the federal government has been largely absent from the policy arena, unable to forge the coalitions necessary to enact climate-change legislation. The respective roles of various levels of government in mitigating and adapting to further climate change continue to be a pressing issue of public policy in the United States.

Scholarly, public, and political discourse tends to downplay the extent to which the *causes* of climate change are regional and local as well as national and global. Global concentrations of greenhouse gases do reflect the sum total of emissions the world over, but most of these emissions are the product of individual choices under the auspices of largely local decision making. Take, for example, decisions with respect to the foods we eat, how and when we choose to heat or cool our homes, and whether and how we travel to work or play.

The *impacts* of climate change are just as diverse and multiscaled as the causes. Coastal areas—especially low-lying coastal areas—are subject to risks from sea-level rise and changes in storm patterns and intensity. The natural and human environments in North America and around the globe vary in ways that make every specific location unique with respect to risks from climate change. The varying impacts of climate change on different US regions, states, cities, and counties help to explain why states and localities have been at the forefront of greenhouse-gas policy, and are likely to continue to be active with regard to climate-change policies.

This book adopts the position that no single policy by a single scale of government can possibly reach and adequately shape all of the choices and actions necessary to mitigate and adapt to climate change. Rather, limiting greenhouse-gas emissions requires many complementary policies at many scales, from local zoning decisions to international trade treaties.

The United States, with a federal form of government, appears well suited to respond to both the causes and impacts of climate change at multiple scales. A federal form of government—the common shorthand used in this volume is *federalism*—refers to the allocation of power among a national government and states or provinces. Federal systems acknowledge different powers, responsibilities, interests, and competencies at different levels of government. When any government acts in a federal system, it may be irrelevant to, consistent with, or inconsistent with the powers and interests of another level of government.

Modern understandings of federalism have increasingly come to recognize that, for many aspects of public policy, multiple sovereigns have both authority and reason to act. They might act together or separately, in harmony or in conflict. As such, most scholars and courts now reject an older conception of clear demarcation of responsibility between the federal government and the states on most matters.

The diversity of possible governmental responses leads directly to the many policy and legal questions elaborated by this volume. The policy reasons to favor or disfavor state or federal actions in response to climate change must be carefully weighed. Because disputes between states and the federal government will often be brought to federal court, it is also critical to illuminate the legal frameworks for resolving such federalism battles. This book, written by lawyers, political scientists, and a climate scientist, provides a current status report. It is intended to help local, state, and federal policy makers, advocates, and judges as they resolve both informal and formal conflicts over climate-change policy in the future.

The approach of the contributors to this volume is to acknowledge and recognize the strengths of American federalism, to identify the challenges it poses for effective governance, and to explore how it can lead to and support robust policy responses to climate change. In doing so, the authors address a number of key policy and governance issues that have received little attention in US climate-change policy debates to date:

- The roles and interactions of states, American Indian tribes, and the federal government as each actively pursues climate-change policies.

- The leeway states and tribes have taken in designing and implementing climate-change policies and how the federal government may exercise its preemption powers to constrain state activity.

- Diverse forms of cooperation and coordination among federal and state public agencies, interest groups, and citizens.

- Climate-change policies, besides cap-and-trade, that encourage cooperation among federal and state governments.

- Climate-change policies that states are best suited and situated to pursue.

- The role of regional state-based collaborations and associations in encouraging cooperation among states.

- The role of federal courts in resolving the inevitable conflicts between state and local actors, Indian tribes, and the federal government over climate-change policies.

Road Map

This volume begins in section 1 with a foundational chapter written by Jonathan Overpeck, Marc Miller, and Diana Liverman—a climate scientist, a law professor, and a social scientist. They explain why climate change should be understood as both a global and a local phenomenon and lay the scientific groundwork for the topical sections that follow.

Section 2, "The Institutional Context," provides a broad overview of federalism, its components, and how it works. Federal systems allow for a blend of diverse approaches within a unifying framework. Robert A. Schapiro introduces readers to different forms of federal systems. James Hopkins discusses how American Indian tribes fit within the federal framework and the special roles they play in responding to and addressing climate change. Kirk Emerson examines how collaboration among governments, interest groups, and citizens in a federal system works in practice and how it can be encouraged and strengthened.

Section 3, "Policy Initiatives Among and Across States," examines the interactions among states as they individually and collectively respond to climate change. Andrew Karch provides a framework for explaining the diffusion of policies across states. Judith Resnik, Joshua Civin, and Joseph Frueh examine how states and localities collaborate through voluntary non-profit organizations that educate, lobby, and support states' collaborative efforts. Edella Schlager explores different types of administrative agreements that states have created to engage in regional efforts to address climate change. David E. Adelman and Kirsten H. Engel focus on the important roles states play in technology adoption and diffusion.

Section 4, "State and Federal Dynamics," focuses directly on relations between the federal government and states. The section interweaves legal and policy analyses to help elucidate the nature of vertical ties among governments. Holly Doremus and W. Michael Hanemann examine the Clean Air Act as a possible model on which national climate-change policy can be based. Daniel A. Farber addresses one of the primary legal questions raised by federalism—preemption—and explores the circumstances and settings under which courts have found that the federal government preempted state activity. Barry G. Rabe examines the experience of states with climate-change policies and how they will shape both federal action and relationships between the federal government and the states.

The concluding chapter highlights policy implications raised across the volume. It focuses on policy implications that require recognition and attention if the states and federal government are to act collaboratively and decisively to address climate change.

In the United States, state and local actors, and those who work with states, have taken the lead in thinking about the implications of climate change for our society and have been the primary actors in creating climate-change policy. One such person is California State Senator Fran Pavley, who wrote the foreword to this volume, and who has been a leader in state-level climate policy. Such leadership occurs in the face of limited federal action. But there is no reason to assume that this will continue to be the case: a federal government can be more or less aggressive in promoting new federal climate-change policies; in promoting new state, local, and regional policies; or in limiting state local and regional policies—even in the absence of a new federal policy in the same area. Congress, in designing federal legislation, should carefully consider the roles of the states and include them as partners in the nation's efforts to address climate change.

Because climate change is one of the defining issues of our time, and is likely to be so for the indefinite future, the legal and policy disputes are also likely to have a defining character. They will reveal the capacity of our political and legal systems to respond to new and immensely complex and diffuse challenges. This book was created to help lay the groundwork for new policy and to provide a framework for resolving disputes to come.

Scientific Background on Climate Change

Chapter 1

Global Climate Change as a Local Phenomenon

Jonathan Overpeck, Marc Miller, and Diana Liverman

In Brief

- Climate change is a global problem driven by human greenhouse-gas emissions that are changing the composition of the global atmosphere and thus affecting temperature and precipitation patterns worldwide. However, the impacts of climate change vary regionally and locally.

- Not only global but also regional to local knowledge and cooperation will be required to adapt successfully to climate change.

- Regional to local climate impacts motivate action by people working at these scales, such as mitigating harms, enhancing the development and deployment of new technologies, providing leadership in driving larger scale policies, and testing policy innovations.

- Some local to regional actors may see economic and other advantages to leading the development of both adaptation and mitigation strategies, whereas others will not have the knowledge, social, or economic resources to act. Regional and local variation also reaffirms the continuing importance of national to international attention to climate change.

Climate change appears to epitomize a global environmental problem. Although the production of human-generated greenhouse gases is unevenly distributed across countries, these gases quickly mix into the overall atmosphere, so it does not matter for global mean climate change where greenhouse gases are produced. In this sense, Earth has one global climate system. Science and policy discussions of climate change often start with global climate models, which are used to assess how much the global mean temperature will increase depending on future alternative human behaviors. The impacts of climate change are also often expressed globally in terms of numbers of species and lives that may be lost or aggregate economic costs.

But the extent to which climate change has been portrayed and discussed as a global phenomenon obscures the significant variation in causes, impacts, and capacities for responses across different regions and localities. This geographic variation has biological and physical dimensions. These include local differences in climate, ecology, biogeochemistry, and hydrology. The geographic variation also has social dimensions, which include economics, demographics, social structures, and institutional and political structures.

Biophysical and social variation takes place at many different geographic, temporal, and sociological scales. Most important for state and local actions in response to climate change, this variation takes place across multiple political scales, including scales that can be influenced by local and regional action. Given that the reality of climate change is no longer a subject of serious scientific debate (see Overpeck spotlight, p. 24), this chapter focuses first on variation in the biophysical nature of climate change and its impacts, and then examines the social dimensions of scale in relation to climate change. Our goal is to highlight the importance of local- to regional-scale decisions about how to address both the adaptation and mitigation challenges associated with climate change.

> What remains of the scientific debate about human-induced climate change? See "The Scientific Consensus with Regard to Human-Induced Climate Change" on page 24.

Regional Variations in the Physical Impacts of Climate Change

Climate theory and models have emphasized that the physical impacts of climate change vary by region. Given continued emissions of greenhouse gases, the entire planet will continue to warm, but some areas will warm faster and more than others. Warming of the oceans is today causing ocean waters to expand and ice to retreat, and this is contributing to significant, documented sea-level rise around the globe.[1] In North America, this sea-level rise could, if left unabated, lead to highly significant impacts in those areas with extensive low-lying lands, such as in Florida, Louisiana, and much of the Southeast coast.[2] Warming is also occurring in environments at high latitudes and elevations. As the Intergovernmental Panel on Climate Change (IPCC) notes, this regional variation "is driven by the uneven distribution of solar heating, the individual responses of the atmosphere, oceans and land surface, the interactions between these, and the physical characteristics of the regions."[3] For North America as a whole, the broader assessment of climate change to come has been summarized by IPCC as a set of likely occurrences:[4]

- In most areas of North America, annual mean warming is likely to exceed global mean warming.

- In northern North America, minimum winter temperatures are likely to increase more than the annual average.

- In the US Southwest, summer temperatures are likely to increase more than the annual average.

- Annual mean precipitation is very likely to increase in Canada and the US Northeast and likely to decrease in the US Southwest.

- In parts of southern Canada, precipitation is likely to increase in winter and spring but decrease in summer.

- Snow season length and snow depth are very likely to decrease in most of North America except in the northernmost part of Canada.

In some parts of the United States, the projected changes have already become quite noticeable. For example, warming and sea ice retreat over the last thirty years have already led to substantial impacts to coastal communities and economic activities in Alaska.[5]

Impacts Already Occurring in the US Southwest

It may be helpful to focus in greater detail on one region to illustrate the different kinds of impacts from climate change that may be seen by residents and ecosystems of a particular place. In parts of the US Southwest, mean annual warming has already surpassed that of most of the rest of the country. Current projections indicate that the headwaters of the Colorado River are likely to continue warming at a rate faster than the global average and than much of the United States.[6] An annual average warming of 5–6°C (about 10°F) is likely by the year 2100 in the absence of significant greenhouse-gas emission reductions.

The climate research community has high confidence that temperatures will continue to rise, and in the Southwest observations have already shown that this translates into not just a hotter future but also a drier one. Continued warming in the US West will reduce snowpack and streamflow, as well as increase moisture stress for plants and vegetation. Temperature increase is a major factor currently causing snow in mountain headwaters to melt, evaporate, and be absorbed by drier soils earlier in the year, thereby reducing the average flow of the Colorado River, which supplies drinking water to much of the region.[7] The observed temperature increases are having a disproportionate impact on the vegetation of the Southwest relative to many other areas of the United States.[8]

This drier Southwest future could also include less precipitation, particularly in winter and spring.[9] On top of this, there is evidence that parts of the southwestern United States and northern Mexico will be persistent climate-change hot spots defined by heightened year-to-year variability in precipitation.[10] Dry areas of the Southwest will have more water troubles—both floods and droughts—in the future.

Studies of tree rings in the region indicate that droughts lasting for decades have occurred many times in the past[11] and must be considered a likely threat for the future—only they may be hotter. Such lessons from the past are sobering news to water planners, and ultimately to modern Southwest civilization writ large, even without considering climate change. Climate systems in the Southwest can evidently shift from periods of relatively abundant precipitation, such as in the 1980s and 1990s, into long-term periods of droughts.[12]

Anthropogenic climate change may exacerbate climate variability; greenhouse gases could force climate systems past a tipping point into a period of more frequent or longer multidecadal droughts of the kind that occurred before humans had such direct impact on the globe's climate. The 2009 report of the US Global Change Research Program, *Global Climate Change Impacts in the United States*, highlights that "the prospect of future droughts becoming more severe as a result of global warming is a significant concern, especially because the Southwest continues to lead the nation in population growth."[13]

Challenges to Water Resources Management

The scarcity of water in the Southwest has for most of human history been a central factor in both individual survival and collective existence. Humans have responded to the key role of water in arid lands by building waterworks and developing particular patterns of life and culture (including law and regulation) in pursuit of steady supplies.

Physical structures and administrative regimes for water supply management have reduced some of the risks of water supply variability due to droughts and floods. But with climate change, the end points of the extremes of precipitation are likely changing (e.g., the frequency of drought and flood is increasing, and droughts are likely becoming more severe), and human systems have limited resilience in their capacities to manage this change. Management systems will need to adapt to the new natural extremes that result from climate change.

For example, seven states in the western region rely on water from the Colorado River: the upper basin states of Colorado, Wyoming, Utah, and New Mexico and the lower basin states of California, Arizona, and Nevada; Mexico also receives an allocation. The complex political, social, and engineering history of allocations of the Colorado River is based on assumptions about the typical amount and timing of water supplies that formed the basis of the Colorado River Compact. The compact assumed, based on a relatively short record of streamflow from wetter-than-average years, that the river could supply 7.5 million acre-feet per year to each of the two basins, plus 1.5 million acre-feet for Mexico. In contrast, we now know that the average flow in the river will not support these allocations.[14] As a result, in many years, more water is allocated than enters the basin from precipitation.

Increases in late-winter temperature and associated decreases in late-season snowpack, as well as other climate-change–related factors, are reducing the already overallocated Colorado River flow, thereby magnifying the water deficit and the political, social, and economic implications of that deficit. Increases in temperature and decreases in precipitation together produce lower supplies than might result from either change alone, and increased temperatures lead to greater evaporation from rivers, lakes, and reservoirs.

Fire and Invasive Species Threaten Ecosystems and Human Systems

Changing air temperature and precipitation regimes also affect water temperature and soil moisture; such impacts can cause a shift in the locations where different plant and animal species survive and change the likelihood and scale of extreme events such as storms, floods, and fire. Warming is likely already causing a significant increase in tree death, large wildfire frequency, wildfire duration, and wildfire-season length across the West.[15]

Likely future changes in the region's wildfire regime will reflect a hotter, drier climate that will directly increase the flammability of fuels and reduce the opportunity for snow or rain to limit the scale of fires that do occur. Researchers have documented significant changes in fire regimes that have already occurred.[16] But wildfire changes are not solely a function of heat and precipitation. Portions of the Sonoran and Mojave deserts are now burning not because of the change in temperature but because of the spread of human-introduced nonindigenous plant species that have transformed the landscape and fundamentally changed the desert ecology. The spread of invasive—and highly flammable—plant species such as buffelgrass[17] and red brome is bringing wildfire into Southwest deserts that are poorly adapted to the large and extreme hot fires generated by these invasive species.

The increase in fire risk from a hotter, drier climate would be substantial if it were limited to wilderness areas of the Southwest. But the combination of climate change, invasive plants, and other human factors greatly expands fire risk both to natural systems and to human structures and populations. This risk increases as human development spreads into new areas in the deserts and the mountains and as invasive species transform areas that would otherwise have only localized burns into flammable systems that can link upland forests with lowland desert ecosystems.

Impacts Projected for Other Regions

A similar story with different emphases and impacts applies to each region, state, and watershed in the United States. Increases in the mean temperature; the volume, timing, and availability of freshwater supplies; frequency of extremes; and other physical dynamics display varying—but in all cases significant—current and/or predicted shifts from climate change.

- For many regions, heat waves will become an ever-increasing threat to human health, with even locations in the Northeast experiencing nearly thirty days per year with temperatures exceeding 100°F by the end of the century if climate change is left unchecked.[18]

- For states with coastlines and regions that rely on marine resources, rising ocean levels and shifting storm dynamics may be the more significant impacts.[19]

- In the Southeast, the greatest climate-change threats are to the availability and timing of water supplies and increasing hurricane intensities.[20]

- In the Upper Midwest, increases in heat waves, floods, droughts, insects, and weeds are posing increasing challenges to managing crops, livestock, and forests.[21]

- In the Northwest, climate-change–related issues include water for consumption and natural systems, as well as for hydropower—water is a critical factor for energy systems throughout the country.[22] Increased insect outbreaks and wildfires and changing species composition in forests are already posing challenges for ecosystems and forest management—and economies—in the Northwest, a trend that is expected to continue.[23]

The implications of changes in temperature and precipitation extend to human consumption and use of resources, industry, power generation, agriculture, and ecosystem functions. The brief story we have told about temperature, precipitation, and fire could be told about other dimensions of natural and human systems. We have not discussed all of the impacts that climate change can have on natural areas, endangered species, disease and human health, energy use and production, cities, or agriculture. Each of these spheres will likely see impacts from climate change that vary at local to regional scales. For example, warmer weather and changing precipitation patterns have led to increased regional outbreaks of tropical diseases such as West Nile virus and dengue fever that have previously been rare or nonexistent in the United States.[24]

The point of this discussion is not to catalog all the impacts of climate change on Earth or human systems. Rather, we have sought to illustrate the significance of local variation, complexity, and interconnectedness of climate-change impacts. The dramatic and varied local and regional impacts of climate change explain and justify the demand for local and regional political and policy responses.

Variation in Social Systems, Vulnerability to Climate-Change Impacts, and Responses

Climate impacts take place not only on the stage of Earth systems but also on a stage set with both the "furniture" (the built environment) of states, cities, towns, roads, and water systems and the "actors," or the people, who that inhabit that stage. Even if the impact of climate change were identical across the globe in terms of temperature and precipitation changes—which it is not—different institutions, groups, economies, and polities would have different knowledge, wealth, political, and institutional capacities to respond to climate change.[25]

As with the variation in Earth systems described in the first part of this chapter, the variations in social systems are complex, interrelated, and uncertain. Social and political systems operate and change through mechanisms quite different in time, scale, and process from those forces that play out and transform Earth systems. The variation in social systems, however, drives home the same point as with Earth systems: the global problem of climate change has profound local impacts and responds to significant and pervasive local differences.

The enormous variation in social endowments and capacities affecting potential responses to climate change makes it far easier to understand why states, towns, nongovernmental organizations, local political leaders, or a group of states might pursue local and regional responses to climate change. Returning to the example of the Southwest, the political landscape is itself complex, with large parts of western states—on the order of 30–75 percent of the total land—owned and managed by the federal government. American Indian tribes also have large landholdings and resource claims, especially claims on water resources. Other political and social pressures come from the presence of a long border with Mexico and deep and intricate ecological and social webs and conflicts across that border.[26] Pressures from climate change on water supply and demand are unlikely to make potential regional disputes any easier.

Local and regional economies are tied directly and indirectly to climate, having different vulnerabilities to climate change depending on resource needs and institutional structures. Agricultural demand for water often dominates water systems and makes other systems—such as cities or natural ecosystems—more vulnerable because of legal and institutional traditions that give agriculture first priority. Numerous industries make direct use of water, often in nonobvious ways. For example, many high-tech industries are especially large consumers of water, as are many energy producers. Lack of access to private or government-assisted insurance and credit, or to other government assistance, can also make farmers and communities more vulnerable to climate impacts. Such vulnerability is powerfully illustrated during natural disasters such as Hurricane Katrina, where poverty, race, and class were strong determinants of the impacts from the storm.[27]

It is not just institutional vulnerabilities and capacities to respond that vary but also individual capacities. Research on countries and communities around the world show that poorer states and communities and poorer individuals have fewer options for adapting to climate threats.[28] The poor are more vulnerable to extreme heat, flash floods, inadequate or expensive heating and cooling of homes, poor communication of disaster warnings, limited access to and affordability of water, and health problems associated with inadequate health care. And individual wealth is in many places unevenly distributed with regard to race, gender, ethnicity, and age. The capacity of individuals to respond to climate impacts will also vary based on the mobility of a person's work skills and reliance on social systems (e.g., those with special needs, the elderly, and the homeless).[29]

Among the southwestern states, vulnerability to climate variations and thus the pattern of impacts is extremely varied, with high levels of poverty and institutional constraints all adding to the challenge of responding. For example, Arizona and New Mexico have some of the highest levels of poverty in the United States, with more than 1.5 million people living in poverty in 2008 (almost 20 percent of their populations).[30]

The Relevance of Locality to Mitigation and Adaptation

The distinction between climate-change responses that strongly implicate national and supranational actors and those that are coherent at local, regional, and state levels in part reflects the distinction between mitigation of, and adaptation to, climate change. *Mitigation* refers to efforts to reduce the concentration of greenhouse gases, whether by reducing human generation or increasing human or natural sequestration. *Adaptive responses* focus on adjustments to natural or human systems, which are designed (or should be designed) either to moderate harm or to exploit potential opportunities.

Mitigation

Mitigation is often assumed to be a large-scale activity, and adaptation to be more local. This distinction, however, can be drawn too quickly. The effort of one region or locality (or even a country, acting alone) to reduce the production of greenhouse gases might seem quixotic, particularly since the mitigation benefits may be shared by all but the costs are borne by a few—for economists, this describes a classic "free-rider" problem.

There are reasons, however, that mitigation efforts by localities might make sense, including geographic variation in the sources of emissions, development and deployment of new technologies, social leadership, benefits in terms of energy security and pollution mitigation, and anticipation of future regulatory regimes and market opportunities. The State of California provides a powerful example of state actions driven by such factors that have spillover effects beyond the state and have significant potential to reduce emissions given the size of the state's economy. All of these reasons are built on complex assumptions about the future costs and benefits of different regulatory regimes for energy, water, and transportation, as well as on future economies and beliefs about social psychology, such as the collective desire for minimizing or accepting risk or the group rewards of being leaders or doing the right thing.

Many mitigation efforts will inherently be regional because of regional advantages and disadvantages in both traditional and alternative energy and resource production. For example, some regions have the sun, wind, tides, or water needed to generate energy. Some regions may be more suited to mitigation efforts because of social factors, including wealth, committed political institutions, expert knowledge, industrial capacity, and the ability to modify housing or transportation strategies.

Even as national or international agreements on mitigation become stronger, many regions, states, and localities are trying to understand their own mitigation options and prepare in ways that minimize deleterious outcomes while maximizing opportunity. And many economic activities are highly geographically concentrated and include massive "sunk" costs, including manufacturing clusters, intensive agriculture, and major cities, increasing the potential for local-government or private-sector efforts to reduce emissions.

Lastly, differences in scale, the obviousness of change and impacts, and the timing of impacts could lead to different levels of political will to address climate change in different locations and in different regions. This could legitimize current and future local, state, and regional programs, as well as programs that go above and beyond future federal programs. Not all geographies have the same risks from climate change, and this is reflected in existing regional response patterns.

Adaptation

It is not hard to understand why a locality, state, or region (or those actors who focus on localities, including nongovernmental organizations, community groups, and individuals) might pursue strategies for adaptation to climate change in order to reduce the impacts of climate change on local landscapes and economies. Adaptive responses are usually undertaken explicitly at the scale of a locality, state, or region. Just as many climate-change impacts are at this subnational scale, so is the self-interest in dealing with them.

Since the biophysical and social contexts and impacts are highly variable by location and at different scales, the adaptive needs and capacities will vary. Adaptive strategies, even those encouraged by federal action, will often require some degree of local knowledge and expertise. The need for local planning and implementation of adaptive responses to climate change has parallels to current responses to natural disasters, where federal insurance and other programs provide some level of response, but myriad local regulations, disaster management plans, and local resources reduce vulnerability to hazards.

The links from state and local action to policies at the federal level are highlighted in recent reports of the US National Academies on America's Climate Choices, which argue for the significance of local responses in reducing emissions and adapting.[31] They emphasize, however, the critical importance of federal actions to coordinate and fill in the gaps in state and local action, including business demands for a more even and predictable landscape of regulation and the federal role in protecting health and national security and in maintaining the research and information systems to support climate decisions. They recommend the need for a "national" response to climate change that coordinates federal action with state and local government, the private sector, and ordinary citizens.

The very idea of national or global adaptive strategies is as odd at first glance as the idea of primarily local efforts at mitigation. However, global adaptation strategies are significant when it comes to the need to assist the most vulnerable countries to adapt, or in the case of globally connected systems of food production, health, or migration. It is a reflection of the extent to which public climate policy debates have focused overwhelmingly on mitigation rather than adaptation that the different reasons why and how localities might want to act in response to climate change have not been more widely discussed.

The Mitigation–Adaptation Nexus

Climate-change mitigation and adaptation are also becoming inexorably linked because adaptation needs are defined by the climate change that cannot, or will not, be mitigated. With climate change already under way, and only limited success in reducing emissions, it is increasingly likely that the world faces average temperature increases of greater than 2°C by midcentury.[32]

Even with the most ambitious mitigation strategies now being discussed, there will still be substantial unmitigated climate change to adapt to across a wide range of systems, including ecosystems, food, water, health, infrastructure, and energy. Adaptation may clash with resource needs for mitigation, including needs for water (e.g., for power generation, urban growth, and agriculture) and land (e.g., for power generation and transmission, agriculture, recreation, and conservation).

Efforts to reach international agreement to limit greenhouse-gas emissions and assist with adaptation have had mixed success, as illustrated by

> What has resulted from recent international negotiations on climate change? See "Climate Governance and Non-Nation-State Actors in the Aftermath of Copenhagen and Cancún" on page 27.

the December 2009 UN negotiations in Copenhagen (see Liverman spotlight, p. 27). But the international climate negotiations also emphasize the increasing significance of local, regional, and nonstate actors in efforts to respond to climate change and develop an international regime.

Policy Laboratories and Interaction Among Governments

Local impacts and local responses offer paths for hope in dealing with such a large, complex, and transformative force as climate change. Treating the global dimensions of climate change as a reason to favor responses at a national level or higher—and to preempt or limit local responses—may eliminate precisely those areas of opportunity that local knowledge, economies, and political institutions can best create.

Justice Brandeis famously celebrated the role of states as laboratories in our federal structure.[33] While states are a familiar political scale at which to celebrate our federal system, modern conceptions of federalism also take account of the different political scales at which effective policy innovation, experimentation, and action may occur and that may be called for by the nature of the problem being confronted. These political scales are both smaller than states—cities, towns, counties, irrigation districts—and larger, including regions and associations of states or cities.

Conclusions

Historically, most discussion about climate-change mitigation has focused on options for national to international policy making, whereas focus on climate-change adaptation has tended to flourish at the more local to regional scales at which climate change is already being felt, or where climate change poses the most serious challenges.

With time, and with an ever-increasing number of tangible climate-change impacts, local to regional actors will likely be among the first to really understand what is at stake and what must be done. This means they will have an ever-increasing motivation to develop effective adaptation strategies, as well as a broadening array of reasons to act with respect to climate-change mitigation. They will provide leadership in reducing the impacts that they know will harm them, and they will act to gain economic or political leadership. Their intimate understanding of what is at stake with climate change gives them a potential advantage over national and global policy actors.

Unfortunately, even though many individuals and institutions at local to regional levels will be affected by climate change, not all at these levels have the human, social, or economic resources to act. Moreover, many adaptation strategies will likely require cooperation, leadership, and economic support across broader geographies, and climate-change mitigation will ultimately require coordinated action at national and international levels. Thus, meeting the climate-change challenge will be a shared responsibility of people operating at all scales of governance, from local to international.

Notes

1. Intergovernmental Panel on Climate Change (IPCC), *Fourth Assessment Report of the Intergovernmental Panel on Climate Change* (Cambridge: Cambridge University Press, 2007).

2. J. T. Overpeck and J. L. Weiss, "Projections of future sea level becoming more dire," *Proceedings of the National Academy of Sciences of the United States of America* 106: 21461–62 (2009).

3. IPCC, *Fourth Assessment Report*, 865.

4. G. A. Meehl, T. F. Stocker, W. D. Collins, P. Friedlingstein, A. T. Gaye, J. M. Gregory, A. Kitoh, R. Knutti, J. M. Murphy, A. Noda, S.C.B. Raper, I. G. Watterson, A. J. Weaver, and Z.-C. Zhao, "Global climate projections," in *Climate Change 2007: The Physical Science Basis. Contribution of Working Group I to the Fourth Assessment Report of the Intergovernmental Panel on Climate Change*, S. Solomon, D. Qin, M. Manning, Z. Chen, M. Marquis, K. B. Averyt, M. Tignor, and H. L. Miller, eds. (Cambridge: Cambridge University Press, 2007), 747–845.

5. T. R. Karl, J. M. Melillo, and T. C. Petersen, eds., "Regional climate impacts: Alaska," in *Global Climate Change Impacts in the United States* (Cambridge: Cambridge University Press, 2009), available at http://www.globalchange.gov/publications/reports/scientific-assessments/us-impacts.

6. IPCC, *Fourth Assessment Report*; Karl et al., "Regional climate impacts."

7. T. P. Barnett, D. W. Pierce, H. G. Hidalgo, C. Bonfils, B. D. Santer, T. Das, G. Bala, A. W. Wood, T. Nozawa, A. Mirin, D. Cayan, and M. Dettinger, "Human-induced changes in the hydrology of the western United States," *Science* 319(5866): 1080–83 (2008).

8. D. D. Breshears, N. S. Cobb, P. M. Rich, K. P. Price, C. D. Allen, R. G. Balice, W. H. Romme, J. H. Kastens, M. L. Floyd, J. Belnap, J. J. Anderson, O. B. Myers, and C. W. Meyer, "Regional vegetation die-off in response to global-change type drought," *Proceedings of the National Academy of Sciences of the United States of America* 102: 115144–48 (2005).

9. Karl et al., "Regional climate impacts."

10. N. S. Diffenbaugh, F. Giorgi, and J. S. Pal. "Climate change hotspots in the United States," *Geophysical Research Letters* 35: L16709 (2008).

11. E. R. Cook, C. Woodhouse, C. M. Eakin, D. Meko, and D. Stahle, "Long-term aridity changes in the western United States," *Science* 306(5698): 1015–18 (2004); D. M. Meko, C. A. Woodhouse, C. A. Baisan, T. Knight, J. J. Lukas, M. K. Huges, and M. W. Salzeer, "Medieval drought in the upper Colorado River basin," *Geophysical Research Letters* 34: L10705 (2007).

12. Cook et al., "Long-term aridity changes."

13. Karl et al., "Regional climate impacts," 129.

14. Karl et al., "Regional climate impacts."

15. A. Westerling, H. Hidalgo, D. Cayan, and T. Swetnam, "Warming and earlier spring increase western US forest wildfire activity," *Science* 313(5789): 940–43 (2006); P. J. van Mantgem, N. L. Stephenson, J. C. Byrne, L. D. Daniels, J. F. Franklin, P. Z. Fulé, M. E. Harmon, A. J. Larson, J. M. Smith, A. H. Taylor, and T. T. Veblen, "Widespread increase of tree mortality rates in the western United States," *Science* 323(5913): 521–24 (2009).

16. For example, Westerling et al., "Warming and earlier spring."

17. J. P. Sands, L. A. Brennan, F. Hernández, W. P. Kuvlesky, Jr., J. F. Gallagher, D. C. Ruthven, and J. E. Pitmann, III, "Impacts of buffelgrass (*Pennisetum ciliare*) on a forb community in South Texas," *Invasive Plant Science and Management* 2:130–40 (2009); M. E. Miller, A. Burquez, and A. Martinez-Yrizar, "Grasslandification in the Sonoran Desert: the case of Pennisetum ciliare" (manuscript).

18. Karl et al., "Regional climate impacts."

19. Overpeck and Weiss, "Projections of future sea level."

20. Karl et al., "Regional climate impacts."

21. Karl et al., "Regional climate impacts."

22. N. Mee and M. Miller, "Here Comes the Sun: Solar Power Parity with Fossil Fuels," *William and Mary Environmental Law Review* 36 (forthcoming 2012); R. Glennon, *Unquenchable: America's Water Crisis and What to Do About It* (Washington, DC: Island Press, 2009).

23. Karl et al., "Regional climate impacts."

24. K. L. Ebi, J. Balbus, P. L. Kinney, E. Lipp, D. Mills, M. S. O'Neill, and M. Wilson, "Effects of global change on human health," in *Analyses of the Effects of Global Change on Human Health and Welfare and Human Systems. A Report by the U.S. Climate Change Science Program and the Subcommittee on Global Change Research*, J. L. Gamble, ed.; K. L. Ebi, F. G. Sussman, and T. J. Wilbanks, authors (Washington, DC: US Environmental Protection Agency, 2008), 39–87.

25. M. L. Parry, O. F. Canziani, and J. Palutikof, *Climate Change 2007: Impacts, Adaptation and Vulnerability. Contribution of Working Group II to the Fourth Assessment Report of the Intergovernmental Panel on Climate Change* (Cambridge: Cambridge University Press, 2007); D. M. Liverman, "Vulnerability and adaptation to drought in Mexico," *Natural Resources Journal* 39: 99 (1999).

26. L. Lopez-Hoffman, E. D. McGovern, R. G. Varady, and K. W. Flessa, *Conservation of Shared Environments: Learning from the United States and Mexico* (Tucson: University of Arizona Press, 2009).

27. S. L. Cutter, C. T. Emrich, J. T. Mitchell, B. J. Boruff, M. Gall, M. C. Schmidtlein, C. G. Burton, and G. Melton, "The long road home: Race, class, and recovery from Hurricane Katrina," *Environment: Science and Policy for Sustainable Development* 48(2): 8–20 (2006).

28. Liverman, "Vulnerability and adaptation"; Parry et al., *Climate Change 2007.*

29. Cutter, S. L., ed. *American Hazardscapes: The Regionalization of Hazards and Disasters* (Washington, DC: National Academies Press, 2001); S. L. Cutter, B. J. Boruff, and W. L. Shirley, "Social vulnerability to environmental hazards," *Social Science Quarterly* 84(2): 242–61 (2003); S. L. Cutter, and C. Finch, "Temporal and spatial changes in social vulnerability to natural hazards," *Proceedings of the National Academy of Sciences of the United States of America* 105(7): 2301 (2008).

30. US Census Bureau, available at http://www.census.gov.

31. National Research Council, *Informing an Effective Response to Climate Change* (2010), available at http://americasclimatechoices.org/panelinforming.shtml; *Adapting to the Impacts of Climate Change* (2010), available at http://americasclimatechoices.org/paneladaptation.shtml; *Limiting the Magnitude of Future Climate Change* (2010), available at http://americasclimatechoices.org/panelmitigation.shtml; and *Advancing the Science of Climate Change* (2010), available at http://americasclimatechoices.org/panelscience.shtml.

32. M. New, D. M. Liverman, and K. Anderson, "Mind the gap," *Nature Reports Climate Change* (12): 143–44 (2009).

33. *New State Ice v. Liebmann*, 285 U.S. 262 (1932) (Brandeis, dissenting); K. Engel and M. Miller, "State governance: Leadership on climate change," in *Agenda for a Sustainable America*, J. C. Dernbach, ed. (Washington, DC: Environmental Law Institute, 2009).

The Scientific Consensus with Regard to Human-Induced Climate Change

Jonathan Overpeck

Although there is still considerable political debate concerning the reality of climate change, the climate science research community is confident in its assertions that climate change is already happening, that it is driven mostly by human activities (e.g., the burning of fossil fuels), and that it will continue to become more significant with time unless actions are taken to reduce greenhouse-gas emissions significantly.

There will always be scientific debate about the details of climate change, but this type of debate—in scientific journals, e-mails, or elsewhere—is intrinsic to science and does nothing to diminish scientific confidence in the reality of climate change as an environmental issue that must be taken seriously. The vast bulk of the scientific literature relating to climate change is not policy prescriptive, but rather forms a foundation of knowledge to be used by the public and decision makers in efforts to deal with climate change.

While the popular perception is that climate change emerged as a topic of concern only in the new millennium, the reality of climate change has been suspected for more than 100 years,[1] and major scientific reports of the last several decades have expressed increasing confidence that human-caused climate change is detectable and likely to be substantial in the future in the absence of efforts to curb greenhouse-gas emissions.[2]

The most recent report of the World Meteorological Organization and the United Nations Intergovernmental Panel on Climate Change was the strongest report yet on the seriousness of the climate-change issue.[3] The US National Academies has weighed in similarly in several recent study reports,[4] and these are also supported by multiple major climate-change reports published by both the G. W. Bush and Obama administrations.[5]

What are the biggest uncertainties with respect to future climate change? As with all science, there are uncertainties with respect to climate-change science. The most important concern is how much climate change will occur in a given region, of what type, and by when.

A primary reason for this uncertainty is the inability to predict future human actions, particularly as they relate to greenhouse-gas emissions. Additional uncertainty exists because global climate models do not agree on some details of what will happen in the future for a given estimate of greenhouse-gas emissions. Nonetheless, the current scientific state-of-the-art is sufficient for informed decision making with respect to climate-change mitigation and adaption.

Does the recent slowing of global warming mean the problem is going away? Although the first decade of the twenty-first century was the warmest of any decade since global temperature measurements were initiated in the nineteenth century, the rate of global warming has been slower since the start of the twenty-first century than over the previous several decades. Does this mean global warming has stopped? Absolutely not. Climate change is change that takes place over decades, not from any one year to the next. Climates of the future will be the result of human-caused greenhouse-gas emissions, but also other smaller climate influences such as variations in the sun, volcanic eruptions, and processes internal to Earth's climate system, such as El Niño or deep-ocean circulation. As a result, in the last 150 years we have experienced several periods of inexorable warming where the rate of warming was either faster or slower than the average of the whole period. The fact remains that Earth has warmed about 0.8°C since the Industrial Period began, and the last decade is the warmest of the entire period.[6]

Notes

1. H. Le Treut, R. Somerville, U. Cubasch, Y. Ding, C. Mauritzen, A. Mokssit, T. Peterson, and M. Prather, "Historical overview of climate change," in *Climate Change 2007: The Physical Science Basis, Contribution of Working Group I to the Fourth Assessment Report of the Intergovernmental Panel on Climate Change*, S. Solomon, D. Qin, M. Manning, Z. Chen, M. Marquis, K. B. Averyt, M. Tignor and H. L. Miller, eds. (Cambridge: Cambridge University Press, 2007), 93–127.

2. Le Treut et al., "Historical overview."

3. Intergovernmental Panel on Climate Change (IPCC), *Fourth Assessment Report of the Intergovernmental Panel on Climate Change* (Cambridge: Cambridge University Press, 2007).

4. US National Research Council, *Ecological Impacts of Climate Change* (Washington, DC: National Academy Press, 2008); and *America's Climate Choices: Advancing the Science of Climate Change* (Washington, DC: National Academy Press, 2010).

5. US Climate Science Program, *Scientific Assessment of the Effects of Global Change on the United States: A Report of the Committee on Environment and Natural Resources,*

National Science and Technology Council (2008); US Climate Science Program, *Weather and Climate Extremes in a Changing Climate. Regions of Focus: North America, Hawaii, Caribbean, and U.S. Pacific Islands. A Report by the U.S. Climate Change Science Program and the Subcommittee on Global Change Research*, T. R. Karl, G. A. Meehl, C. D. Miller, S. J. Hassol, A. M. Waple, and W. L. Murray, eds. (2008); T. R. Karl, J. M. Melillo, and T. C. Petersen, eds., "Regional climate impacts: Alaska," in *Global Climate Change Impacts in the United States* (Cambridge: Cambridge University Press, 2009), available at http://www.globalchange.gov/publications/reports/scientific-assessments/us-impacts.

6. IPCC, *Fourth Assessment Report*; Karl et al., "Regional climate impacts."

Climate Governance and Non-Nation-State Actors in the Aftermath of Copenhagen and Cancún

Diana Liverman

International negotiations under the United Nations Framework Convention on Climate Change (UNFCCC) have always provided a space for local government and nonstate actors such as businesses, scientists, and environmental groups to participate in the process of framing the international climate regime.

The 2009 United Nations Climate Change Conference and Conference of the Parties (COP 15), held in Copenhagen, saw thousands of people and organizations join official government negotiators for a two-week attempt to agree on a response to the risks of climate change. Side events included a conference of city mayors, art exhibitions, and full-day workshops focusing on forests, agriculture, business, indigenous peoples, oceans, and development. State and regional governments participated through representatives from states and cities from countries such as the United States, Brazil, and Mexico.

Analyses of the relationship between cities and the international climate regime start from the empirical observation that cities are associated with up to 70 percent of global greenhouse-gas emissions and in many parts of the world are responsible for managing key sectors such as transportation and housing. Federal systems often delegate environmental management to states and counties, including regulation of lands, transport, and air quality. International networks, such as the World Mayors Council on Climate Change and the Cities for Climate Protection initiative of the International Council for Local Environmental Initiatives, seem to be important in sharing best practices, providing input into international negotiations, and working with the private sector.

In the developing world, private-sector investment in carbon-offset projects under the Clean Development Mechanism, as well as assistance for adaptation and forest protection, can also involve local and state government in the development and approval of carbon-mitigation and climate-adaptation projects. The Clean

Development Mechanism is a provision under the Kyoto Protocol that allows countries with commitments to emission restrictions under the protocol to offset some of their emissions through the implementation of emission-reduction projects in developing countries. For example, the Brazilian states of Amazonas, Pará, Mato Grosso, and Amapá have signed a memorandum of understanding with the states of California, Wisconsin, and Illinois to work together on tropical forest protection and to make tropical forest projects eligible for carbon credits that could be used for compliance within the United States.

The interests of state and local government in the full range of climate issues— emission targets, offsets, forest protection, adaptation, and funding mechanisms— provide multiple points of engagement with the international climate regime and drove their interests in the outcome of Copenhagen.

Although attention at Copenhagen focused on the struggle over who would cut emissions and when, negotiators were also working on detailed drafts for international agreements over technology transfer; reform of the Clean Development Mechanism; monitoring, reporting, and verification of commitments; forest protection; adaptation; and overall funding mechanisms—all with significant implications for non-nation-state actors.

The negotiations concluded with little in the way of binding decisions—the so-called Copenhagen Accord was only noted (rather than accepted as a decision of the UNFCCC) and included weak commitments to keep climate change under 2°C, for voluntary targets, and for financing without clearly designated additional sources of funds. Detailed agreements on forests and adaptation had to wait for the next COP (COP 16) in Cancún at the end of 2010.

Many local governments, climate-aware corporations, and environmental and humanitarian nongovernmental organizations were deeply disappointed that the outcome provided little in the way of support for state and local government actions, a wavering carbon price, and inadequate commitment for adaptation. For example, local actors hoped to benefit from an international agreement that would promote financial flows for mitigation and adaptation at the local level through decarbonization and adaptation projects, including forest protection. Some of these hopes were restored by the Cancún Accord of December 2010, which included proposals for a new Green Fund, assistance for forest protection, and institutional frameworks for adaptation funding that would support action by national, state, and local actors in response to climate change.

The Institutional Context

The Institutional Context

The jurisdictional complexity of international climate-change response efforts is echoed by the complexity of the US federal system of government, within which domestic efforts at mitigation and adaptation take place. Some would call the US federal system "messy": a census of US governments (including local and special districts) counts thousands of jurisdictions, each with its own institutions and constitution, certain degrees of independence and autonomy, and some shared authorities. A result of this wide range of jurisdictions with overlapping and shared powers is a dynamic tension between self-rule and shared rule.[1] Self-rule allows a jurisdiction to make laws and rules regarding its citizens without interference, while shared rule means that one jurisdiction may directly affect another through overlapping powers. In climate-change policy, shared rule is exhibited when states cooperate to achieve a shared goal, such as agreeing upon how to share the costs of investing in a regional electricity grid that ties into new solar and wind power generation.

The challenge of federalism is to build on the strengths of having governments responsive to the interests and values of their citizens while also encouraging governments to coordinate and cooperate over shared interests and concerns. In the United States, the challenge posed by the tension between self-rule and shared rule is how to ensure that its almost 90,000 governments not only attend to their own concerns but also energetically collaborate to address common challenges and mandates.

Encouraging the energetic pursuit of commons ends, as Robert A. Schapiro points out in chapter 2, has sometimes been attempted within the legal system by simplifying and ordering, so as to reduce the number of governments that need to cooperate around any given issue. The impulse to tidy up the messy federal system has taken two forms: creating fewer governments through consolidation (e.g., combining county and city governments) and establishing clear jurisdictional boundaries (e.g., in which the national government deals exclusively with foreign and national matters and states deal exclusively with regional issues). In explaining the notion of federalism, Schapiro encourages us to resist the impulse to tidy up and instead to embrace what he terms *polyphonic* federalism—"multiple, independent sources of political authority." Broad overlap in the exercise of authority between the federal and state governments in addressing a complex subject such as climate change, according to Schapiro, supports multiple approaches to problem solving ("plurality"), dialogue, and redundancy, each of which in turn encourages policy experimentation, learning, and resilience in the face of such challenges.

We embrace the concept of polyphonic federalism in this book because we believe it describes federalism as it is actually practiced in the United States and that the concept is particularly well suited to address the messy and complex problems created by climate change. As Jonathan Overpeck, Marc Miller, and Diana Liverman note in chapter 1, the sources of, impacts from, and solutions to climate change occur at multiple, overlapping scales. While national greenhouse-gas reduction standards may eventually provide a common floor for all jurisdictions, how that floor is met and exceeded will vary across the country. For example, western states may be better suited to solar power, and coastal states to wind power. Furthermore, people and governments in low-lying coastal areas will adapt to sea-level rise differently from how the intermountain West will adapt to declines in winter snow-pack and a changing hydrologic regime. Polyphonic federalism holds the potential to support coordination among jurisdictions to develop regionally tailored approaches to problems that spill over boundaries.

Federalism, resting as it does on self-rule and shared rule, constantly presents citizens and government officials with questions about who should make authoritative decisions, what the scope of their decision-making authority should be, and how they should be held accountable. For instance, in relation to environmental law, James Hopkins asks who decides the scope and context of tribal jurisdiction. As he describes in chapter 3, the answer has varied historically: at times, tribes have been treated as sovereign nations; at other times, as dependent wards of the federal government or as states; and more commonly today, as all three. When polyphonic impulses have been ascendant, as appears currently to be the case, tribes have experienced many more opportunities to exercise authority, develop a sense of autonomy, invest in the capacity for self-rule, experiment with different types of policies, and collaborate with other jurisdictions.

These opportunities have become apparent in relation to a variety of environmental issues, such as the development of water-quality standards as well as responses to climate change. Hopkins illustrates how American

Indians have been among the first Americans to be affected directly by climate-change impacts. The experiences of Native American tribes in land management, adaptation to climate-change impacts, and working with other governments and organizations will affect how the United States responds to climate change and provide many opportunities for states to learn from tribes.

While federalism is complex and messy, it is certainly not a free-for-all. The US federal system is structured not only by constitutions, statutes, and legal doctrines but also by practice, experience, and, for its thousands of governments, the necessity of coordination and collaboration. In particular, the practice of collaborative management may prove beneficial in dealing with climate change, described by Kirk Emerson in chapter 4 as "a dilemma for which solutions are uncertain, over which there is disagreement on the best approaches, and that exceeds the boundaries and abilities of one jurisdiction or authority to resolve."

Emerson notes that collaborative management holds many potential benefits for states and localities, including the promise of pooled resources, shared risk, and increased policy compliance. But when it comes to climate change, just as there is no one-size-fits-all impact, policy, or government, there is no one-size-fits-all method of collaborative management. Given the premium that climate change and federalism place on coordination, it is vital to begin to experiment more explicitly with and understand what types and forms of collaborative management work well in what types of situations. As such, Emerson describes conditions for fostering consensus and conflict resolution that are conducive to collaborative management and that can therefore best support climate-change mitigation across jurisdictions. Echoing Hopkins, Emerson emphasizes the role of accountability and the appropriate delegation of authority. For instance, in developing a climate adaptation plan for a national forest, how much authority should forest officials exercise, and how much decision making should be turned over to the many groups and governments with an interest in the forest—from states and counties to timber companies and environmental groups? And given that most collaboratives are voluntary—members are not legally bound to the commitments they make to one another—how can a collaborative ensure that its members follow through with their agreements? For instance, a group of northeastern states and eastern Canadian provinces agreed to meet specific regional greenhouse-gas emission-reduction targets over a period of years. If those targets are not met, can citizens in the region hold this collaboration of states and provinces accountable, and if so, how? These are issues that require additional consideration, especially in the context of climate change and increasing reliance on cross-jurisdictional collaborations.

Taken together, the chapters in this section establish the overarching legal and policy context for the volume. They introduce themes related to the practice of US federalism that carry throughout the book as the challenges and opportunities of climate change are explored in more depth.

Note

1. D. Elazar, *Exploring Federalism* (Tuscaloosa: University of Alabama Press, 1987).

Chapter 2

The Varieties of Federalisms

Robert A. Schapiro

In Brief

- Polyphonic federalism is characterized by multiple, independent sources of political authority—such as federal and state—whose scopes are not defined by subject matter, and of which no type of conduct is categorically beyond the boundaries of their authorities.

- Dual federalism, in which government regulation is divided into exclusively federal and state enclaves with no overlap, was the dominant model of federalism in the United States until around 1937.

- Polyphonic federalism allows multiple entities to have authority over a given topic, facilitates learning from the practices and experiences of others, and fosters redundancy with multiple entities seeking the same policy end.

- Climate change, a global phenomenon having variable local impacts, demands both global and local responses and thus is well suited to a polyphonic federalist policy approach.

Federalism generally refers to a system of governance in which power is allocated among a central government and subunits, such as states, provinces, or territories. However, in legal theory and in practice, multiple conceptions of federalism have arisen over time. While all notions of federalism concern the allocation of authority among the states and the national government, the method, characteristics, and benefits of that allocation vary widely. As an indication of that variety, the concept of federalism has been championed by a diverse group of Supreme Court justices with radically differing legal philosophies. This common support for federalism among justices with fundamentally different approaches to the law emphasizes both the changing nature of the problems that federalism confronts and the flexibility of the concept itself. The issue of global climate change presents a contemporary example of how evolving conceptions of federalism can offer valuable approaches to new problems.

Much attention has focused on the role of courts in enforcing federalism. The more fundamental question, though, concerns the proper way to allocate power among the states and the national government, no matter what institution is effecting that allocation. The proper distribution of power is a question for officials at all levels and in all branches of government. Federal policy makers in Congress and in administrative agencies must decide on the role of states and the federal government in devising and implementing solutions to problems, such as climate change. For their part, states must decide how to develop their policies in light of the action or inaction at the federal level. After the states and the federal government adopt their policies, the courts stand ready to resolve any conflicts between the federal and state regulations and to ensure that neither the federal nor the state initiatives violate provisions of the US Constitution. All of these decisions, by state and federal policy makers and by courts, involve understandings of the proper interaction of state and federal governments. Thus, all of these actions depend on conceptions of federalism.

To provide a basis for understanding how federalism can address climate change, this chapter focuses on two influential conceptions of the proper distribution of power: dual federalism and polyphonic federalism. Building on this foundation, I then outline the advantages of polyphonic federalism in addressing the challenges of climate change.

Conceptions of Federalism

Dual Federalism: A Strict Separation of Power

Dual federalism focuses on dividing government regulation into exclusively federal and state enclaves. In this view, federal and state power should not overlap, for each enjoys complete dominion within its designated subject area. Dual federalism requires deciding which topics properly belong to which level of government and then guarding the boundaries against attempted state or federal trespasses. Supporters of dual federalism draw from the text of the Constitution, which grants power to the national government in the form of legislative authority in Article I, section 8, and then suggests, by means of the Tenth Amendment, that all other authority rests exclusively with the states. However, in the years following the adoption of the Constitution, it became clear that the language of the Constitution did not define impermeable boundaries between state and federal domains. To take a notable example, the Constitution granted to Congress the power to regulate commerce "among the several states."[1] States, though, also traditionally regulated goods flowing in interstate commerce.

The theory of dual federalism did not keep pace with the changing social situation in the United States. In the late nineteenth and early twentieth centuries, both the states and the federal government sought to regulate the potentially deleterious effects of industrialization, such as unsafe and unsanitary working conditions, child labor, low wages, long hours, and other abusive workplace practices. Congress and state legislatures enacted legislation to address harms that crossed the boundaries between state and national domains. The Supreme Court attempted at first to adhere to a dual federalism conception by striking down the state and federal actions that veered over the state–federal border. However, in the increasingly interconnected world of commerce, drawing clear lines between national and local became very difficult. The Court attempted various formal labels in a vain effort to maintain the boundary; it distinguished between commerce and manufacturing, between direct effects on commerce and indirect effects on commerce, between regulations that were really economic and those that were really social, and between the regulation of goods still in their original packages and those that had been unbundled.

In the wake of the Great Depression, this categorical approach led the Court into a confrontation with President Franklin Roosevelt. The Court invoked the dual federalism framework to strike down important components of President Roosevelt's New Deal program. President Roosevelt believed that these decisions imperiled his plan for helping the nation to recover from its economic crisis. Following his reelection in 1936, President Roosevelt proposed his "court-packing" plan, which would have allowed him immediately to add six justices to the Supreme Court. Congress refused to endorse the proposal, but in 1937 the Court began to take a more deferential approach to President Roosevelt's initiatives. Retirements soon allowed him to add his own nominees to Court, and the new justices gave much greater discretion to state and federal legislatures.[2] The Court largely ceased policing a formal boundary between state and federal domains. These developments famously led Edward Corwin to note the "Passing of Dual Federalism."[3]

Although dual federalism of the pre-1937 variety appears to have ended, the project of dividing authority among states and the national government remains. The contemporary Supreme Court appears to be embracing dual federalism once again, based on some of its recent federalism decisions. Thus, possession of guns in schools, or mere interpersonal violence, is outside of the boundaries of federal authority.[4] These topics lie so close to the heart of state prerogative that concurrent federal regulation is not permissible. By the same token, addressing the fate of foreign Holocaust-era insurance policies lies so close to the core of federal authority that it lies beyond the realm of state power.[5] Climate-change issues do not fit easily into this dualist framework. The problems and potential solutions are both global and intensely local, as noted in chapter 1. For this reason, the dualist approach might threaten climate-change initiatives. For example, courts might construe state implementation of international climate-change agreements to constitute unconstitutional invasions of an exclusively federal realm.

Polyphonic Federalism: Overlapping Authority

In light of the inadequacies of the dual model of federalism, policy makers and scholars have developed alternative conceptual frameworks that reject a rigid division between state and federal realms. One prominent, though limited, example of a more flexible understanding of federalism is *cooperative federalism*.

Tracing back to the New Deal, or perhaps earlier,[6] cooperative federalism acknowledges and endorses close relationships between the state and national governments in a variety of areas. The term *cooperative federalism* sometimes broadly describes any arrangement in which states and the federal government exercise a functional overlap of authority. In this sense, cooperative federalism is the opposite of dual federalism, which generally insists on a division of functions.[7] However, cooperative federalism more commonly refers to a system in which states implement a federal plan or at least regulate in accordance with general federal policies.[8] Thus, it is the federal government that sets the overall regulatory objectives. States act as agents, determining means rather than ends. States often enjoy considerable flexibility in deciding how to implement the federal objectives.[9] Cooperative federalism plays an especially important role in the field of environmental law. Pollution control laws, in particular, often involve plans designed to induce states to implement federal standards.[10] In a cooperative model, federal action does not preempt state participation in the field. However, the state role remains subsidiary to the federal. Although states enjoy broad authority over policy implementation, they may have little control over policy formulation.

Neither dual federalism nor cooperative federalism adequately describes the actual dynamic relationship of the states and the federal government in the contemporary United States. Contrary to the assumptions of dual federalism, states and the federal government exercise extensive concurrent authority. Climate change presents one example among many of this broad policy overlap. In areas ranging from health care to securities fraud, from education to crime, intersecting state and federal regulation has become the norm. Further, the role of the states has not followed the model of simply implementing federal policy, as cooperative federalism would suggest. In the area of climate change, for example, in periods of federal inaction, the states sought to counteract the federal inertia. Opposition, rather than obedience, to federal plans has motivated state regulatory efforts.

In other work, I have suggested an alternative conception of federalism that would acknowledge a broad role for the interaction of the states and the federal government and would not license a return to pre-1937 judicial activism in the federalism arena.[11] I have termed this approach a "polyphonic" conception of federalism. Drawn from music theory, polyphony refers to the simultaneous combination of independent melodic lines, as in a fugue. Polyphony represents a useful trope for federalism in that it emphasizes the independence and autonomy of the different musical lines, which together form the overall musical composition. The polyphonic approach notes the broad overlap of federal and state policy initiatives and emphasizes the benefits of this concurrence, which advances the values of plurality, dialogue, and redundancy.

In the polyphonic conception, federalism is characterized by the existence of multiple, independent sources of political authority. The scope of this political authority is not defined by subject matter. No kind of conduct is categorically beyond the boundaries of state or federal jurisdiction; the federal and state governments function as alternative centers of power. A polyphonic conception of federalism thus resists the idea of defining enclaves of state power protected from federal intrusion. Whereas dualist federalisms insist on dividing state and federal realms of authority, the key elements of polyphonic federalism are the protection of the institutional integrity of multiple sources of power and the promotion of the dynamic interaction of those centers of authority. What is essential in a polyphonic regime is the ability of states to formulate and express their views on a wide range of policies. The focus of polyphonic federalism is structural; it safeguards the legislative, judicial, and administrative apparatus of the state, rather than defining the particular jurisdictional boundaries of state authority. Instead of asking whether some activity belongs on the state or federal side of a line, polyphonic federalism asks how the overlapping power of the state and federal governments can best address a particular issue.

In its embrace of overlapping state and federal power, polyphonic federalism strives to advance a conception of intergovernmental relations that fits with the realities of contemporary society. In the United States, the distinction between the "truly local" and the "truly national" has disappeared. As discussed below, climate change represents a striking example of this blurring of boundaries. Climate change is a global phenomenon with causes and effects in every locality. In other areas as well, problems transcend geographical borders yet remain intensely local. The concepts of "truly local" and "truly national" do not reflect or illuminate contemporary policy issues. A conception of federalism that rests on such a distinction has no foundation.

The Benefits of Polyphonic Federalism

Polyphonic federalism offers a powerful approach to addressing issues because it facilitates the key values of plurality, dialogue, and redundancy. These principles promote innovative and effective policies. This section explores these values and how polyphonic federalism promotes them. The following section explains the special benefits of the polyphonic approach in confronting problems of climate change.

Plurality: Multiple Entities with Authority over a Given Topic

Polyphonic federalism emphasizes the value of plurality. Two heads are better than one, and ensuring the possibility of both a federal and a state approach significantly broadens the perspectives brought to bear on an issue.

As in all conceptions of federalism, the states may offer their own policy prescriptions. States have the ability to test novel approaches, and interstate competition provides an incentive for states continuously to seek new and improved ways of operating. Supreme Court Justice Louis Brandeis memorably characterized the states as "laboratories," in which different social policies can be tested on a small scale, rather than at the national level.[12] One can think of a variety of contemporary policies, such as charter schools or community policing, that originated in one or a few states and are subject to borrowing, revision, or rejection in others. As discussed in the next section, climate change has benefited from exactly this state-by-state experimentation. For example, states have enacted various policies to encourage energy efficiency, especially for residential and commercial buildings. New York adopted a property-assessed clean energy program that provides long-term, low-interest loans to property owners for clean forms of energy and energy-efficient technologies, such as double- or triple-pane windows. The loan is paid through a property tax assessment. In contrast, Illinois established energy efficiency targets for its utilities, requiring electric utilities, for instance, to reduce energy usage by 2 percent of the amount of electricity delivered by 2015.[13] Successful policies will reap rewards as people and businesses flock to the innovating state. Thus, optimal social policy can be determined scientifically, rather than by top-down bureaucratic speculation.

Polyphonic federalism adds the federal laboratory to this collective search for best practices. Because the polyphonic approach refuses to draw a sharp division between state and federal responsibilities, the states and the national government confront the same challenges. Hence, they can learn from each other's experiences. States and the national government also can experiment with shared approaches to problems. The overlap and interconnection of state and federal policies allow for valuable dialogue and a greater range of potential policy prescriptions.

With the overlap of federal and state power comes the possibility of multiple approaches to a particular problem. The different institutional frameworks in which state and federal governments operate give them varying perspectives. Their different geographical scope also may give them divergent strengths and weaknesses. Some solutions may work better when imposed nationally, while others function more efficiently on a local scale.[14] The states and the federal government may attempt differing approaches to address particular issues. For example, many methods exist for trying to ensure environmental protection and workplace safety. The federal government may seek to impose some firm national baselines, while the states may experiment with additional safeguards or alternative implementation schemes (see Doremus and Hanemann, chapter 9). Complex problems can benefit from a variety of responses.

Dialogue: Learning from the Practices of Others

In addition simply to increasing the opportunities for legal protection, the concurrence of federal and state authority provides a valuable opportunity for dialogue. The states and the federal government can attempt alternative means of preventing employment discrimination or defining the fundamental right to privacy. Dialogue magnifies the value of plurality. Not only can each government try different responses to common problems, but also the different regulators can learn from each other. In their account of democratic experimentalism, Michael Dorf and Charles Sabel have emphasized the importance of bottom-up problem solving.[15] Regulators can learn from the best practices of other regulatory regimes. As Andrew Karch discusses in chapter 5, the diffusion of policies from one jurisdiction to another provides a critical vector for policy development in the United States.

The interaction of state and federal regulators may produce a regulatory scheme superior to what either level of government would produce on its own. For example, Kirsten Engel has demonstrated how the development of national low-emission vehicle standards arose from such a productive dialogue.[16] California devised its own standards to require the sales of lower-emission cars. Other states considered adopting the California standards, which led the US Environmental Protection Agency to work with the auto industry to produce alternative regulations, more stringent than the existing national standards. The resulting regulatory scheme represented an advance on what state or federal regulators had conceived separately.[17]

Dialogue facilitates regulatory innovation. The optimal regulatory scheme develops and changes over time, with constant interaction from a variety of forces, including information generated by other regimes. State tort suits may produce information of great value to federal regulators.[18] Like a musical composition, federalism consists in multiple participants contributing to an unfolding, dynamic process. Kirk Emerson notes in chapter 4 that collaborative management, which is based on dialogue, is becoming increasingly common as agencies and jurisdictions seek cooperative solutions to climate-change impacts.

Indeed, even if Congress were to mandate a uniform policy preempting state law, state action may nevertheless play a valuable role in a federalist system. State enactments that conflict with federal law may constitute important symbols of opposition.[19] Even if a state policy cannot become legally binding, the existence of a potential alternative system reminds officials and citizens of the possibility of choosing other solutions. A state law can provide an important protest, a powerful criticism of the federal approach. That kind of officially stated opposition can, in time, help to produce a transformation in federal policy. That change might take the form of adopting the state alternative, or the federal government might simply allow local variance. This kind of protest has occurred among states frustrated with the lack of federal action on climate change. As Edella Schlager notes in chapter 7, three regional initiatives have implemented or are planning to implement greenhouse-gas cap-and-trade systems and have explicitly justified their actions by pointing to the inaction of the federal government.

Redundancy: Multiple Entities Seeking the Same Policy End

Polyphonic federalism involves the states and the federal government addressing the same policy challenges, thus incorporating redundancy, which is an important value in complex systems. A multiplicity of regulators proves useful not only when they each offer valuable, distinctive approaches but also when one regulator fails to perform its task. By contrast, a system of divided, nonoverlapping responsibilities, such as dual federalism, has difficulty in rectifying lapses by particular actors.

Yochai Benkler has noted the array of benefits that flow from redundancy, especially when the multiple layers afford distinctive perspectives:

> Redundancy provides important values in terms of the robustness and innovativeness of a system. Having different people produce the same component makes the production system more resistant to occasional failures. Moreover, having different people with different experience and creative approaches attack the same problem will likely lead to an evolutionary model of innovation where alternative solutions present themselves.[20]

Redundancy makes systems both more resilient and more innovative. Polyphonic federalism embraces the overlap of federal and state authority to take advantage of these benefits.

David E. Adelman and Kirsten H. Engel (see chapter 8) have drawn on the analogy to ecosystems to highlight the value of the regulatory overlap promoted by a polyphonic understanding of federalism.[21] They emphasize that a search for a single point of optimization can leave a system fragile and incapable of adapting to changing circumstances. In contrast, more complex, adaptive systems promote higher levels of resilience and innovation. Building on this study of natural systems, Adelman and Engel advocate regulatory solutions that incorporate multiple levels of governance, as opposed to policies that seek to identify a single, most efficient level of regulation. As with investing in the stock market, they emphasize the value of a diversified regulatory portfolio, in contrast to a strategy that relies on a single regulatory tool.

State and federal law may provide alternative forms of relief. The potential regulatory redundancy constitutes a fail-safe mechanism, an additional source of protection if one or the other government should fail to offer adequate safeguards.[22] The lapse may occur because one government does not address an issue at all or because it fails to enforce regulations that facially apply. In recent years, climate change has become the paradigmatic example of the value of state policy initiatives in the face of federal regulatory inaction.[23]

Federalism and Climate Change

The issue of climate change offers a dramatic example of the benefits of a polyphonic, as opposed to a dualist, understanding of federalism. Dual federalism strives to divide state from federal authority and to categorize problems as "truly local" or "truly national." Climate change reveals the incompleteness and futility of this dual approach. Is climate change local or national? Do states differ fundamentally in the risks they face and in the values they are pursuing, or do all states face a similar, widespread phenomenon that requires a broad-based solution? Though the questions frame supposed alternatives, in fact the dichotomies are false. The answers are affirmative for each query. Climate change is a global phenomenon with differing local manifestations. The responses have been, and will likely continue to be, both local and global. A polyphonic approach acknowledges that the problems of climate change do not fit neatly into local or national or global packages. Polyphonic federalism recognizes the need to develop intersecting global, national, and local responses to issues that cross jurisdictional boundaries.

Geography certainly does matter. As emphasized, for example, by Jonathan Overpeck, Marc Miller, and Diana Liverman in chapter 1, adaptation issues will vary widely by locality. Effective responses, however, will require broad coordination. As many other chapters in this volume demonstrate, mitigation requires a global understanding of the problem and cannot be addressed solely by local action. Nevertheless, state initiatives have proved valuable, at least in raising public awareness and in providing small-scale tests for potential broad responses.

With regard to mitigation, state plans have proved useful not because states are fundamentally different, as dualists are wont to stress, but because in key regards states are fundamentally the same. Thus, a state's adoption of renewable energy portfolio standards, requiring energy suppliers to include a certain percentage of renewable power, can provide a model for other states.[24] The political and scientific dynamics are sufficiently similar such that state-based policies may indeed be scalable. In this instance, it is the similarities that make a federalist approach so valuable. As the polyphonic framework emphasizes, it is the plurality, dialogue, and redundancy that make federalism useful, all of which require a basic commensurability of the conditions in various states.

In this regard, polyphony builds on one of the most traditional and longstanding tropes of federalism, the idea of states as laboratories.[25] Laboratories represent multiple approaches to a single problem. They differ from each other only in the particular solutions tested, not in their method or goals. They all follow the scientific method, a discipline that demands commensurability and reproducibility, not singularity.

Climate change illustrates the appeal of some of the underlying conceptions of dualism. Global warming does have differential impacts on different states. Place matters. However, the scalability and reproducibility of the solutions demonstrate a great benefit of federalism from a polyphonic perspective. The leadership that states have sometimes shown in promoting mitigation strategies illustrates the power of the polyphonic approach. Climate change is both a local and a global concern. Dualist approaches, rooted in conceptions of sameness and difference, cannot account for the complexities that climate change presents. Polyphony, by contrast, rejects the dichotomy of national and local and insists on the valuable interaction of regulators, local, state, national, and global. Climate change clearly fits more comfortably into this polyphonic paradigm.

Conclusion

Theories of federalism will not solve problems of climate change. However, theories of federalism may help, or hinder, the search for effective policy solutions. While dualist conceptions of federalism sometimes figure prominently in opinions of the US Supreme Court, the dualist perspective is far from inevitable. Polyphony provides a descriptively more accurate and normatively more attractive account of how power may be allocated among the states and the national government. Polyphonic federalism enhances principles of plurality, dialogue, and redundancy, which can make the political system more innovative and adaptive. From within a dualist framework, the key question is which issues belong essentially to the states and which belong essentially to the national government. From a polyphonic conception, the key question is how the states and the national government can best exercise their overlapping powers so as to advance policy goals. The chapters in this book help to answer that question.

One might ask why the right answer is not just to have the national government determine optimal policy and then to enforce that plan uniformly throughout the United States. That kind of dualist solution would obviate the need for complex calculations of intersecting state and national power. Of course, the next question might be how we can be sure that the policy is optimal and that a uniform federal implementation strategy will be accurate and effective. Polyphonic federalism does not establish the optimal substantive policy, but it provides a valuable way to get to the best achievable result. We would have little use for polyphony, or for any kind of federalism, if we knew all the answers and if the political system functioned perfectly. But those assumptions are as heroic as the assumption that the global climate system will fix itself.

Notes

1. U.S. Const., art. I, §8.

2. W. E. Leuchtenburg, *The Supreme Court Reborn: The Constitutional Revolution in the Age of Roosevelt* (1995); R. A. Schapiro, "Must Joe Robinson Die? Reflections on the 'Success' of Court Packing," 16 Const. Comm. 561 (1999).

3. E. S. Corwin, "The Passing of Dual Federalism," *36 Va. L. Rev. 1* (1950).

4. *United States v. Morrison*, 529 U.S. 598, 627 (2000); *United States v. Lopez*, 514 U.S. 549, 568 (1995).

5. *Am. Ins. Ass'n v. Garamendi*, 539 U.S. 396 (2003): 421.

6. See Harry N. Scheiber, "American Federalism and the Diffusion of Power: Historical and Contemporary Perspectives," *9 U. Tol. L. Rev. 619* (1978): 676; see also Harry N. Scheiber, "Federalism and Legal Process: Historical and Contemporary Analysis of the American System," *14 Law & Soc. Rev. 663* (1980): 679–83; Daniel J. Elazar, "Cooperative Federalism," in *Competition Among States and Local Governments: Efficiency and Equity in American Federalism*, Daphne A. Kenyon and John Kincaid, eds. (Washington, DC: Urban Institute Press, 1991), 67; Daniel J. Elazar, "Theory of Federalism," in *Encyclopedia of the American Constitution*, vol. 3, Leonard W. Levy and Kenneth L. Karst, eds. (New York: Macmillan Reference, 2000), 1006.

7. See Joseph F. Zimmerman, "National-State Relations: Cooperative Federalism in the Twentieth Century," *31 Publius J. Federalism 15* (2001): 15, 18.

8. See Philip J. Weiser, "Towards a Constitutional Architecture for Cooperative Federalism," *79 N.C. L. Rev. 663* (2001): 665.

9. See Weiser, "Towards a Constitutional Architecture," 670–72.

10. See Robert L. Fischman, "Cooperative Federalism and Natural Resources Law," *14 N.Y.U. Envtl. L. J. 179* (2005): 187–89.

11. R. A. Schapiro, *Polyphonic Federalism: Toward the Protection of Fundamental Rights* (2009); R. A. Schapiro, "Toward a Theory of Interactive Federalism," *91 Iowa L. Rev. 243* (2005).

12. *New State Ice Co. v. Liebmann*, 285 U.S. 262, 311 (1932) (J. Brandeis, dissenting).

13. Pew Center on Global Climate Change, US Climate Policy Maps, available at http://www.pewclimate.org/what_s_being_done/in_the_states/state_action_maps .cfm, accessed June 7, 2010.

14. P. E. Peterson, *The Price of Federalism* (1995): 17–20.

15. M. C. Dorf and C. F. Sabel, "A Constitution of Democratic Experimentalism," *98 Colum. L. Rev.* 267 (1998).

16. K. H. Engel, "Harnessing the Benefits of Dynamic Federalism in Environmental Law," *56 Emory L. J.* 159 (2006).

17. Engel, "Harnessing the Benefits," 168–69.

18. W. W. Buzbee, "Asymmetrical Regulation: Risk, Preemption, and the Floor/Ceiling Distinction," *82 N.Y.U. L. Rev.* 1547 (2007); R. Rabin, "Reassessing Regulatory Compliance," *88 Geo. L. J.* 2049 (2004): 2068–70.

19. J. A. Gardner, "State Constitutional Rights as Resistance to National Power: Toward a Functional Theory of State Constitutions," *91 Geo. L. J.* 1003 (2003): 1032–54.

20. Y. Benkler, "Coase's Penguin, or, Linux and the Nature of the Firm," *112 Yale L. J.* 369 (2002): 423.

21. D. E. Adelman and K. H. Engel, "Adaptive Environmental Federalism," in *Preemptive Choice: The Theory Law, and the Reality of Federalism's Core Question,* ed. W. W. Buzbee (Cambridge University Press, 2008).

22. R. M. Cover, "The Uses of Jurisdictional Redundancy: Interest, Ideology, and Innovation," *22 Wm. & Mary L. R.* 639 (1981): 656–57; R. M. Cover and A. Aleinikoff, "Dialectical Federalism: Habeas Corpus and the Court," *86 Yale L. J.* 1035 (1977): 1042–46; M. Landau, "Federalism, Redundancy and System Reliability," *3 Publius J. Federalism* 173 (1973): 188–89.

23. K. H. Engel, "State and Local Climate Change Initiatives: What Is Motivating State and Local Governments to Address a Global Problem and What Does This Say About Federalism and Environmental Law?" *38 Urb. Law.* 1015 (2006): 1016; Pew Center on Global Climate Change, *Learning from State Action on Climate Change* (2008): 12, available at http://www.pewclimate.org/docUploads/States% 20Brief%20(May%202008).pdf (on file with the Harvard Law School Library).

24. D. E. Adelman and K. H. Engel, "Adaptive Federalism: The Case Against Reallocating Environmental Regulatory Authority," *92 Minn. L. Rev.* 1796 (2008): 1846–49; M. D. Nichols, "California's Climate Change Program: Lessons for the Nation," *27 UCLA J. Envtl. L. & Pol'y* 185 (2009).

25. *New State Ice Co. v. Liebmann.*

Chapter 3

Tribal Sovereignty and Climate Change

Moving Toward Intergovernmental Cooperation

James Hopkins

In Brief

- Climate-change impacts directly affect the resources, communities, and cultural identity of tribal governments, but defining the role of tribal governments in addressing these impacts calls into question who decides the scope and content of tribal jurisdiction.

- Historically, state governments and the federal government sought ownership of Indian lands, and Congress and the courts privatized Indian lands and limited tribal authority, treating tribes as dependent nations and providing little opportunity for them to manage their natural resources as autonomous actors.

- In the 1970s, US Environmental Protection Agency recognized tribal governments as the primary parties for making environmental decisions and managing environmental programs on Indian lands and successfully lobbied Congress to recognize tribes as states for purposes of environmental laws.

- Recently, tribes have accessed US courts and international bodies seeking relief from climate-change impacts on human rights grounds. Although tribes' success in court has been limited to date, their efforts illustrate the proactive approach of tribal governments in addressing climate change.

Native American imagery and stereotypes hold unique and contradictory places in popular culture, many of which transcend discussions of environmental regulation and climate-change policy. On one hand, there is the stereotype of the American Indian as a noble savage: the watchful steward of the land in its natural state. In this image, the American Indian does not tinker with the ecosystem but coexists in a special albeit passive harmony. This is the well source for popular myths about how the natural world works; the stereotype assumes that any Native American within arm's reach can take us back to find the simple answers to what we do not know about the mysterious ordering of nature and how to preserve it. This stereotype was powerfully illustrated in 1971 by the efforts of the not-for-profit Keep America Beautiful Inc., an organization focused on the development of a national ethic of cleanliness. The "Crying Indian" commercial, played by the Greek-American actor Iron Eyes Cody, focused the attention of millions of Americans on their personal practices that contributed to littering.[1]

On the other hand, there is the stereotype of the American Indian as a savage—untrustworthy—whose tribal contemporaries pursue illegitimate business interests such as casinos. This stereotype assigns a negative attribute to the actions of tribal governments and delegitimizes their sovereignty on the false pretense that they manipulate Native American cultural identity for self-interest and financial gain.[2] The cause and consequence are by no means arbitrary: at times American jurisprudence has vigorously trammeled upon the distinct legal and cultural identity of Native Americans, overlooking cooperative efforts by tribal governments that are choosing to find sustainable economies to end poverty, fostering economic self-determination, and working with Congress on progressive ways to manage precious tribal resources. Indeed, American Indian law and policy actively engage this stereotype. Lorie Graham has noted that "Americans may have a hard time acknowledging—despite the lip service paid to tribal sovereignty—that at the core of most Indian law decisions today is a historically rooted negative mythology of cultural inferiority and Indian savagery."[3]

Beneath the veil of these stereotypes lies a rich and complex story that explains resource management systems and their inner workings between tribal, state, and federal governments. When examined more closely, stereotypes and popular nomenclature, both romantic and damning, noble and ignoble, fall to the side to reveal a resilient tribal cultural context shaped by episodic and contradictory forces around one core question: Who decides the scope and content of tribal jurisdiction? Discussion regarding the law's response to climate change tends to overlook tribal governments completely, yet they play a significant role juxtaposing federal and state actors who all too often are viewed as the dominant institutions for reform. Tribal governments manage significant natural resources in critical habitats (e.g., arid lands of the Southwest), even though, as Bethany Berger observes, Native Americans have historically fallen at the bottom of leading socioeconomic indicators in the country.[4]

The impact of climate change directly affects the resources, communities, and cultural identity of tribal governments, but defining the role of tribal governments in addressing these impacts requires recognition of them as a third level of government that functions concurrently within the federal system. With respect to climate-change policy, recognition and understanding of the role of tribal governments create new challenges of direction, controversies, and exciting opportunities by cracking open the presumptive federal–state duopoly over planned responses, adaptation, diffusion, innovation, mitigation, and the role and application of science. Recognition of tribal authority, however, is not without intergovernmental tensions and struggles; the process has been endlessly frustrated by the US Supreme Court, which, as S. James Anaya claims, "has propagated a demeaning myth of conquest and diminished the impact of the indigenous point of view in the resolution of relevant conflicts."[5]

This chapter explores and addresses the role of tribal governments within the climate-change debate. First, it examines the historic and legal framework that defines tribal sovereignty and the emergence of tribal sovereignty within the context of environmental federalism. The chapter highlights significant gaps in tribal jurisdiction arising from federal policy over matters relevant to climate-change policy and describes how tribes respond strategically, including appeals to international human rights law. Next, the chapter explores the potential adaptation of tribal governments to climate-change policy by analyzing and comparing experiences with water management programs under the Clean Water Act of 2002[6] and other federal environmental protection statutes designed to empower tribal resource management in partnership with the US Environmental Protection Agency (EPA). Finally, it explores two issues that will likely influence tribal resource management in the future in light of climate change. First, continued resource depletion on tribal territory may affect the scope and content of tribal jurisdiction by providing the basis for a stronger set of claims to limited tribal resources. Second, emerging independent actors such as nongovernmental organizations play a unique role in contributing to strategic tribal resource management projects.

The History of Tribal Sovereignty

The status of tribal sovereignty in American jurisprudence is the culmination of an epic legal narrative that reflects distinct policy shifts between the federal government and federally recognized Indian tribes. Two themes emerge, however, from the historic shifts in federal Indian policy: the overarching or plenary authority of Congress over Indian lands and affairs, on one hand, and the interpretation by the US Supreme Court with regard to tribal governments as domestic dependent nations on the other. Just as federal Indian law and policy have ranged widely in scope and application, the landscape that defines Indian country is equally diverse. According to the 2009 *Federal Registrar*, 564 Indian tribes are federally recognized in the United States,[7] of which 229 are federally recognized Native Alaskan Villages. Indian trust lands are a unique form of land tenure and are the touchstone of tribal land holdings that span the contemporary landscape and include arid lands, boreal forests, high plains, canyons, and watersheds; they abut national and state parks, military bases, urban areas, and a wide variety of other environs with valuable and unique ecosystems.

The indigenous homelands that predate European contact were bound through complex customary legal systems whose diverse intersocietal frameworks illustrated the richness of Native American societies across North and South America. The fortunes of Native Americans and tribal governments shifted dramatically in concert with federal Indian policy, which is categorized into five distinct eras: treaty making (1789–1871); allotment and assimilation (1871–1928); the Indian New Deal, or Indian Reorganization era (1928–45); the termination era (1945–61); and the era of self-determination (1961 to present).[8]

1789–1871: Treaty Making

The origins of federal plenary authority can be traced back to the treaty-making era. Following the American Revolution, tribes engaged in treaty making with the federal government on a nation-to-nation basis, seeking mutual friendship, respect, and recognition of one another's autonomy. Treaties were made between the executive branch and a specific tribe or group of tribes based upon the foregoing mutuality and set aside significant tracts of indigenous territory. Inherent powers of tribal self-government were held by the tribe in reserve, and the treaty affirmed tribal authority over specific demarcated territory.

Recognizing tribal authority within a treaty defined early federal–tribal relations and continues to apply in situations where the scope of tribal authority is juxtaposed between state and federal laws and the courts. For instance, in 1999, a majority decision by the US Supreme Court upheld the fishing rights of the Mille Lacs Indian Band in *Minnesota v. Mille Lacs Band of Chippewa Indians*, contrary to arguments made by the State of Minnesota that it retained jurisdiction to regulate.[9] In 1837, the United States entered into a treaty with several Chippewa Bands to purchase their land in exchange for guarantees, including "the privilege of hunting, fishing, and gathering wild rice, upon the lands, the rivers, and the lakes included in the territory ceded."[10] Minnesota argued in 1999 that events leading up to its admission into the Union in 1858 had resulted in the loss and removal of these treaty rights, but the provisions of the 1837 treaty were held by the majority of the Supreme Court to guarantee the Chippewa Bands a usufructuary right to fish despite subsequent changes to their territory.

The use of treaties ended by 1871, brought about by westward expansion and burgeoning pressure by settlers and local governments for Congress to open up tribal lands for development. Despite a sharp change in federal policy over plenary authority to acquire Native American lands as well as the removal of Native American populations onto reservations, treaties are regarded as foundational agreements that shape the federal–tribal relationship. The end of the treaty-making era reflected the plenary role sought by Congress over Indian lands and affairs. Vexed by the president's exclusive treaty-making portfolio, Congress reacted harshly to their exclusion and used its control over federal money to amend the Indian Appropriations Act, cleverly requiring the president to have congressional consent prior to spending any new treaty dollars. This action had the practical result of terminating all future treaty making with Indian tribes.[11]

1871–1928: Allotment and Assimilation

The allotment and assimilation era from 1871 to 1928 was characterized by federal policies that imposed plenary authority over Indian lands and affairs. Emerging jurisprudence on the sweeping scope of plenary power further undermined tribal authority to govern within the reservation boundaries. Congress and the Supreme Court foreclosed comanagement opportunities in the wake of westward settlement and new state governments seeking to exert their own authority and control on tribal lands. The policy shift to allotment and assimilation had staggering consequences: in 1887, approximately 138 million acres constituted Indian trust lands for Native Americans;[12] this figure has since plummeted to approximately 55 million acres.[13]

The most significant federal statute during the allotment and assimilation era was the Dawes Act of 1887,[14] which struck a blow to tribal land holdings by parceling off yeoman's tracts to both tribal and nontribal individuals and transferring large tribal land holdings into federal surplus trust lands.[15] The continued westward expansion by non-Indians placed the question of Indian title and the residual powers of tribal governments squarely on the congressional agenda. Newly elected members were concerned that their citizens could not access the vast resources held on treatied lands and reservations, so Congress, through the Dawes Act, sought to make possible the privatization of these holdings along with the assimilation of tribal governments by undermining their territorial base and ability to govern over non-Indians within the reservation boundaries. Judith Royster observes that, "as non-Indian settlement of the trans-Mississippi West burgeoned, federal policy shifted from the removal of tribes" to "the isolation of tribes in pockets of lands carved out of aboriginal territories."[16] The result is the modern checkerboard of reservation land holdings among communal, tribal, and nontribal landowners. The allotment policy officially ended in 1934, but Royster's conclusion describes its significance as "the greatest and most concerned attack on the territorial sovereignty of the tribes."[17]

1928–1945: The Indian New Deal

Despite the lasting footprint of these allotments on tribal lands, the inherent and reserved powers of tribal governments remained intact following the end of the allotment era into the emergence of President Franklin Roosevelt's policy of the Indian New Deal in 1928. In 1934, the Indian Reorganization Act sought to restore expropriated treaty lands; the statute provided a widely adopted model for tribal governance that emphasized the separation of powers and a framework for tribal government to interface with the growing array of federal services that were responsible for Indian affairs.[18] The statute formally ended the federal policy with regard to allotment and surplus lands and established a mechanism for tribal governments to reclaim some of the lands that had been taken away. Section 465 allows the US secretary of the interior to acquire new lands and place them into trust, including lands located beyond the reservation boundary, and add them to the reservation.[19] In 1977, the final report by the American Indian Policy Review Commission found that between 1936 and 1974, approximately 595,157 acres were returned to tribal governments through this mechanism.[20]

The Indian Reorganization Act prevented further allocation of individual title of tribal lands, but it did not quiet the title of existing allotees. Thus, while lands were put into trust for tribal governments, questions over the rights of non-Indian fee owners who found themselves inside the reservation set the stage for a new struggle over the scope of tribal authority. For example, a 2001 US Supreme Court decision strictly limited tribal sovereignty in relation to non-Indian fee lands. The Court held in *Atkinson Trading Co., Inc. v. Shirley* that the Navajo Nation did not have jurisdiction over non-Indian fee lands upon which a small non-Indian business operated; the owners defeated the Nation's attempts to levy a tribal sales tax, further limiting the scope of tribal authority within the reservation boundaries.[21]

The failure of the New Deal era to reconcile prior allotments created a legacy that illustrates the episodic policy shifts that highlight the lack of a singular or static federal Indian policy. As Charles Wilkinson explains, "There are a number of scattering forces that push Indian law away from any center," and most notable is the shifting role of federal Indian policy.[22] Absent a unitary legal doctrine, Wilkinson's "splintering influences" are pervasive, with disputes growing over treaties, federal statutes, the role of race, precise location of lands and resources, third-party interests in common resources, and myriad other factors.[23] With respect to any unitary doctrine, plenary power within the five policy eras suggests a constitutional interpretation by Congress different from treaty interpretation and that its oversight is part of a broader power "to regulate commerce with foreign Nations, and among the several States, and with the Indian Tribes."[24] The absence of an interpretative anchor and the encroachment of federal plenary authority resulted in a jurisprudence that is, in Wilkinson's view, "not what American Indians would choose."[25]

1945–1961: Termination of Federal Recognition

Federal Indian policy made yet another dramatic shift at the dawn of the cold war, when Congress decided that terminating the federal trust responsibility would empower tribes to assimilate. So Congress began to identify prospective tribes and withdraw federal recognition through targeted legislation. The significance of how this policy reflected congressional intent to end the distinct status of Native Americans was captured by Royster: "Termination was assimilation with a vengeance."[26] Approximately 109 tribes were subjected to congressional legislation that withdrew federal recognition, thereby cutting off financial support for tribal communities and releasing tribal trust lands.[27] For example, in 1954 Congress enacted the Menominee Indian Termination Act with the expectation that the tribe would create a small corporation and function much like a county government subject to the laws of Wisconsin.[28]

The most significant action with regard to tribal termination was the passage of Public Law 280.[29] Enacted by Congress in 1953, the law gave certain states, including Wisconsin and California, broad civil and limited criminal jurisdiction over Indian tribes. However, it contains an important caveat that protects tribes from being deprived "of any right, privilege, or immunity afforded under Federal treaty" concerning hunting and fishing.[30] The Menomonee Tribe was a signatory to the Wolf River Treaty of 1854 and successfully argued before the US Supreme Court in *Menominee Tribe of Indians v. United States* in 1968 that despite the termination of the federal relationship, the treaty rights to hunt and fish were still in force and effect.[31] The *Menominee* decision was indicative of the shifting tribal–federal relationship. The legal framework set forth under termination was cumbersome, and states often were unable to adequately oversee new jurisdictional matters that pertained to tribes.

1961 to Present: Self-Determination and the Creation of Domestic Dependent Nations

In 1964, federal policy toward Indian tribes began to change once again when the "Great Society" initiatives under President Lyndon Johnson began to fund tribal communities, as impoverished constituents in the fight against poverty, through the Economic Opportunity Act.[32] By 1968, recognition of the status of marginalized Native Americans on poor reservations coincided with growing awareness about race, civil rights, and class struggle in the United States more generally. In 1970, President Nixon formally denounced termination, describing Native Americans as the most deprived and isolated minority group in the nation.[33] Nixon championed new federal legislation that was designed to empower tribal governments with management over specific areas that were of the utmost importance to sustainable community development. For example, the genesis of modern tribal police and healthcare programs dates to the 1975 passage of the Indian Self-Determination and Education Assistance Act,[34] which gave tribal governments the option to control federally funded programs where the tribe had jurisdiction. And yet, given the dramatic shift in federal policy by Congress during this new era, what could tribes expect with regard to judicial perspectives on tribal regulatory authority?

Early American jurisprudence affirmed federal control over Indian lands and Indian affairs when the US Supreme Court promulgated the doctrine of tribal sovereignty in the landmark Marshall trilogy, three cases that were delivered between 1823 and 1832.[35] Chief Justice John Marshall envisioned tribal sovereignty through international law's own lens of antiquity: discovery, war, conquest, wardship, and dependency afforded to the victor the spoils of nationhood. The Marshall trilogy affirmed the autonomy of Indian tribes but made it dependent upon federal plenary oversight. Federal Indian law's origin with regard to the legitimacy of tribal governance was timed to

American history itself as Marshall's vision of tribal sovereignty was tied to Native American subjugation under English and then American law. His decisions recognize Native American sovereignty prior to European contact, but with discovery and conquest their autonomy was diminished, and within the American legal system tribes held a collective status as domestic dependent nations: wards that were dependent upon federal protection by the growing numbers of non-Indians who craved their lands and resources.

This jurisprudential footprint remains today and continues to narrow the scope of tribal authority over lands and resources. As domestic dependent nations, the jurisdictional powers of tribal governments are under constant pressure from judicial interpretation. The patchwork of landholdings resulting from allotment illustrates this vulnerability when non-Indian landowners within reservation boundaries reject tribal jurisdiction. This issue was tackled in 1981 by the US Supreme Court in *Montana v. United States*, where the Crow Tribe attempted to prohibit all hunting and fishing by nonmembers, including fee holders of non-Indian property within the reservation.[36] Tribal hunting and fishing rights were included in their original treaty of 1851; however, the Crow Tribe's territory had been reduced significantly with successive shifts in federal policy aimed at assimilating tribal governments and diminishing Indian title.[37] When the Tribe attempted to regulate fishing and hunting over non-Indian landowners within the reservation, the Court held that tribes could regulate only with express congressional delegation and intent. Congressional delegation and a tribe's inherent retention of its tribal power could be validly executed under one of two exceptions, known commonly as the *Montana* exceptions:

1. When a consensual relationship has been entered into between the tribe and the non-Indian, such as a commercial contract, a lease, or a partnership. In these instances, the non-Indian has acquiesced to tribal jurisdiction of the tribe, thus being subject to the tribal code as it applies to their dealings (i.e., taxation and licensing).

2. When the tribe's political integrity, economic security, or health and welfare, is directly affected by the non-Indian's conduct, or where the core tribal governmental interest is affected.

Unfortunately, the Supreme Court has narrowly construed this second exception, as illustrated by several cases. In *Montana* the Court found that nothing in the conduct of non-Indian hunters and fishers threatened the Crow Tribe's political or economic well-being "as to justify tribal regulation," and accordingly, the Tribe lacked regulatory jurisdiction over the nonmembers and their conduct on non-Indian lands.[38] Similarly, in 1997, the US Supreme Court held in *Strate v. A-1 Contractors* that a state highway that intersected tribal land was not under tribal authority.[39] The highway was originally a US Army road that was granted as a right-of-way and never sold. Incredibly, the Court held that the easement gave the highway attributes of non-Indian fee land—similar to the land in *Montana*—because the highway was open to the public and maintained by the state.[40] The Court concluded that the tribe had not retained a "gate-keeping right" over the land.[41]

With respect to climate change, the Supreme Court's interpretation of tribal sovereignty exposes a potential weakness in seeking to build and enforce alternative models to the federal–state duopoly that has dominated the climate-change discourse. That is, if tribal governments are unable to enforce their laws within the reservation proper regardless of tribal membership, the jurisdictional quagmire suggests that tribes lose. The Supreme Court's perspective on the scope and content of tribal jurisdiction leaves very little recourse for tribal governments hoping to secure their rights as a legitimate third sovereign to the environmental protection arena. The court's reliance on congressional plenary power, observes Angela Riley, "assumed that Congress's management of Indian affairs is proper pursuant to its plenary power, and Congress has freely exercised that authority, both in favor of and against tribal interests."[42] This approach overlooks the centrality of land in defining Native American culture and fails to explore the purpose behind a tribe's exercise of authority. As Dean Suagee observes, "Tribal cultures are deeply rooted in the natural world; therefore, protecting the land and its biological communities tends to be a prerequisite for cultural survival. While tribal officials tend to have a wide range of reasons for developing environmental regulatory programs, the survival of tribal culture is usually one of the main reasons."[43]

Federal plenary authority has exerted vast power over Indian affairs. Consequently, little collaborative comanagement has occurred between tribal and federal governments; instead, the courts have a history of reducing and limiting tribal sovereignty. Federal jurisprudence has resulted in Indian lands being pursued for non-Indian profit, offered narrow views of the tribes' natural resources as potential commodities, and promoted the general attitude that tribes are dependent entities, with little room for tribes to be genuinely autonomous actors in managing their natural resources. Going forward, important collaborative comanagement opportunities exist that can inform a richer and more pluralistic jurisprudence as it relates to climate change. As potential working models, these opportunities suggest a practical recognition of the constituent connection between the rights of Native Americans and the topography of the land itself, where proximity to abutting reservation lands, its history with respect to the tribe and the chain of title, places the subject matter within the ambit of the tribe's cultural fabric and customary understanding of the world. The role of the environment in shaping Native American cultural identity and the rights that flow from this connection make the issue of climate change all the more pressing. As Rebecca Tsosie explains, the tort-based approach to categorizing environmental harm from climate change limits a proper impact assessment because indigenous perspectives view consequences inseparable from the physical, spiritual, and cultural destruction of a people.[44]

Federal Environmental Laws and Tribes as States

Environmental laws at the federal level establish national standards for protecting and restoring a wide range of subjects in the environment. These standards act as a basic floorboard in terms of what states and tribes must adhere to. The US EPA's regulatory and enforcement role in the protection and maintenance of air quality, safe drinking water, waste management, and hazardous materials does not prohibit states and tribal governments from filling in gaps or establishing higher standards. A key policy goal of federal environmental laws is to create cooperative systems that incentivize the implementation of local, regional, and state environmental protection measures. The transboundary aspects of these laws, however, necessitate the US EPA's broad oversight, bringing to the fore the issue of federal plenary power over tribal governments, but with a unique cooperative approach. The US EPA has an established track record of promoting tribal environmental regulation, and according to Suagee, the US EPA policy complements tribal policy and perspective that reflects the centrality of land and the environment within Native American culture: "Tribal cultures are deeply rooted in the natural world; therefore, protecting the land and its biological communities tends to be a prerequisite for cultural survival. While tribal officials tend to have a wide range of reasons for developing environmental regulatory programs, the survival of tribal culture is usually one of the main reasons."[45] Policies of the US EPA with regard to tribal regulatory powers further illustrate Royster's compelling reference to tribal governments as the "third sovereign" as it reflects both their inherent sovereignty and the strength that tribal authority derives from federal pollution control statutes and, as we will discuss, over state jurisdiction.[46]

In 1970, the emergence of a US EPA tribal policy began in earnest with the consultation framework established within the National Environmental Policy Act.[47] In 1984, the stage was set for important legislative developments that became a watershed for tribal authority over the environment. First, the US EPA adopted the widely touted "Policy for the Administration of Environmental Programs on Indian Reservations"[48] in direct response to legitimate tribal criticism of the agency's previous oversight of tribal sovereignty and the need for tribal governments to enact their own environmental protections. The policy recognized tribal governments as "the primary parties for setting standards, making environmental policy decisions and managing programs for reservations, consistent with Agency standards and regulations."[49] Second, the US EPA's successful lobbying of Congress to authorize the treatment of Indian tribes as states (TAS) effected legislative amendments to several key EPA-administered statutes. Those that enable the application of tribal authority under TAS provisions are the Clean Water Act (CWA), Clean Air Act (CAA),[50] Safe Drinking Water Act (SDWA),[51] National Historic Preservation Act,[52] and the Comprehensive Environmental Response, Compensation and Liability Act.[53] All were amended to include TAS, although TAS under the CAA and SDWA are program specific, whereas TAS under the CWA is largely inclusive of the entire statute.

The importance of TAS as it applies to CWA came to the fore in 1996 in *Albuquerque v. Browner*,[54] which involved a challenge by the City of Albuquerque to a decision by the US EPA to require the city to meet the more stringent CWA standards of a downstream Indian tribe.[55] The City of Albuquerque's wastewater treatment facility was situated along the Rio Grande less than six miles upstream of Isleta Pueblo's reservation boundary. The city's discharge limits under the National Pollutant Discharge Elimination System (NPDES) were set by the US EPA; however, while the US EPA revised the facility's discharge limits to meet New Mexico's more stringent standards, Isleta Pueblo filed for TAS recognition pursuant to § 518(e) of the CWA.[56] The US EPA, having granted this recognition, successfully tailored the city's facility NPDES permit to meet the even more stringent standards set by Isleta Pueblo. In doing so, the US EPA recognized the tribe's rights to set stricter standards just as individual states do, and upheld the higher standards.

Browner provides a powerful illustration of the courts interpreting congressional plenary power from a purposive perspective; inquiring into the statute's objective and intent can define the scope of tribal regulatory authority relative to the statute's aims and objects. In *Browner* the inquiry was in regard to the purpose of congressional statutory protection conferred on behalf of the Isleta Pueblo pursuant to the CWA's TAS provision. This was evident when Albuquerque unsuccessfully argued that the designated downstream use of the water was not prescribed and thus not protected by the CWA. Justice Edwin Mechem, however, considered the purpose of the CWA, which is to "restore and maintain the chemical, physical, and biological integrity of the Nation's waters through reduction and elimination of pollutant discharge into those waters."[57] Although Isleta Pueblo refused to fully disclose the water's designated use on the basis that it concerned sacred religious ceremonies, the Court concluded that it involved ingestion of water not unlike a fishable or swimmable standard of protection.[58]

The result of this decision is a unique and vital extension of tribal sovereignty beyond the territorial limits of the reservation and where the regulation of a common resource is concerned. Moreover, because Albuquerque and the Isleta Pueblo were governed concurrently by the NPDES, and the US EPA carried ultimate jurisdiction pursuant to environmental federalism, the TAS assignment for Isleta Pueblo did not undermine the CWA federal–state partnership as TAS subsumed tribal–state jurisdiction in a manner consistent with federal environmental law. Specifically, in this instance, the CWA's legislative objective rationally connected the national and transboundary aspects of the regulated area through TAS, and the result is an important remedy against regulatory gap: a situation where all but one party are subject to the same regulation over a common resource. To put the matter differently, the jurisdictional controversy would be no different had Isleta Pueblo caused the point-of-source discharge in contravention of the CWA; its legislative objective is geared toward empowering both tribal and state governments to pursue higher standards and ensuring that neither party is precluded from seeking US EPA review under the TAS CWA system.

The Environmental Justice Approach to Tribal Sovereignty

Expanding from US EPA's model, how can we more broadly develop a workable approach to climate-change policy that recognizes the unique history of the tribes and tribal sovereignty and appropriately balances tribal interests with national environmental interests? This section examines the role of social justice or environmental justice (EJ) as it relates to tribal sovereignty and climate change, and the concurrent emergence of related international human rights concerns. Both themes approach the role of causation broadly, in contrast with the narrow tort-based approach in determining environmental harms. *Browner* coincided with a renewed interest by EJ scholars to focus on the deepening relationship between tribes and the federal government as Congress increased its efforts to protect tribal control over environmental regulation on the reservation. EJ scholars monitor how systemic institutional problems, including access to justice, can cause disparate environmental impacts due to socioeconomic status, gender, race, or political power. An example of the EJ approach is to perform such an assessment on a local community. According to Sarah Krakoff, "environmental justice for tribes must be consistent with the promotion of tribal self-governance," and a just framework is one that protects and achieves tribal "authority to control and improve the reservation environment."[59] Krakoff's definition advocates for a deeper appreciation of the reasons why tribal economic development projects are controversial from an environmental protection perspective. Native Americans criticize the EJ approach for ignoring the context through which tribal governments are forced to make decisions. According to Suagee, tribes have difficulty applying this approach to controversial decisions about developing their natural resources, and while "people in the EJ movement are genuinely interested in learning about tribal concerns and finding ways to deal with these issues that are acceptable to tribal peoples, a blind spot with respect to tribes is a common affliction."[60]

EJ does, however, raise important issues that federal Indian law fails to address in light of the narrow application of plenary power. When courts rule in favor of Congress and indirectly favor third-party lease holders on tribal lands, such as mining companies, what can tribes do? In reviewing the federal framework, Mary Wood observes the impact that uranium mining has had on the Navajo reservation and concludes, "In assessing whether federal approval decisions adequately protect the usable tribal land base, courts should also consider the ever-present externalities resulting from pollution that accompanies many forms of industrial development. Serious pollution becomes a form of land confiscation every bit as consequential to tribal interests as outright condemnation."[61] In this regard, the issue of causation and environmental harm illustrates why tribal governments exert authority to protect their land and way of life despite the absence of procedural protections. By expanding the range of factors that institutions should consider in determining the scope of tribal authority, EJ scholars provide a useful window through which we can begin to examine a more comprehensive approach to adjudicating competing interests over common resources.

Adjudicating Indigenous Rights Pertaining to Climate Change

In 2007, the United Nations General Assembly adopted the United Nations Declaration on the Rights of Indigenous Peoples (UNDRIP).[62] The event affirmed significant and emerging developments in the field of international human rights law as it pertains to the rights of indigenous peoples and communities worldwide. In general, once indigenous communities have exhausted their domestic remedies within the nation-state system, they can seek recourse to international and regional human rights decision-making bodies, which recognize that indigenous communities can suffer loss of land, cultural identity, and the ability to self-govern under domestic systems (see Anaya spotlight, p. 71).

UNDRIP adds to the growing jurisprudence that is being shaped by indigenous petitioners seeking relief from human rights abuses before international and regional human rights decision-making bodies. In addition, UNDRIP can establish procedural standards in relation to institutional responses by nation-states seeking to comply with international human rights, a significant point in regard to climate-change policy. For example, Article 32 of UNDRIP establishes the rights of indigenous peoples to "determine and develop priorities and strategies for the development or use of their lands or territories" and requires states to "consult and cooperate in good faith" before approving the development of "any project affecting their lands or territories" with "effective mechanisms for just and fair redress for any such activities."[63]

How do international human rights standards affect indigenous peoples and climate-change policymaking? See "Incorporating Rights of Indigenous Peoples in Climate-Change Initiatives" on page 71.

UNDRIP is inclusive of all parties: it recognizes and safeguards against the rights of others in several provisions, including discrimination, and concludes with Article 46(3), which reads, "The provisions set forth in this Declaration shall be interpreted in accordance with the principles of justice, democracy, respect for human rights, equality, nondiscrimination, good governance and good faith."[64] UNDRIP can play an important role in shaping domestic climate-change policy. As a tool for renewed domestic claims and international petitions, however, the issues of remoteness and causation cannot be overlooked when characterizing climate change as a tort-based claim with respect to loss of environment, resources, and cultural identity. US courts have placed limits, as demonstrated by *Native Village of Kivalina and City of Kivalina v. ExxonMobil Corp. et al.*, in which an Alaskan Native village filed a nuisance suit against twenty-four defendant oil companies, claiming they were responsible for climate-change impacts that are affecting their communities.[65] On September 30, 2009, the US district court granted a summary motion for dismissal in favor of the oil companies.[66] While the court did not dispute the claim that the Village of Kivalina could become submerged due to melting ice and rising sea levels, it could not find causation necessary to allow the Tribe standing for a nuisance suit, and accordingly, the Tribe lacked a justifiable cause of action.

Remoteness and causation were also issues with regard to the human rights petition filed by the Inuit Circumpolar Conference (ICC) before the Inter-American Commission on Human Rights (IACHR), asserting within the normative framework of international human rights law that climate change infringed and breached the petitioners' human rights guaranteed under the Organization of American States (OAS) system.[67] On November 16, 2006, IACHR denied consideration and admissibility of the human rights petition filed by the ICC.[68] Unlike in *Kivalina*, in which the indigenous claimants named specific oil companies as tortfeasors, the ICC petition sought human rights protections and relief from global warming caused by the United States of America.[69] The IACHR's letter to the petitioners stated that the claims did not enable the IACHR to determine "whether the alleged facts would tend to characterize a violation of rights protected by the American Declaration."[70] In short, the UNDRIP may be best viewed as a forward-looking document that can establish progressive benchmarks to a new regulatory system, given the current limits of liability for the purposes of making a determination under the OAS system and international human rights law more generally.

The caveat to this, however, is the recognition that customary law is an evolutionary process. It is significant to note that the ICC petition created awareness and strengthened coalitions within the petitioner group; it also raised the IACHR's understanding of the issues. The fact that the IACHR was able to continue a hearing on the substance of the issues advanced the discourse on indigenous human rights law as it relates to climate change.

In a similar vein, on April 24, 2009, the Indigenous Peoples' Global Summit on Climate Change issued the Anchorage Declaration that explicitly prescribes how the organization will uphold the fundamental human rights affirmed by the UNDRIP "in all decision-making processes and activities related to climate change."[71] This critical document strengthens the human rights framework on climate change and the rights of indigenous peoples, and while several nations—including the United States and Canada—did not vote in support of it, it has become part of the international human rights framework.[72] Prior to the ICC petition, the recognition of international human rights of indigenous peoples and indigenous communities arose from cases involving the infringement or denial of traditional land tenure, and the issue of climate change will remain an important issue before the IACHR and other international decision-making bodies.[73]

Options for Tribal Representation in Climate-Change Policy

The limits of tribal sovereignty and domestic dependent nationhood beg the question: What alternatives do tribal governments have when considering a response to climate-change policy? Federal environmental law relies on cooperation among parties as a means to govern and manage resources. An earlier section discussed the limits of tribal sovereignty as defined by federal Indian law; however, the subsequent analysis of TAS strongly suggests that federal environmental law can intercede to recognize and strengthen claims for tribal authority where the depletion of a resource is integral to tribal identity, whether or not the resource crosses outside the reservation boundary. The EJ approach and the growing field of international indigenous human rights law shed important light on the limits of viewing climate change as a narrowly defined tort-based cause of action. These approaches also provide instructive reference points in structuring an institutional response that focuses on inclusion of tribal perspectives and meaningful tribal participation within the regulatory context. It is important to note that TAS already places stringent requirements on tribal governments seeking to obtain and secure a TAS designation by the US EPA; that tribes with TAS designation already come to the regulatory table with peer reviewed capacity adds further support to an inclusive regulatory model.[74]

Interagency Efforts Advance Tribal Interests

With respect to the climate-change policy and tribal governments, independent federal research agencies and nongovernmental organizations can play unique roles in strategic tribal resource management projects and advancing tribal claims. For example, in 2009 the National Center for Atmospheric Research under the National Oceanic and Atmospheric Administration (NOAA) testified before Congress to advance a National Climate Service and create an integrated organization to produce authoritative information on climate change "that would enable decision-makers to manage climate-related risks and opportunities, along with other local, state, regional, tribal, national, and global impacts."[75] In 2009, the National Climate Service was announced, emphasizing the need to work among agencies at the federal, state, and tribal levels. In another initiative, the US Department of the Interior issued a Secretarial Order in September 2009 that established the Climate Change Response Council, which is responsible for developing multiyear management plans to increase understanding of climate change and its impact across all Interior bureaus, with particular emphasis on the impact to tribes.[76]

The ability of tribal governments and their agencies to interface between federal and state governments within a cooperative framework is not new or unique. For example, the restoration of the lake trout population in Lake Superior has been viewed as a model for federal–state–tribal comanagement; it began in 1996 with a partnership between the interstate fishery committee and the Great Lakes Indian Fish and Wildlife Commission (GLIFWC) and continues to implement a multitude of tracking techniques for a range of trout species.[77] With an established record of success, GLIFWC's delegated jurisdiction by the eleven-member, federally recognized Ojibwe tribes in Wisconsin, Michigan, and Minnesota readily lends itself to integrating with such organizations as the National Climate Service. GLIFWC illustrates the potential role that can be played by tribal agencies with established records of success and a history of effective comanagement. The prevalence of tribal organizations that aggregate over a common cause and in conjunction with independent agencies and intergovernmental bodies offers significant opportunities for developing law and policies with regard to climate-change responses.

Looking Ahead: Growing Recognition and Hope for Greater Equity

Many scholars have studied the domestic-international aspects of federal Indian law and EJ issues concerning indigenous claims for "climate justice"—rights to protection from climate change caused by others. Within international indigenous human rights law, the customary framework is shifting as numerous agencies and organizations are beginning to apply existing international human rights instruments to the issue. The absence of a human rights discourse with respect to indigenous peoples and climate change has not been quietly set aside: S. James Anaya, United Nations Special Rapporteur on the Rights of Indigenous Peoples, has characterized the lack of discourse with regard to indigenous communities and the impacts of climate change as deplorable.[78] Indeed, there is a sense of urgency behind this observation, as illustrated by the president of Bolivia's announcement that his country will take a lead role in addressing climate change from the indigenous community perspective and host a World Conference on Climate Change. Bolivia has officially extended invitations to the conference through its Permanent Mission to the United Nations and the Secretariat of the UN Permanent Forum on Indigenous Issues.[79]

Native Americans and tribal governments cover a broad cross section of society and geography and are culturally diverse. The climate-change claims made under tribal sovereignty cross into the international human rights framework, in part reflecting the systemic law and policy barriers posed by congressional plenary power and tribal authority being consistent with domestic dependent nationhood.

With respect to climate-change policy, tribal governments oppose the normative presumption of a federal–state duopoly. Having a better understanding of the tribe's unique role will help inform future discourse as it applies to environmental federalism, including their ability to anchor jurisdictional rights to cooperative resource management agreements and the preservation of TAS status—with the real potential of moving toward a tripartite system of governance over common resources.

Environmental federalism offers a unique opportunity to revisit the frustrating jurisprudence that courts seem to generate all too frequently. *Browner* illustrates how Congress and the US EPA can direct judicial interpretation through a federalist perspective in a manner that is consistent with their respective fiduciary duties and responsibilities toward Native Americans, while protecting tribal regulatory control over transboundary and common resources. The recognition of TAS status is further evidence that tribal governments can change the practices of underperforming governmental actors along patterns of use that may not readily fit into common understandings and practices. However, they can be properly interpreted with analogy to other prescribed categories under the CWA. The ability of tribal governments to form strategic coalitions and pursue international venues in asserting their claims is an area of further consideration in developing effective responses to climate change. The expertise contained in many tribal management organizations fosters the development of new partnerships and highlights the sophistication of tribal governments and their responsiveness, further supporting a regulatory discourse that is inclusive and participatory and that provides meaningful process to all parties concerned. Moreover, it puts to rest the stereotype of American Indian environmental stewardship as depicted by Iron Eyes Cody and offers a more active and equitable institutional portrayal of effective tribal environmental and resource management.

Abbreviations Used in This Chapter

CAA	Clean Air Act
CWA	Clean Water Act
EJ	environmental justice
GLIFWC	Great Lakes Indian Fish and Wildlife Commission
IACHR	Inter-American Commission on Human Rights
ICC	Inuit Circumpolar Conference
NOAA	National Oceanic and Atmospheric Administration
NPDES	National Pollutant Discharge Elimination System
OAS	Organization of American States
SDWA	Safe Drinking Water Act
TAS	tribes as states
UNDRIP	United Nations Declaration on the Rights of Indigenous Peoples
US EPA	US Environmental Protection Agency

Notes

1. Iron Eyes Cody as told to C. Perry, *Iron Eyes, My Life as a Hollywood Indian* (New York: Everest House, 1982).

2. R. A. Williams, Jr., *Like a Loaded Weapon: The Rehnquist Court, Indian Rights and the Legal History of Racism in America* (Minneapolis: University of Minnesota Press, 2005): 8 and n.15.

3. L. M. Graham, Book Review: "The Racial Discourse of Federal Indian Law," 42 *Tulsa L. Rev.* 103 (2006): 104.

4. B. Berger, "Red: Racism and the American Indian," 56 *UCLA L. Rev.* 591 (2009): 595, citing US Comm'n on Civil Rights, *A Quiet Crisis: Federal Funding and Unmet Needs in Indian Country* (2003): 8, 34–35, 42, 67–69, 83–84.

5. S. J. Anaya, "The United States Supreme Court and Indigenous Peoples: Still a Long Way to Go Toward a Therapeutic Role," 24 *Seattle U. L. Rev.* 229 (2000): 235.

6. *Clean Water Act*, §§ 101–607, 33 U.S.C. §§ 1251–387 (2002).

7. 74 Fed. Reg. 40281 (2009).

8. D. H. Getches, C. F. Wilkinson, and R. A. Williams, Jr., *Cases and Materials on Federal Indian Law*, 5th ed. (St. Paul, MN: Thomson/West, 2005).

9. 526 U.S. 172 (1999).

10. 526 U.S. 172 (1999).

11. Ch. 120, 16 Stat. 566 (1871), 25 U.S.C. § 71 (1982).

12. F. S. Cohen, *Felix S. Cohen's Handbook of Federal Indian Law*, ed. R. Strickland (Charlottesville, VA: Bobbs-Merrill, 1982): 138.

13. S. J. Czerwinski, *Native American Housing—Homeownership Opportunities in Trust Lands Are Limited* (GAO Rep., Feb. 24, 1998).

14. 24 Stat. 388 (1887).

15. J. Royster, "The Legacy of Allotment," 27 *Ariz. St. L. J.* 1 (1995): 7.

16. Royster, "Allotment," 6.

17. Royster, "Allotment," 6.

18. 25 U.S.C. §§ 461–79 (1988).

19. 25 U.S.C. § 465 (1988).

20. American Indian Policy Review Commission, *Final Report* (1977): 309–10.

21. 532 U.S. 645 (2001).

22. C. F. Wilkinson, *American Indians, Time, and the Law* (1987): 3.

23. Wilkinson, *American Indians*.

24. U.S. Const., art. I, § 8, cl. 3.

25. U.S. Const., art. I, § 8, cl. 3.

26. Royster, "Allotment," 18.

27. C. F. Wilkinson and E. R. Biggs, "The Evolution of the Termination Policy," 5 *Am. Indian L. Rev.* 139 (1977): 151.

28. 25 U.S.C.S. §§ 891–901.

29. Pub. L. No. 83-280, 67 Stat. 588 (1953) (codified as amended at 18 U.S.C.S. § 1162 (1988)(criminal) and 28 U.S.C.S. § 1360 (1988)(civil)).

30. Pub. L. No. 83-280, 67 Stat. 588 (1953).

31. 391 U.S. 404 (1968).

32. Pub. L. No. 88-452, 78 Stat. 508 (codified as amended at 42 U.S.C.S. §§ 2991–94 (1994)).

33. *Special Message to the Congress on Indian Affairs*, Pub. Papers 564 (1970).

34. 25 U.S.C.S. §§ 450–58 (1994).

35. *Johnson and Graham's Lessee v. McIntosh*, 21 U.S. 543 (1823), *Cherokee Nation v. Georgia*, 30 U.S. 1 (1831), and *Worcester v. Georgia*, 31 U.S. 515 (1832).

36. 450 U.S. 544 (1981).

37. 450 U.S. 544 (1981).

38. 450 U.S. 544 (1981).

39. 520 U.S. 438 (1997).

40. 520 U.S. 438 (1997).

41. 520 U.S. 438 (1997): 456.

42. A. R. Riley, "(Tribal) Sovereignty and Illiberalism," 95 *Calif. L. Rev.* 799 (2007): 828.

43. D. B. Suagee, "Legal Structure and Sustainable Development: Tribal Self-Determination and Environmental Federalism: Cultural Values as a Force for Sustainability," 3 *Wid. L. Symp. J.* 229 (1998): 234.

44. R. Tsosie, "The Climate of Environmental Justice: Taking Stock: Indigenous People and Environmental Justice: The Impact of Climate Change," 78 *U. Colo. L. Rev.* 1625 (2007): 1674.

45. Suagee, "Legal Structure."

46. J. V. Royster, "Environmental Federalism and the Third Sovereign: Limits on State Authority to Regulate Water Quality in Indian Country," *Water Resources Update* (Autumn 1996): 17, available at http://www.ucowr.siu/edu/updates/pdf/V105_A4.pdf.

47. 42 U.S.C. § 4321.

48. US EPA, "EPA Policy Statement for the Administration of Environmental Programs on Indian Reservations" (Nov. 8, 1984) available at http://www.epa.gov/tp/pdf/indian-policy-84.pdf.

49. US EPA, "EPA Policy Statement," p. 2.

50. 42 U.S.C. § 7412.

51. 42 U.S.C. § 300f.

52. 16 U.S.C. § 470.

53. 42 U.S.C. § 9601.

54. 865 F. Supp. 733 (*Browner*).

55. 33 U.S.C. § 1342.

56. 33 U.S.C. § 1377(e).

57. 33 U.S.C. § 1251(a).

58. *Browner*, at 740.

59. S. Krakoff, "Tribal Sovereignty and Environmental Justice," in *Justice and Natural Resources: Concepts, Strategies, and Applications*, K. M. Mutz, G. Bryner, and D. Kenney, eds. (Island Press, 2002): 161.

60. D. Suagee, "Dimensions of Environmental Justice in Indian Country and Native Alaska, Second National People of Color Environmental Leadership Summit—Summit II," *Resource Paper Ser.* (October 23, 2002): 2.

61. M. C. Wood, "Protecting the Attributes of Native Sovereignty: A New Trust Paradigm for Federal Actions Affecting Tribal Lands and Resources," 1 *Utah L. Rev.* 109 (1995): 148.

62. Declaration on the Rights of Indigenous Peoples, G.A. Res. 61/255, U.N. Doc. A/RES/47/1 (Sept. 12, 2007).

63. Declaration on the Rights of Indigenous Peoples.

64. Declaration on the Rights of Indigenous Peoples.

65. *Native Village of Kivalina and City of Kivalina v. ExxonMobil Corp., et al.* (case C 08-1138 SBA).

66. *Native Village of Kivalina and City of Kivalina v. ExxonMobil Corp., et al.*

67. Submitted by S. Watt-Cloutier, "Petition to the Inter-American Commission on Human Rights Seeking Relief from Violations Resulting from Global Warming Caused by Acts and Omissions of the United States, with the Support of the Inuit Circumpolar Conference," *ICC Petition* (December 7, 2005).

68. Letter from Ariel E. Dulitzky, Assistant Executive Sec'y, Organization of American States, to Paul Crowley, Legal Rep. (Nov. 16, 2006), available at http://graphics8.nytimes.com/packages/pdf/science/16commissionletter.pdf (on file with the author).

69. S. Watt-Cloutier, "Petition."

70. Letter from Dulitzky.

71. "The Anchorage Declaration, 24 April 2009," in *Report of the Indigenous Peoples' Global Summit on Climate Change*, available at http://www.indigenoussummit.com/servlet/content/home.html.

72. J. Hopkins, "The Struggle for Uniformity: the UN Declaration and Beyond," 9 *Geo. J. Int'l. Aff.* 75 (2008).

73. *The Mayagna (Sumo) Indigenous Community of Awas Tingni*, Inter-Am. Ct. H.R. (Ser. C) No. 79 (August 31, 2001), reprinted in 19 *Ariz. J. Int'l Comp. L.* 395 (2002).

74. *Awas Tingni* (2001). See Suagee, "Dimensions of Environmental Justice."

75. Testimony by Eric J. Brown, Director of the National Center for Atmospheric Research, Chair of the Climate Services Coordination Committee, Climate Working Group of the NOAA Science Advisory Board, for a hearing titled "Expanding Climate Services at the National Oceanic and Atmospheric Administration (NOAA): Developing the National Climate Service," Subcommittee on Energy and Environment, Committee on Science and Technology US House of Representatives (May 5, 2009).

76. University Corporation for Atmospheric Research, Office of Governmental Affairs, "Washington Update: Climate Adaptation Activities at the Department of Interior," News Release (February 12, 2010).

77. Great Lakes Indian Fish and Wildlife Commission, "Lake Superior Trout Restoration Proclaimed a Major Victory: Stocking Put on Hold in Some Areas to Foster Self-Sustainable Lake Trout Populations," Lake Superior News Release (April 8, 1996).

78. Press Conference by Special Rapporteur on Indigenous Rights (October 19, 2009), available at http://www.un.org/News/briefings/docs/2009/091019_Indigenous.doc.htm.

79. Letter from the Chargé d'affaires a.i. of the Permanent Mission of the Plurinational State of Bolivia to the United Nations addressed to the Secretary-General (January 12, 2010), available at http://www.un.org/esa/socdev/unpfii/documents/N1021114.pdf.

Incorporating Rights of Indigenous Peoples in Climate-Change Initiatives

S. James Anaya

Addressing climate change necessitates a major undertaking on the part of governments concerned with advancing human rights conditions and taking positive steps to improve those conditions for indigenous peoples worldwide. With an estimated population of 370 million worldwide, indigenous peoples are situated in some of the locations most vulnerable to the impacts and consequences of climate change, particularly in terms of biodiversity, the environment, and the livelihoods of indigenous communities.[1]

Governments engaging in reform initiatives meant to mitigate or adapt to climate change should view the process as an opportunity to identify and promote best practices at the domestic level that are consistent with international human rights standards and, in doing so, turn their attention to the standards addressed in the United Nations Declaration on the Rights of Indigenous Peoples (UNDRIP).

A common problem facing indigenous peoples throughout the world is that states (i.e., nation-states) often fail to adequately consult with indigenous peoples on decisions that affect them. UNDRIP emphasizes the duty of states to consult with indigenous peoples in the context of legislative reforms that touch upon indigenous subject matter and in the context of natural resources development. The pursuit of effective and meaningful consultation with indigenous peoples is grounded in core UN–based human rights treaties and should not be viewed as a barrier to development or to achieving consensus when addressing the complexities of climate-change adaptation and mitigation.

Climate-change policy can be developed and implemented in a manner that is consistent with a state's obligation to protect and preserve the rights of indigenous communities and indigenous peoples. Consultation, from this perspective, can be viewed as a mechanism for institutional adaptation through a process that seeks to incorporate and act upon the input of indigenous communities. Given the proximity of many indigenous communities to vulnerable environments, along with the common occurrence of resource extraction in these same areas, consultation with indigenous groups is needed in order to create buy-in and offers governments a measurable standard of success when implementing new laws and policies.

The standards required under UNDRIP are significant given the context of climate change and the environment overall. For example, where a resource development project results in the relocation of an indigenous group, UNDRIP requires that the state obtain prior consent from the indigenous community. In the same vein, storage or disposal of toxic waste within indigenous lands requires prior consent.

The principle of consultation is designed to build dialogue through which the parties can work in good faith toward consensus and also ensure the legitimacy of the decision-making process as reflecting all the parties concerned.

The mechanisms envisioned by UNDRIP should give rise to new institutional frameworks that reflect a long-term dialogue between states and indigenous communities with an emphasis on cooperative partnerships that can mitigate the contributing factors associated with climate change and, at the same time, protect, promote, and advance the rights of indigenous peoples.

States will need to commit adequate human and financial resources to achieve these objectives. In doing so, they will generate a measure of reconciliation—a realization of historic justice—from within the process itself. This process includes an emphasis on training and working nationally and locally to bring together state agencies and indigenous leaders to strategize and initiate implementation of policies to address climate-change causes and impacts in the spirit of reconciliation that UNDRIP represents.

Note

1. The content of this spotlight is based on J. Anaya, "Promotion and Protection from All Human Rights, Civil, Political, Economic, Social and Cultural Rights, including the Right of Development: Report of the Special Rapporteur on the Situation of Human Rights and Fundamental Freedoms of Indigenous Peoples, James Anaya" (July 15, 2009), A/HRC/12/34, available at http://daccess-dds-ny.un.org/doc/UNDOC/GEN/G09/145/82/PDF/G0914582.pdf?OpenElement.

Chapter 4

Collaborative Public Management and Climate Change

Kirk Emerson

In Brief

- Collaborative public management is particularly useful in addressing such problems as climate change that a single agency or organization cannot adequately address on its own.

- Collaborative public management within a federal system involves bringing together many actors with differing views on the nature of climate-change problems and possible solutions and having them share information, invest in problem-solving capacity, and jointly deliver services or pursue other shared courses of action.

- For collaboration to persist and succeed, the benefits of cooperation must exceed the costs of participation.

- The benefits of collaborative public management vary. In highly conflictual situations, collaboration supports conflict resolution, the building of social capital, and policy compliance. In situations of significant scientific uncertainty or ambiguous policies, collaboration supports learning and risk sharing.

As many of the authors in this book have suggested, the significant dimensions of global climate change and corresponding policy measures may lend themselves to a different kind of federalism—one that is less categorical or unidirectional and more multifaceted and collaborative (see Schapiro, chapter 2; Resnik, Civin, and Frueh, chapter 6; Adelman and Engel, chapter 8; Doremus and Hanemann, chapter 9; and Rabe, chapter 11). This new form of multilevel collaborative governance could "[build] on the respective strengths of both state and federal governments and [engage] in active policy learning across governmental levels" (Rabe, chapter 11).

Exploring polyphonic or collaborative federalism raises important practical questions beyond the doctrinal questions of presumption and sovereignty under traditional federalism discourse. How do we effectively manage policies that work across federal and state jurisdictions? How do we communicate and share resources, let alone authorities? How do we make decisions when legal power may be ambiguous and political power dispersed? How do we resolve conflicts if there is no single, final authority? How do we incentivize action, enforce compliance, and sanction laggards without a hierarchy of legal power and authority? And finally, how do we assure that our combined greenhouse-gas emission reductions actually meet our agreed upon targets?

The practice of collaborative public management, an emerging form of cross-jurisdictional and cross-sector management, responds to some of these questions and may prove useful in implementing many climate-change policies in the context of multilevel, collaborative federalism. As such, collaborative public management among federal and state agencies and authorities warrants careful scrutiny, targeted improvements and considerably more support. This chapter highlights key management challenges posed by climate change and collaborative federalism, describes collaborative public management and its potential for addressing these challenges, discusses specific opportunities for which collaborative management could be useful, and raises concerns that must be addressed if collaborative management is to be an effective approach to implementing climate-change policies in the future.

The Challenge of Managing Climate Change

Climate change, along with the complexity of associated global interdependencies, has been referred to variously as the ultimate global commons challenge and the ultimate collective action problem. It is also the ultimate "wicked" policy dilemma—a dilemma for which solutions are uncertain, over which there is disagreement on the best approaches, and that exceeds the boundaries and abilities of one jurisdiction or authority to resolve.[1]

While the vast majority of scientists around the world are convinced of the severity of projected climate change and volatility, considerable uncertainty remains about when, where, and to what extent climate-change impacts will be felt and efforts at mitigation will take effect, particularly at local and regional scales. Despite enormous strides in climate science and related fields, we will need continued knowledge generation, translation, and dissemination to compel and inform public and private action to mitigate and adapt to global warming and its impacts.

We will also need a corresponding level of policy generation, experimentation, and recalibration. Lacking one "silver policy bullet," a portfolio of policy strategies and instruments working on many different fronts and at different scales is needed. This volume demonstrates the extent to which many states have already been developing their climate-change policy portfolios. While the federal government will follow suit eventually, it is unlikely to claim a monopoly on all climate policy initiatives, and its own success will depend not simply on the regulatory compliance of states, but on their willing and active cooperation.

Most policy experts acknowledge the massive complexity of shifting away from our carbon-based economy and the resulting challenges of stimulating, coordinating, and accounting for effective policy responses. All sectors of the economy are implicated,[2] and technological innovation will need to be stimulated at the state and federal levels (see Adelman and Engel, chapter 8). We have shifted our economies in the past—from whale oil to petroleum, from horse and buggy to automobile, from lamp light to rural electrification, and from land lines to cell phones. Today's challenge is how to accelerate the shift from an oil economy to a sustainable economy, and from a consumer society to conserving communities, in time and at a sufficient scale to bend the global warming trajectory.

The enormous costs of such shifts, in the midst of the current worldwide economic downturn, make the prospects of ambitious climate-change policies particularly daunting. Further, conflicts over who should bear those costs and how they should be distributed will be matched by future competition for increasingly scarce energy and water resources. Climate-change policy is presently fraught with conflict, which will undoubtedly be exacerbated by the disproportionate weight of climate-change impacts expected to fall on the most vulnerable populations. Domestic conflicts within the United States will likely be overshadowed by international tensions and disproportionate effects of climate change on less developed and therefore more vulnerable countries, particularly in the southern hemisphere. The impacts on water supplies and agricultural productivity, as well as coastal communities, "could easily contribute to social tensions, violent conflicts, humanitarian emergencies, and the creation of ecological refugees."[3]

The complexity and interdependence of these climate-change–related challenges transcend the capacity of any state or federal governmental unit acting on its own authority. In the United States, the key question, following Robert A. Schapiro's theory of polyphonic federalism, then becomes "how the states and the national government can best exercise their overlapping powers so as to advance policy goals" (chapter 2). Exercising their collective authorities, how can these different governmental units effectively manage the challenges of climate change together?

The Practice of Collaborative Public Management

Daniel A. Farber (chapter 10) reminds us that our current national environmental policy directs all levels of government to work together toward sustainable environmental conditions. Environmental policy has been one of the primary seedbeds for the evolving practice of collaborative public management in the twentieth century. As models of federalism began to shift, so did management approaches. With the Clean Air Act came cooperative federalism and improvements in intergovernmental relations. With subsequent requirements for environmental cleanup and restoration came federal, state, and local partnerships and collaboration in forest restoration, habitat conservation planning, and "brownfields" cleanup and redevelopment.

At its most basic, collaborative public management (hereinafter referred to as collaborative management) "is a concept that describes the process of facilitating and operating in multiorganizational arrangements to solve problems that cannot be solved, or solved easily, by single organizations. Collaboration means to co-labor, to achieve common goals, often working across boundaries and in multi-sector and multi-actor relationships."[4] By definition, collaborative management operates within a complex environment of multiple authorities in various interagency, intergovernmental, or cross-sector relationships. These relationships function as networks of interactions maintained through formal and informal, direct and electronic communications. Collaborative management occurs in a broad range of policy arenas, including social service delivery; local economic development, crisis planning, and contracting; environmental protection and natural resources management; forest management; and open spaces preservation. It has been put to use in organizations such as law enforcement agencies, the Veterans Health Administration, and the Department of Homeland Security.[5]

The practice of collaborative management initially developed in reaction to top-down hierarchical management regimes of command and control. However, as Michael McGuire cautions, collaborative management should not be juxtaposed as an independent substitute for top-down, hierarchical administration.[6] Rather, the multiactor, multijurisdictional, complex policy environment requires better coordination and integration of the numerous authorities and structures—top-down, bottom-up, and across. Lisa Blomgren Bingham, Rosemary O'Leary, and Carl Carlson refer to this model as "lateral public management" and connect it to more responsive, participatory forms of collaborative governance that include private stakeholder engagement and public deliberation.[7]

Over the past twenty years, collaborative management practice has evolved through experience and scholarship in intergovernmental cooperation, network management, and conflict management.[8] Today, the primary operating principle behind collaborative management is reciprocity, which helps cultivate sufficient exchange value, shared capacity, and legitimacy to get work done. While this does not deny the legal or political reality of power relations, collaborative management operates in the face of multiple sources of power and within the necessary limits of substantive and administrative laws. While the practice of collaborative management often relies on voluntary engagement across lines of authority, collaborative management can also be induced and incentivized. Transparent rules of exchange, open access to information, fair and equitable treatment, consensual decision-making rules, and shared norms of communication are among the best practice dimensions of collaborative management.[9]

Those who study collaborative management note specific benefits that can derive from its use in complex, cross-institutional settings, including improved coordination of activities, leveraging and pooling of resources, increased social capital, conflict management (prevention, reduction, and resolution), knowledge management (its generation, translation, and diffusion), shared risk in policy experimentation, and increased policy compliance.[10] Which of these benefits accrue depends in part on the primary functions of the collaborative management system, sometimes referred to as networks. Robert Agranoff identifies four collaborative network types by their function: *informational networks* share information and explore possible solutions and policy options; *developmental networks* include information exchange and education for its members, who implement actions within their own organizations; *outreach networks* also deliver programmatic strategies or capacity-building tools to members; and in *action networks* members work together and jointly pursue a shared course of action or the shared delivery of services.[11] H. Brinton Milward and Keith G. Provan distinguish similar network functions of service implementation, information diffusion, problem solving, and community capacity building among public, nonprofit, and for-profit organizations.[12]

Table 4.1. Collaborative Management by Function, Structure, and Process

Functions	Structures	Process mechanisms
Information diffusion *Example:* Environmental Council of the States, Climate and Energy Subcommittee	Informal networks, joint research and education projects	Networking technologies (shared databases, Web-based meeting spaces, Web sites, editing tools), conferences
Policy development and problem solving *Example:* Midwestern Greenhouse Gas Reduction Accord	Advisory committees, reciprocity arrangements, coalitions	Policy dialogues and deliberative forums, joint fact-finding, visioning
Outreach/capacity building *Example:* US Conference of Mayors Climate Protection Agreement	Alliances, campaigns, coalitions	Public education, consensus building, conflict resolution
Action/service provision *Example:* Climate Action Registry	Memoranda of understanding, administrative agreements, joint ventures, compacts, partnerships	Collaborative planning and monitoring, adaptive management

Based on H.B. Milward and K.G. Provan, *A Manager's Guide to Choosing and Using Collaborative Networks* (Washington, DC: IBM Center for the Business of Government, 2006).

Table 4.1 summarizes some of the structures (institutional arrangements) and process mechanisms frequently employed for a range of collaborative management network functions, following Agranoff and Milward and Provan. This framework is useful for describing collaborative management at work more broadly in the climate-change policy arena.

Information Diffusion

At the most basic functional level of information diffusion, any number of groups and committees network across institutions and jurisdictions to provide access to climate-change research, policy, and best practices through conferences, webinars, and Web site information portals. In some cases, these information-diffusion initiatives are embedded in larger networks, such as the Environmental Council of the States (ECOS), a national association of state and territorial environmental agency leaders. ECOS's Air Committee has a Climate and Energy Subcommittee that meets twice a year to exchange information and best management practices, discuss shared concerns and vet possible solutions, track federal activity, and consider needed outreach.[13]

Policy Development/Problem Solving

The most prominent climate-change policy development networks are regional interstate collaborations: the Regional Greenhouse Gas Initiative, the Western Climate Initiative, and the Midwestern Greenhouse Gas Reduction Accord.[14] Such policy development networks often begin as informal coalitions and lead to formal executive commitments, new institutional arrangements including working groups and advisory committees, and finally state-enabling legislation. For example, after considerable policy discussion and public dialogue, the Midwestern Greenhouse Gas Reduction Accord was signed by nine midwestern governors and two Canadian premiers in November 2007. They agreed to establish a midwestern greenhouse-gas reduction program, reduce emissions in their states, and set up a working group to recommend implementation measures for a regional cap-and-trade program suited to the economies and resources of the Midwest. The working group represents diverse sectors—business, labor, agriculture, energy, environmental advocacy groups, and academia—and collaboratively manages its tasks through agreed-upon design principles and procedural ground rules.[15]

Outreach/Capacity Building

The US Conference of Mayors Climate Protection Agreement illustrates a growing outreach and capacity-building network. Initiated by Seattle Mayor Greg Nickels after the February 2005 signing of the Kyoto Protocol, the agreement commits mayors to work toward reducing their cities' emissions to 7 percent below 1990 levels by 2012 and to pressure their states, the federal government, and Congress to adopt climate-change policies consistent with the Kyoto Protocol. The US Conference of Mayors formally endorsed the agreement in 2005 and set up the Mayors Climate Protection Center two years later to enlarge the network and "equip all cities with the knowledge and tools that ultimately will have the greatest impact" on reducing global warming.[16] The center facilitates information exchange, conducts surveys, and issues reports and awards for best practices of large and small municipalities to reduce emissions and conserve energy. As of December 2009, 1,016 mayors had signed on to the agreement across the fifty states, the District of Columbia, and Puerto Rico.[17]

Action/Service Provision

The Climate Registry exemplifies a service network of corporate, nonprofit, and governmental partners. It is a "nonprofit collaboration among North American states, provinces, territories and Native Sovereign Nations that sets consistent and transparent standards to calculate, verify and publicly report greenhouse-gas emissions into a single registry."[18] It grew out of state legislative action that created the California Climate Action Registry and now links with other state-sponsored reporting efforts, such as the Eastern Climate Registry. Described as a "bottom-up approach to emissions accounting," the Climate Registry provides for collaborative development of new and modified accounting protocols through stakeholder engagement and public input processes.

As these examples illustrate, the practice of collaborative management varies considerably by function.

The Implementation of Federal–State Climate-Change Policy

Collaborative management may well be a broadly useful management approach to climate change, but where specifically might it facilitate the federal and state governments to work together to mitigate and manage the impacts of climate change? One place to start is with some of the findings from research on policy implementation. First, we have learned not to rely exclusively on centralized policy direction without taking into account the context, capacities, and contributions of managers engaged in implementation and stakeholders affected by the policy. Implementation occurs as "a continuum located between central guidance and local autonomy."[19] Collaborative management may be useful across this continuum, given its emphasis on engaging public and private interests that can influence policy development and implementation.

Second, we have learned that policy implementation begins with policy formulation and evolves over time with "policy learning" by multiple actors working through complex public and private policy networks.[20]

Collaborative management explicitly recognizes and builds on such networks, enabling the generation and diffusion of knowledge, policy innovation, feedback, and adaptation.

Third, the level of conflict around policy goals can affect implementation; building consensus can be instrumental to effective implementation.[21] Collaborative management works to anticipate and manage differences and forge agreement and buy-in among parties, interest groups, and institutions. As the policy context shifts and evolves, the preferred implementation strategy may change as well. Policy conflict and ambiguity around policy goals and instruments are dimensions particularly useful to consider when designing policy and charting implementation strategies.[22]

Table 4.2 is a matrix of four different policy contexts based on different levels of policy conflict and ambiguity. Each quadrant presents likely implementation strategies based on the major policy driver in that context. For example, in the upper left quadrant where conflict over a given policy is low and the policy goals and chosen instruments are clear and straightforward, administrative implementation makes sense and is determined primarily by the level of resources available to spend on implementation. Where conflict is high, yet the proposed policy prescription is unambiguous, as in the upper right quadrant, then power relations among the policy advocates are likely to determine political implementation. Where there is little policy conflict, yet the policy goals or effective instruments are unknown or uncertain, as in the lower left quadrant, then contextual factors become salient and conducive to more experimental implementation methods. Finally, where conflict and ambiguity are both high, implementation tends to be more symbolic and differentiated at the local level where strong coalitions will play out their influence. The implications of each of these four scenarios for federal and state action on climate change are described in more detail below. In each of these four contexts, collaborative management may bring different value to policy implementation (shown as "CM value").

Low Conflict, Low Ambiguity

In the context of low policy conflict and low ambiguity, collaborative management may enhance the early stages of administrative implementation through information diffusion, coordination, and resource leverage. The Climate Registry fits this scenario. As the registry's infrastructure for tracking and auditing incentives is refined through cumulative use and gradual

Table 4.2. Context and Value of Collaborative Management (CM) for Climate-Change Policy Implementation

Policy ambiguity	Policy conflict	
	Low	High
Low	**Administrative implementation** *Major driver:* resources *CM value:* diffusion/coordination and resource leverage *Examples:* standardization for green building codes or emission registry, incentives to modernize grid	**Political implementation** *Major driver:* power *CM value:* compliance *Examples:* permitting of coal-bed methane production wells, cross-boundary infrastructure planning
High	**Experimental implementation** *Major driver:* contextual conditions *CM value:* knowledge management and shared risk *Examples:* comanagement, adaptive management and collaborative monitoring, joint facilities planning	**Symbolic implementation** *Major driver:* coalition strength *CM value:* social capital formation and conflict management *Examples:* climate-change action plans, negotiated use permits on public lands

Based on R.E. Matland, "Synthesizing the Implementation Literature: The Ambiguity-Conflict Model of Policy Implementation." *Journal of Public Administration Research and Theory* 5(2) (1995): 29.

adoption by states, federal adoption becomes increasingly likely. The initial voluntary and collaborative nature of the registry will give way to more bureaucratic and standardized, if not mandated, implementation, through which coordination will become routine over time.

Another low-conflict, low-ambiguity example is the proposed provision within leading federal climate-change bills for the US Department of Energy (DOE) to assert new authority to ensure that all states adopt energy efficiency standards for new buildings.[23] Collaborative management might be helpful to the states and DOE as they negotiate minimum or enhanced energy standards and as states negotiate with local municipalities over new building code requirements. Implementation of this policy would require coordination among local governments to adopt and enforce consistent local building codes and develop a compliance system for state and DOE certification. Once such a policy is in place, however, collaborative management may not add significant value.

High Conflict, Low Ambiguity

Collaborative management may be less likely to contribute where high policy conflict and low policy ambiguity exist. This is the context for federal and state policy decisions concerning the permitting of controversial energy production, such as coal-bed methane wells or offshore oil drilling, where the relative costs and benefits are unambiguous. Here, the driver of conflict is most often the exercise of power through the political process. Collaborative engagement to mitigate impacts, such as occurs through collaborative National Environmental Policy Act (NEPA) review processes, would be useful, but the level of disagreement over the policy aims and effects makes cooperation difficult.

Another example is permitting for interstate energy infrastructure. Siting interstate energy transmission lines, for example, to connect to dispersed renewable energy sources, generates considerable conflict within and among states and federal land management agencies. Section 216 of the US National Energy Act of 2005 provided the Federal Energy Regulatory Commission (FERC) with "backstop" permitting authority to incentivize states to resolve these conflicts in a more timely manner.[24] The powerful threat of imminent FERC action could enable states, applicants, other federal agencies, and stakeholders to collaborate more effectively over such siting decisions. Recent litigation over Section 216 of the Act, however, has led some congressional leaders to propose stronger preemptive siting authority for FERC, such as the commission already has for gas pipelines, liquefied natural gas facilities, and hydroelectric facilities.[25]

High Ambiguity, Low Conflict

Collaborative management may contribute most significantly to climate-change policy implementation when the impacts or effectiveness of policy interventions are less well known or less certain, as presented in the lower half of table 4.2. This ambiguity may be the result of incomplete or contested science, untested policy options, or significant differences in local or regional factors that are not easily handled in a one-size-fits-all national policy approach. Knowledge management becomes key under these conditions.[26]

Comanagement and adaptive management strategies for natural resources have developed partly in response to these kinds of complex, uncertain conditions. These strategies aim to integrate evolving science into more flexible, experimental management regimes.[27] Comanagement has focused on the institutional partnerships and power-sharing arrangements between communities, resource users, nongovernmental organizations, and government agencies, while adaptive management has focused on the role of scientific and institutional learning and experimentation needed to adapt to changing or uncertain complex resource systems.[28] Both interrelated management arenas are at the forefront of the study of adaptation to climate-change impacts through social and ecological resilience and sustainable development.[29]

The collaborative management and monitoring of forest restoration illustrate this scenario where place-based approaches and changing conditions require more flexibility and experimentation.[30] Climate change is affecting our forests, particularly in the American West, through increased temperatures, drought, and related insect infestations and greater incidence and intensities of wildfire. In 2000, the US Congress authorized and funded the Collaborative Forest Restoration Program (CFRP) as a pilot implementation area to provide cost-share grants to stakeholders promoting forest restoration projects on federal, tribal, state, county, or municipal forest lands in New Mexico. Proposed restoration activities varied considerably according to geographic and ecological conditions as well as community demographics. CFRP specifically required restoration projects and multiparty monitoring to "include a diverse and balanced group of stakeholders in their design and implementation."[31] Based in large part on the success of CFRP, in 2009 Congress established the Collaborative Forest Landscape Restoration (CFLR) Program "to encourage the collaborative, science-based ecosystem restoration of priority forest landscapes" across the National Forest System.[32] CFLR will fund up to $40 million a year in collaborative restoration and monitoring projects, where eligibility depends on collaboration of federal, state, local, and tribal governments.

> Oregon's Lakeview Biomass Project illustrates collaborative, risk-sharing mitigation in action. For more on this, see "The Lakeview Biomass Project: Sharing the Risk" on page 95.

Another contribution that collaborative management can provide under this experimental implementation arena is in the sharing of risk when investing in innovative policies, such as alternative energy facilities. Collaborative solutions and joint implementation can spread risk and improve project accountability, for example, with the Lakeview Biomass Project (see Emerson spotlight, p. 95).

High Ambiguity, High Conflict

Finally, under conditions where policy conflict and ambiguity are both high, the likelihood of executing assertive federal mandates is low and symbolic implementation more probable. This might well be the current situation facing national cap-and-trade legislation. Here, one of the contributions collaborative management can offer is in building social capital through the myriad climate action planning processes occurring at the local and state government levels, some of which include or implicate federal resources and authorities. At last count, the Pew Center on Global Climate Change had inventoried thirty-six states as having some form of climate action plan in place or in progress.[33] Most of these planning efforts are guided by representatives from the public and private sectors throughout the state, such as members of blue-ribbon commissions, advisory committees, or technical working groups. These collaborative efforts are primarily geared toward reaching consensus on general goals, in some cases emission targets, and prioritizing areas for future study, investment, and action. These might be considered initially as symbolic initiatives only, influenced by the power of coalitions within the states. Or they might be viewed as formative starting points or frameworks to guide future commitments—the best that can be accomplished under these conditions as policy is just being developed. Collaborative management can be helpful in fostering shared learning and building mutual trust while forming the basis for future action-oriented alliances.

Extending beyond symbolic implementation, however, when conflict and ambiguity in this quadrant are moving toward administrative or judicial adjudication, collaborative management can also be called on to reengage parties to try to work through impasse and negotiate mutually beneficial outcomes. Increasingly, administrative tribunals, such as the US Department of Interior's Board of Land Appeals, and federal district courts refer or direct parties to mediation and other forms of environmental conflict resolution. Sometimes this leads to improved working relationships and arrangements for future ongoing cooperation.[34] Among the projects of the US Institute for Environmental Conflict Resolution of the Morris K. Udall and Stewart L. Udall Foundation are numerous such cases, in particular involving federal and state land managers and other parties over resource management decisions, such as habitat conservation plans, timber sales, public access, special use permits, and off-road vehicle use.[35]

A useful illustration of the use of conflict resolution occurred in the aftermath of a 2007 decision by the Fishlake National Forest to reauthorize eight grazing allotments in the Tushar Mountains in southwest Utah. Seven conservation organizations appealed the final Record of Decision on an environmental impact statement decision. An alternative collaborative management strategy proposed by the Utah Farm Bureau and the Grand Canyon Trust brought the federal and state agencies, the permittees, scientists, and other stakeholders to the table. The group conducted joint fact-finding and reached consensus on recommendations for future management practices, including ongoing collaborative scientific investigations, joint monitoring, and oversight meetings of the parties. A Resolution Agreement was signed in the spring of 2009 and the appeal withdrawn.[36]

Drawing on table 4.2, depending on the contexts, collaborative management may be more or less useful in fostering intergovernmental cooperation for mitigation and adaptation to climate change. Collaborative management will not resolve the ongoing debate over the right balance between federal and state authority and autonomy; however, it may be a valuable instrument for making progress on the imperatives of climate change under certain conditions.

Future Challenges and Recommendations

Collaborative management poses several challenges to policy makers and public managers. According to John Bryson and Barbara Crosby, "Cross sector collaborations are difficult to create and even more difficult to sustain because so much has to be in place or work well for them to succeed."[37] Collaborative management is designed to respond to opportunities and difficulties that a single agency or organization cannot adequately address on its own. However, collaborative management is not cost free. Dedicated leadership and resources are necessary to build and maintain these shared collaborative frameworks. The value added from shared functions must exceed the energy expended. When the interdependencies or other incentives for collective action are absent, or once joint missions are indeed accomplished, then the overhead costs of collaboration may no longer be justified.

Among the many political, legal, and institutional challenges posed by collaborative management, two in particular warrant attention in the context of federal–state cooperation over climate-change policies. The first addresses the issue of authorities to collaborate, and the second addresses issues of accountability and performance.

Legal Authorities for Collaborative Management

As previously discussed, collaborative management among federal and state governments can occur through informal channels and voluntary networks. However, if it is to assist in experimental implementation or conflict management, where it likely will be most useful with respect to climate change, certain legal authorities will be needed. Several federal laws authorize federal agencies and personnel to collaborate with states and local governments and with representative stakeholders and the public at large:

- Administrative Procedures Act of 1946[38]
- Freedom of Information Act of 1966[39]
- Federal Advisory Committee Act of 1972[40]
- Administrative Dispute Resolution Act of 1990, as amended in 1996[41]
- Regulatory Negotiation Act of 1996[42]
- Alternative Dispute Resolution Act of 1998[43]
- Environmental Policy and Conflict Resolution Act of 1998, as amended in 2003[44]

Several recent federal executive policy directives also support collaborative management in the environmental policy arena and more broadly, including Executive Order 13352, "Facilitation of Cooperative Conservation" (August 4, 2004);[45] Office of Management and Budget and President's Council on Environmental Quality, "Memorandum on Environmental Conflict Resolution and Collaborative Problem Solving" (November 28, 2005);[46] and Presidential Memorandum, "Transparency and Open Government" (January 21, 2009).[47]

In addition, numerous other procedural guarantees and guidelines embedded in specific substantive laws, judicial interpretation, and administration regulation inform intergovernmental cooperation. NEPA, for example, provides for public notice and comment and encourages public input and involvement throughout the environmental review process.[48] NEPA guidance and guidelines issued by the President's Council on Environmental Quality provide for and encourage cooperation among federal agencies, states, and tribes.[49] Other chapters in this book look more closely at some of these legal authorities.

Unfortunately, these legal authorities and policy directives and guidance are not widely known or fully employed. Whether the general practice of collaborative management requires more explicit authority is currently being debated internally at the Office of Management and Budget as staff works on President Obama's directive to assure more open and transparent government.[50] Some argue that numerous authorities already exist and the barriers to collaboration lie elsewhere. Bingham and others suggest a new legal framework is needed to answer key questions:

- Delegation: How can agency staff fully participate in collaborative networks in a way that addresses the legal concern that they might be delegating their legislatively granted authority to act or make decisions to others?

- Authorization to collaborate and the Freedom of Information Act: How do we ensure that collaborative management activities address the need for transparency in government?

- Authorization to involve the public in collaborative public management: How do we foster broader public engagement that extends beyond public comment and input processes?

- Accountability: How do we ensure that collaborative management is accountable to public agency authorities and to the public interest at large?[51]

Fostering collaborative management at the federal and state levels will likely require more than clarifying authorities. Incentives such as leadership directives and personnel policies will be needed, as well as adequate resources to encourage agency executives and senior managers to initiate collaborative intergovernmental action. Nonetheless, this must start by ensuring the legal framework is in place and being used appropriately.

Accountability and Performance

Accountability for individuals and agencies is a central concept in public administration and a rather straightforward one in a hierarchical bureaucratic structure. Lines of authority, roles, and responsibilities are clear, standardized, usually unidirectional, and easily scalable. Accountability becomes more complicated in the context of collaborative management. Many agencies, not one, share responsibility for success or failure. Public managers, while still accountable to the public, must serve their own agency's mission and take on shared responsibility for collaborative outcomes. As Donald Kettl points out, "It is hard to use vertical structures to hold individuals accountable when they are working in increasingly horizontal partnerships."[52] Serving many masters requires explicit and forthright communication and deliberation about individual and shared requirements and responsibilities. Suppressing those obligations or interests jeopardizes the building of shared trust and social capital discussed above.

Internal and external transparency are essential in large part because of these accountability demands. Explicit norms, ground rules, charters, and memoranda of understanding clarifying individual and joint responsibilities and decision-making roles not only streamline collaborative processes but also function to produce accountability. Over time, collaborative structures become institutionalized and accountability issues become more stable and embodied in instruments of incorporation, commissions, and formal authorities. Scholars of common-pool resources have focused at length on the development, use, and enforcement of rules and organizational structures for collaborative resource management.[53]

Accountability is not only *to* someone but *for* something. And in the context of climate-change mitigation, collaborative management must be accountable for its performance in meeting greenhouse-gas emission-reduction targets. The imperative for climate-change mitigation requires us to invest public resources in what works. This requires us to make, chart, and reward progress. "An accountable collaborative . . . needs a measurement system to document its results and how those results change over time. It also needs a 'managing for results' system that links the data it measures to specific actors and interventions, to provide critical performance information to its stakeholders, and that uses the information to improve its operations."[54]

More attention will need to be placed on these performance metrics and how to track them through cross-sector collaboration. Collaboration scholarship to date has focused primarily on describing or prescribing collaborative processes or structures. Performance has been measured most often as process outputs (e.g., public meetings held, attendance at workshops) and interim outcomes (e.g., agreements reached, working relationships improved) rather than substantive and longer term performance outcomes and impacts (e.g., improved environmental quality or resource condition, implementation of recommended actions, emission standards met or exceeded).[55] While several conceptual and methodological challenges make this difficult, collaborative management must be held accountable for its performance and develop more effective evaluation tools to measure progress and success.

Conclusion

The imperative of climate change calls for action across all levels of government and throughout the private sector. As we explore the limits and possibilities within the US federal system for effective responses to climate change, it behooves us to learn more about how to manage across jurisdictional and sectoral boundaries. These management challenges are compounded by the complexity and uncertainty of future climate conditions. Collaborative public management, drawing on intergovernmental relations, network management, and conflict management, offers useful approaches and lessons for operating in complex, cross-boundary settings.

Collaborative public management takes many forms and employs diverse processes depending on the tasks at hand, be they information diffusion, policy development, outreach and capacity building, or direct action or service provision. The value that collaborative public management can bring to climate-change policy implementation may vary, depending on the extent to which there is policy conflict and ambiguity. Attention to the challenges of legal authorities and accountability and performance will strengthen the contribution that collaborative management can make to effective policy responses to climate change.

Notes

1. H. Rittel and M. Webber, "Dilemmas in a General Theory of Planning." *Policy Sciences* 4(2) (1973): 14.

2. T. R. Karl, J. M. Melillo, and T. C. Peterson, eds., *Global Climate Change Impacts in the United States* (Cambridge: Cambridge University Press, 2009).

3. J. G. Speth, *Red Sky at Morning* (New Haven, CT: Yale University Press, 2004).

4. A. Agranoff and M. McGuire, *Collaborative Public Management* (Washington, DC: Georgetown University Press, 2003): 4.

5. K. G. Provan and H. B. Milward, "A Preliminary Theory of Interorganizational Effectiveness: A Comparative Study of Four Community Mental Health Systems." *Administrative Science Quarterly* 40(1) (1995): 33; A. Ebrahim, "Institutional Preconditions to Collaboration: Indian Forest and Irrigation Policy in Historical Perspective." *Administration and Society* 36 (2004): 34; S. Nicholson-Crotty and L. O'Toole, "Public Management and Organizational Performance: The Case of Law Enforcement Agencies." *Journal of Public Administration Research and Theory* 14(1) (2004): 18; R. F. Durant, Y.-P. Chun, B. Kim, and S. Lee, "Toward a New Governance Paradigm for Environmental and Natural Resources Management in the 21st Century." *Administration and Society* 35 (2004): 39; C. A. Berry, G. S. Krutz, B. E. Langner, and P. Budetti, "Jump-Starting Collaboration: The ABCD Initiative and the Provision of Child Development Services through Medicaid and Collaborators." *Public Administration Review* 68(3) (2008): 10.

6. M. McGuire, "Collaborative Public Management: Assessing What We Know and How We Know It." *Public Administration Review* 66(Supplement) (2006): 10.

7. L. B. Bingham, R. O'Leary, and C. Carlson, "Frameshifting Lateral Thinking for Collaborative Public Management." *Big Ideas in Collaborative Public Management*, L. B. Bingham and R. O'Leary, eds. (Armonk, NY: M.E. Sharpe, 2008): 3–16.

8. D. S. Wright, *Understanding Intergovernmental Relations* (Belmont, CA: Duxbury Press, 1988); R. Agranoff and M. McGuire, "American Federalism and the Search for Models of Management." *Public Administration Review* 61(6) (2001): 10; H. B. Milward and K. G. Provan, "How Networks Are Governed." *Governance and Performance: New Perspectives*, C. J. Heinrich and J.L.E. Lynn, eds. (Washington, DC: Georgetown Press, 2000); L. B. Bingham and R. O'Leary, eds., *Big Ideas in Collaborative Public Management* (Armonk, NY: M.E. Sharpe, 2008); R. O'Leary and L. B. Bingham, eds., *The Promise and Performance of Environmental Conflict Resolution* (Washington, DC: Resources for the Future, 2003).

9. H. B. Milward and K. G. Provan, *A Manager's Guide to Choosing and Using Collaborative Networks* (Washington, DC: IBM Center for the Business of Government, 2006); C. Carlson, *A Practical Guide to Collaborative Governance* (Portland, OR: Policy Consensus Initiative, 2007); R. O'Leary and L. B. Bingham, *A Manager's Guide to Resolving Conflicts in Collaborative Networks*, Networks, Collaboration, and Partnership Series (Washington, DC: IBM Center for the Business of Government, 2007).

10. W. D. Leach and P. A. Sabatier, "To Trust an Adversary: Integrating Rational and Psychological Models of Collaborative Policy Making." *American Political Science Review* 99(4) (2005): 12; R. Agranoff, "Collaboration for Knowledge: Learning from Public Management Networks." *Big Ideas in Collaborative Public Management*, L. B. Bingham and R. O'Leary, eds. (Armonk, NY: M.E. Sharpe, 2008): 162–94; Provan and Milward, "A Preliminary Theory," 33; T. L. Cooper, T. A. Bryer, and J. W. Meek, "Citizen-Centered Collaborative Public Management." *Public Administration Review* 66(suppl): 12 (2006); K. Emerson, P. J. Orr, D. L. Keyes, and K. M. McKnight, "Environmental Conflict Resolution: Evaluating Performance Outcomes and Contributing Factors." *Conflict Resolution Quarterly* 27(1) (2009): 38.

11. Agranoff and McGuire, *Collaborative Public Management.*

12. Milward and Provan, *A Manager's Guide.*

13. Environmental Council of the States (2009), available at http://www.ecos.org/section/committees/air/climate_change/ (last visited December 2009).

14. See Barry G. Rabe, chapter 11 this volume, for further discussion on these regional initiatives.

15. Western Climate Initiative (2009), available at http://midwesternaccord.org (last visited December 2009).

16. US Conference of Mayors Climate Protection Center (2009), available at http://www.usmayors.org/climateprotection/about.htm (last visited February 2010).

17. US Conference of Mayors Climate Protection Center.

18. Climate Registry (2009), available at http://www.climateregistry.org/about.html (last visited February 2010).

19. H. Pulzl and O. Treib, "Implementing Public Policy." *Public Policy Analysis Theory Politics and Methods*, F. Fischer, G. J. Miller, and M. S. Sidney, eds. (Boca Raton, FL: CRC Press, 2007): 100.

20. F. W. Scharpf, "Interorganizational Policy Studies. Issues, Concepts and Perspectives." *Interorganizational Policy Making, Limits to Coordination and Central Control*, K. I. Hanf and F. W. Sharpf, eds. (London: Sage, 1978): 345–70; P. A. Sabatier and H. C. Jenkins-Smith, *Policy Change and Learning: An Advocacy Coalition Approach* (Boulder, CO: Westview, 1993); Pulzl and Treib, "Implementing Public Policy."

21. D.S.V. Meter and C. E. Van Horn, "The Policy Implementation Process, a Conceptual Framework." *Administration and Society* 6 (1975): 43; S. Winter, "Integrating Implementation Research." *Implementation and the Policy Process: Opening up the Black Box*, D. J. Palumbo and D. J. Calista, eds. (New York: Greenwood Press, 1990): 19–38; Pulzl and Treib, "Implementing Public Policy."

22. R. E. Matland, "Synthesizing the Implementation Literature: The Ambiguity-Conflict Model of Policy Implementation." *Journal of Public Administration Research and Theory* 5(2) (1995): 29; P. deLeon and L. deLeon, "What Ever Happened to Policy Implementation? An Alternative Approach." *Journal of Public Administration Research and Theory* 12(4) (2002): 26.

23. American Clean Energy and Security Act, 2009, H.R. 2454; Clean Energy Jobs and American Power Act, 2009, S. 1733.

24. National Energy Act, 2005, P.L. 109-58.

25. *Piedmont Envtl. Council v. FERC*, No. 07-165 (2009), 388237: 4th Cir.

26. R. Agranoff, "Collaboration for Knowledge."

27. C. S. Holling, *Adaptive Environmental Assessment and Management* (New York: John Wiley & Sons, 1978); C. J. Walters, *Adaptive Management of Renewable Resources* (Caldwell, NJ: Blackburn Press, 1986); E. Ostrom, *Governing the Commons: The Evolution of Institutions for Collective Action* (Cambridge: Cambridge University Press, 1990); F. Berkes, J. Colding, and C. Folke, eds., *Navigating Social-Ecological Systems: Building Resilience for Complexity and Change* (Cambridge: Cambridge University Press, 2002).

28. D. Armitage, F. Berkes, and N. Doubleday, eds., *Adaptive Co-Management: Collaboration, Learning, Multi-level Governance* (Vancouver: University of British Columbia Press, 2007).

29. C. Folke, S. Carpenter, T. Elmqvist, L. Gunderson, C. Holling, B. Walker, J. Bengtsson, F. Berkes, J. Colding, K. Danell, M. Falkenmark, L. Gordon, R. Kasperson, N. Kautsky, A. Kinzig, S. Levin, K.-G. Mäler, F. Moberg, L. Ohlsson, P. Olsson, E. Ostrom, W. Reid, J. Rockström, H. Savenije, and U. Svedin, *Resilience and Sustainable Development: Building Adaptive Capacity in a World of Transformations*. Scientific Background Paper on Resilience for the Process of the World Summit on Sustainable Development (Stockholm: Environmental Advisory Council to the Swedish Government, 2002).

30. USDA Forest Service, "Chapter 2020—Ecological Restoration and Resilience." *FSM 2000—National Forest Resource Management* (Washington, DC: USDA Forest Service, 2008).

31. Community Forest Restoration Act, 2000, P.L. 106-393, Title VI.

32. Omnibus Land Management Act, 2009, S. 22, Title IV: Forest Landscape Restoration.

33. Pew Center on Global Climate Change, Map of Status of State Climate Action Plans (2009), available at http://www.pewclimate.org/what_s_being_done/in_the_states/state_action_maps.cfm (last visited March 2010).

34. Emerson et al., "Environmental Conflict Resolution," 38.

35. US Institute for Environmental Conflict Resolution, "ECR Project Briefs" (2009), available at http://ecr.gov/Projects/Projects.aspx (last visited March 2010).

36. US Institute for Environmental Conflict Resolution, Tushar Allotments Collaboration (Tucson: US Institute for Environmental Conflict Resolution, 2009), available at http://tushar.ecr.gov/ (last visited March 2010).

37. J. M. Bryson and B. C. Crosby. "Failing into Cross-Sector Collaboration Successfully." *Big Ideas in Collaborative Public Management*, L. B. Bingham and R. O'Leary, eds. (Armonk, NY: M.E. Sharpe, 2008): 55–78.

38. Administrative Procedures Act, 1946, P.L. 79-404.

39. Freedom of Information Act, 1966, P.L. 89-554, 80 Stat. 383; amended 1996, 2002, 2007.

40. Federal Advisory Committee Act, 1972, P.L. 89-554, 80 Stat. 383; amended 1996, 2002, 2007.

41. Administrative Dispute Resolution Act, 1990, P.L. 104-320, as amended 1996.

42. Regulatory Negotiation Act, 1996, P.L. 104-320.

43. Alternative Dispute Resolution Act, 1998, P.L. 105-315.

44. Environmental Policy and Conflict Resolution Act, 1998, P.L. 105-156, amended 2003, P.L. 108-160.

45. President George W. Bush, "Executive Order 13352 of August 4, 2004: Facilitation of Cooperative Conservation." *Federal Register* 69(167) (2004): 52989.

46. Office of Management and Budget and President's Council on Environmental Quality, "Memorandum on Environmental Conflict Resolution" (November 28, 2005), available at http://www.ecr.gov/Resources/FederalECRPolicy/MemorandumECR.aspx.

47. President Barack Obama, "Memorandum of January 21, 2009: Transparency and Open Government." *Federal Register* 74(15) (2009): 4685.

48. National Environmental Policy Act, 1969, P.L. 91-190.

49. Office of Management and Budget and President's Council on Environmental Quality, "Memorandum on Environmental Conflict Resolution"; President's Council on Environmental Council, *Collaboration in NEPA—A Handbook for NEPA Practitioners* (Washington, DC: President's Council on Environmental Quality, 2007); President's Council on Environmental Quality, "Memorandum for Heads of Federal Agencies concerning Cooperating Agencies in Implementing the Procedural Requirements of NEPA." 40 C.F.R. §§ 1501.6 and 1508.5 (2002).

50. Obama, "Transparency."

51. L. B. Bingham, "Legal Frameworks for Collaboration in Governance and Public Management." *Big Ideas in Collaborative Public Management*, L. B. Bingham and R. O'Leary, eds. (Armonk, NY: M.E. Sharpe, 2008).

52. D. F. Kettl, "Managing Boundaries in American Administration: The Collaboration Imperative." *Public Administration Review* 66 (2006): 15.

53. Ostrom, *Governing the Commons*; E. Ostrom, *Understanding Institutional Diversity* (Princeton, NJ: Princeton University Press, 2005).

54. S. Page, "Measuring Accountability for Results in Interagency Collaboratives." *Public Administration Review* 64(5) (2004): 15, as cited in J. M. Bryson, B. C. Crosby, and M. M. Stone, "The Design and Implementation of Cross-Sector Collaborations: Propositions from the Literature." *Public Administration Review* 66(Supplement) (2006): 44.

55. A. Conley and M. A. Moote, "Evaluating Collaborative Natural Resource Management." *Society and Natural Resources* 16 (2003): 15; Emerson et al., "Environmental Conflict Resolution"; Koontz, T. M., and C. W. Thomas, "What Do We Know and Need to Know about the Environmental Outcomes of Collaborative Management?" *Public Administration Review* 66 (supplement) (2006):10.

The Lakeview Biomass Project

Sharing the Risk

Kirk Emerson

The Lakeview Biomass Project is one of many Oregon Solutions projects, administered by the National Policy Consensus Center at Portland State University.[1]

Located in rural Lake County, Oregon, the Lakeview Stewardship Unit of the Fremont–Winema National Forest encompasses close to 500,000 acres. Lakeview suffers from the multiple climate-related stressors of drought, insect and disease epidemics, and hot-burning catastrophic fires. Past fire suppression policies have taken their own toll with the encroachment of western juniper on historic rangelands. Managing these unhealthy forest conditions requires costly thinning of small-diameter trees and the removal of fire-prone brush and western juniper.[2]

Previously, the piled biomass was disposed of through controlled open burns that degraded air quality and released significant amounts of carbon into the atmosphere. The idea for a biomass energy facility originated as a way to address forest health issues and became an integrated solution providing not only for forest management but also for renewable energy and rural economic development. A diverse set of project partners from local government, state and federal agencies, businesses, nonprofits, and other local stakeholders shared interests in ecosystem restoration, renewable energy production, and local employment and job creation. Once their vision and objectives were in place, Oregon governor Ted Kulongoski designated the Lakeview Biomass Project Team an Oregon Solutions project and appointed the dean of the Oregon State University College of Forestry and a Lakeview County commissioner, both respected and impartial leaders, to serve as project coconveners. This multisector team comanaged the project to make efficient use of available resources, accelerate the pace of the project, deal quickly with challenges as they arose, raise awareness of the initiative on a statewide level, and help engage effective partners.

Within six months, all Lakeview Biomass Project Team members had signed a Declaration of Cooperation[3] that included an implementation plan for a

13-megawatt biomass facility that will consume 250,000 gigatons of forestry biomass material from regional lumber mills and the national forest. The biomass facility was sited on public land and will provide steam to the nearby Fremont Sawmill and create sixty new jobs in the community. Commercial operation is scheduled to start in 2012.

While there was strong interest in moving forward with biomass projects elsewhere in Oregon, few proposals succeeded in overcoming the political, economic, and institutional barriers to such innovation. In this case, the risk was spread across many parties and minimized through an integrative solution offering multiple outcomes: an economically viable biomass energy facility producing clean energy, improved resilience of forestlands and rangelands, reduced carbon dioxide emissions, reduced risk and cost of wildfire in and around human communities, and new jobs for a struggling rural economy, suited to the skills of forest-sector workers.

Notes

1. Oregon Solutions. "Community Governance System" (2010). National Policy Consensus Center, Portland State University, available at http://www.orsolutions.org/about.htm#community (last accessed February 28, 2011).

2. Oregon Solutions. "Overview of Lakeview Biomass" (2011). National Policy Consensus Center, Portland State University, available at http://www.orsolutions.org/central/lakeviewbiomass.htm (last accessed February 28, 2011).

3. Lakeview Biomass Oregon Solutions Team. "Declaration of Cooperation: Lakeview Biomass Energy Facility" (2006). Oregon Solutions, Portland State University, available at http://www.orsolutions.org/docs/LakeviewBiomassDOC.pdf (last accessed February 28, 2011).

Policy Initiatives Among and Across States

Policy Initiatives Among and Across States

In the United States, state and local governments have been actively engaged in debating and developing climate-change policies for almost two decades. The federal government's absence from, and at times hostility to, climate-change debates and activities have spurred responses by thousands of sub-national governments, especially states. Individual states have not acted in isolation. Rather, they interact, whether incidentally or intentionally, taking common positions, learning from one another about best practices, or engaging in joint action and implementation of specific policies. Thus, to better understand state-level climate-change policy initiatives, the chapters in this section elaborate the multiple ways states interact and how such interaction affects the climate-change policies they adopt.

Andrew Karch (chapter 5) begins this section by examining how policy diffuses among the states, such that one state's officials learn of an innovative policy adopted in another state and consider adopting it—or a modified version—in their own. Policy diffusion is an outcome, in part, of what Robert A. Schapiro in chapter 2 refers to as dialogue. Variables in the dialogue within a state, such as the party in control of its legislature or its economic prowess, greatly influence whether that state adopts a particular climate-change policy. In turn, as Karch argues, the political calculus of elected officials—shaped by dialogue, time constraints, and reelection considerations and by the interests of key constituents and public opinion—is central to policy diffusion. In building their political agendas, officials search for information shortcuts—timely, readily accessible information, particularly by examining what other jurisdictions are doing. At the same time, reelection considerations mean that policy diffusion leads not to policy uniformity but instead to policy experimentation. For instance, as noted by several authors in this volume, one of the most popular types of climate-change policy embraced by states is the renewable portfolio standard, yet not one of the more than thirty standards is exactly like another. This variation, experimentation, and diffusion of similar yet distinct climate-change policies are the result of polyphonic federalism in practice.

States' interactions are by no means confined to the process of policy diffusion; some states and localities intentionally engage in collective action to realize common ends. One important vehicle for this is what Judith Resnik, Joshua Civin, and Joseph Frueh in chapter 6 call translocal organizations of government actors, or TOGAs. Although they do not speak with one voice for their members, TOGAs have been influential actors in advancing sub-national climate-change policy activities. As Resnik and colleagues explain, the membership of professional organizations such as the US Conference of Mayors transcends a single jurisdiction. TOGAs also transcend simple categorization—because their members are government officials, they are not typical nonprofits, but neither are they government organizations. They are entirely voluntary, and they have no governmental decision-making authority. So once again, as is typical of a polyphonic federal system, we are confronted with multiple ways of defining the role of specific types of actors, such as TOGAs.

Through TOGAs, subnational government officials have petitioned state and national governments to take specific policy actions, such as through policy statements promoting action on climate change. In addition, they have held conferences and workshops to educate their members on different climate-change issues and policy innovations and have engaged with federal agency officials around planning regional and national infrastructure, such as the identification of renewable energy zones in support of alternative energy projects. In support of a well-functioning polyphonic federal system, Resnik and colleagues argue that more careful attention should be paid to TOGAs in legal and policy processes, such as allowing them standing to intervene in court cases or establishing a process whereby federal agencies formally consult with TOGAs as they craft their management plans, administrative rules, and programs.

TOGAs have also spawned regional climate-change initiatives whereby groups of states develop common goals, objectives, and implementation actions. Edella Schlager documents in chapter 7 how western, midwestern, and northeastern states have jointly engaged in initiatives focused on energy policies—alternative energy, energy efficiency, and alternative forms of transportation—that are crafted to match the particular economic and social circumstances of the member states. For instance, via a joint action plan, one TOGA planted the seeds for the formation of the northeastern Regional Greenhouse Gas Initiative (RGGI), a carbon cap-and-trade system.

Climate-change initiatives such as the RGGI are created through administrative agreements among the states, which are flexible arrangements used to collaborate and act collectively to solve specific problems or realize specific benefits. While it is easy to point to specific instances of climate-change initiatives and the administrative agreements they are based on, it is much more difficult to categorize them in the constellation of associations, organizations, and governments common to federal systems. Through administrative agreements, self-governing entities engage in shared governance without sacrificing their autonomy. Schlager more clearly defines administrative agreements by contrasting them with a common form of shared government provided for in the US Constitution, the interstate compact.

Cooperative climate-change initiatives allow states to realize benefits that they could not achieve individually. The regional energy initiatives Schlager describes are vital mechanisms for spurring states' economic development while ensuring the stability and security of energy supplies. In addition, states use climate-change initiatives to position themselves in relation to the federal government and to influence and shape national climate-change policies.

Any discussion of subnational climate-change mitigation begs the question: Can state action around climate change really make any difference? Aside from two or three states, such as California or Texas, each state represents a very small percentage of global emissions. Will state action have any appreciable effect on climate change? Are particular types of policies better suited for states? These are the issues addressed by David E. Adelman and Kirsten H. Engel in chapter 8. As these authors note, the development and widespread adoption of a variety of technologies will be required in order to sufficiently reduce greenhouse-gas emissions to avoid dangerous climate-change impacts. States are well positioned to engage in technology development and adoption by creating incentives for businesses and consumers to adopt energy-efficient and alternative energy technologies.

Potential technology pioneers—either innovators or early adopters of existing technologies—face risks and costs that may discourage much-needed investment in technologies. This is where states have a role to play. States, and not the federal government, have historically devised and enforced building codes and have engaged in business and residential zoning. More strict building codes, according to Adelman and Engel, would encourage builders and owners to invest in more efficient heating and cooling systems and other technologies. Furthermore, states have long regulated electric utilities; requiring utilities to produce a portion of their electricity through clean technologies using renewable portfolio standards is just another in a long line of regulatory innovations by states and an example of the many policies Adelman and Engel discuss by which states can encourage technology adoption.

Once the federal government adopts climate-change policies, state actions will complement and enhance federal efforts. Federal action will likely entail setting greenhouse-gas emission reduction goals, a national greenhouse-gas cap-and-trade system, and renewable energy requirements. State regulations encouraging clean technology adoption will make it easier for states, businesses, and consumers to meet and respond to such federal action. For instance, a national cap-and-trade system will likely increase the price of electricity, but if homeowners have invested in more energy-efficient heating and cooling systems and appliances because of state subsidy programs and building codes, the effects of increased electricity prices will be lessened.

The federal government has been woefully absent from climate-change policy debates and action. However, it is only one among thousands of governments in the United States, and as the chapters in this section point out, thousands of governments have been engaged in climate-change policies. States, in particular, have experimented and adopted dozens of different types of climate-change policies. In so doing, they learn from the experiences of each other and borrow policies; they work collectively through professional associations both to support policy innovation and learning and to influence the actions of other governments. Furthermore, they combine forces by engaging in administrative agreements that promote technology innovation and technology adoption. It is by transforming how energy is generated and used that states are likely to have the greatest effect in mitigating climate change.

Chapter 5

Policy Diffusion and Climate-Change Policy

Andrew Karch

In Brief

- The policy diffusion process requires public officials, who are constrained by time and reelection interests, to become aware of innovative public policies, gather salient information about such policies, and customize them in order to gain constituent support.

- Focusing events and national government activity can move policy innovations that address climate change onto the agenda by increasing their visibility and political salience.

- Professional organizations, policy research institutes, and think tanks are important diffusion mechanisms that provide detailed information to policy makers about a program and its effectiveness elsewhere, suggestions for avoiding pitfalls faced by early adopters, and analysis of its political impacts.

- A clear understanding of diffusion mechanisms will allow policy makers and other interested parties to better predict when diffusion is most likely to occur and where efforts to overcome the obstacles to diffusion should be directed.

In the absence of strong national leadership in the United States, the fifty states have taken the lead in climate-change policy. The actions of state governments have received relatively limited attention from the press and political scientists, yet they touch on virtually every policy sector relevant to the generation of greenhouse gases, including energy, air quality, transportation, agriculture, and natural resources.[1] In chapter 8, David E. Adelman and Kirsten H. Engel argue that state policy makers have strong incentives to promote the spread of effective technologies and policy experience to other governments precisely because climate change is a global problem.

The process through which innovative policy ideas spread from one jurisdiction to another is known as policy diffusion. Diffusion is not the mere fact of increasing incidence. It does not occur when officials in multiple jurisdictions adopt the same public policy innovation completely independently, nor does it occur when later adopters are unaware of the existence of the innovation elsewhere. Instead, diffusion implies that extant versions of a public policy affect the likelihood that it will be adopted in other jurisdictions.

The topic of diffusion is inherently significant in an era of rapid technological change and instantaneous communication and is especially important in a policy arena in which the states have taken on such a crucial policy-making role. Understanding how political forces can facilitate or hinder the spread of policy innovations will help lawmakers and interested observers understand why some climate-change policies spread widely and others are confined to a limited number of states. This chapter uses insights from recent research in political science and illustrative examples to speculate both about why some climate-change policies have diffused more widely than others and, more tentatively, about what the future may hold in this critical policy arena.

Why Does Policy Diffusion Occur?

The question of why policy diffusion occurs is deceptively simple. A public policy can diffuse for a multitude of reasons; competition, emulation, and politics are among the primary driving forces.

Competition advances policy diffusion in several ways. Officials might believe that the failure to adopt an innovative program will put their state at a competitive disadvantage, pressuring them to keep up with their colleagues in other jurisdictions. Competition might be especially likely to affect the diffusion of innovations in climate-change policy as lawmakers are motivated to adopt "green" policies because of their direct economic advantages. The adoption of state-level renewable portfolio standards, for example, creates business opportunities for companies that are involved in renewable energy generation. Such positive effects may also benefit the state as a whole. In chapter 11, Barry G. Rabe describes how many states have framed programs that would reduce greenhouse gases as being in their economic interest. Officials in Texas, for example, framed the expanded utilization of renewable energy sources as a benefit for economic development, and Nebraska pursued carbon sequestration due to its potential to provide both additional income and better soil conservation for farmers.

In contrast, policy innovations that are viewed as inimical to job growth or economic development more generally might be confined to a limited number of jurisdictions. In the 1990s such states as Michigan, Colorado, Florida, and Louisiana framed climate-change action in these terms and depicted it as a threat to the state economy.[2] These examples illustrate how competition can facilitate or hinder policy diffusion by pressuring officials to adopt or not adopt innovative programs that exist elsewhere.

A policy innovation might also diffuse because officials observe an existing successful version elsewhere and try to copy its success in their own jurisdiction. Emulation is a specific form of imitation, such that officials believe they should adopt an innovative program because it will allow them to achieve a substantive policy objective. Emulation is driven by the perceived success of a policy, with later adopters attempting to equal or surpass the positive achievements of early adopters. This idea resonates with the notion that states can function as "laboratories of democracy" in which policy makers experiment with innovative approaches to societal problems.[3] If a new approach is successful, officials in other states can learn from the experiment and enact the program, as seems to have occurred in the context of the Children's Health Insurance Program, where state officials have emulated policies that proved effective at addressing the needs of uninsured poor children and lowering program costs.[4] If a new approach is unsuccessful, in contrast, officials elsewhere can learn not to enact the program. The concept of emulation implies that policy making is a rational process of trial and error, an appealing notion that characterizes the states as testing grounds for new policy ideas.

The scientific concerns involved in evaluating public policies are often superseded by political imperatives, meaning that policy making is rarely the pragmatic and rational process described by emulation. It is extraordinarily difficult to evaluate public policies along objective dimensions that will satisfy everyone. Although developments along a particular dimension might convince some observers of a policy's success, others might use different criteria to judge its effectiveness.

Such disagreements are common in the context of climate-change policy, where innovative programs sometimes pose trade-offs between such policy goals as energy production, agricultural production, and environmental protection. The politicization of policy-relevant research further demonstrates how political imperatives and policy making interact to make emulation difficult. Partisan and ideological differences lead to controversies about climate-change science and policy as opponents debate the appropriate interpretation of existing research. A series of leaked e-mails among climate scientists, for example, drew varied reactions from the advocacy community in the weeks leading up to the 2009 global summit in Copenhagen.

Policy-relevant research can be employed as part of a broader strategy to set or limit the political agenda. It can serve as a political tool to establish the viability or undesirability of an innovative program. Finally, an election or the imminent end of a legislative session can force policy makers to make a decision about a public policy before all of the relevant data have been gathered and analyzed. Under such circumstances, they might be willing to pass judgment on a program in the absence of a scholarly consensus about its effectiveness. For all of these reasons, understanding why policy diffusion occurs requires a deeper appreciation for the interaction between political imperatives and the policy-making process.

Understanding Policy Diffusion: A Process-Oriented Approach

Policy diffusion is profoundly affected by two major constraints that state officials face: insufficient time to complete the many tasks for which they are responsible, and the need to retain constituent support to win reelection. Overscheduled officials must prioritize their tasks, among them, acquisition of information about a policy innovation. They begin with the most accessible information and search sequentially for that which requires more effort.[5] They are influenced by models that grab their attention and rely on information that is timely, accessible, and salient. As a result, lawmakers rely on resources that consistently provide policy-relevant information without requiring a huge time investment.

If elected officials wish to remain in office, they must be attentive to their constituents' opinions. Electoral calculations can affect policy diffusion because they make it more likely that decision makers will be drawn to versions of innovative policies supported by voters (or organizations that can mobilize large numbers of voters). But although public opinion controls the general ideological direction of policy, it does not force elected officials to comply with specific demands.[6] Furthermore, while reelection-minded officeholders are likely to be attentive to public opinion, they do not always receive clear signals about how to proceed, particularly in the context of environmental policy, where a variety of inconsistent ballot propositions have been put forth. Supporters of innovative environmental programs therefore must define the terms of debate in ways favorable to their cause if they

Table 5.1. Policy Diffusion: A Process-Oriented Approach

Process	Relevant constraint	Influential diffusion mechanisms	Example
Agenda setting	Time constraints	Focusing events	Kyoto Protocol
Information generation	Time constraints	Professional associations	US Conference of Mayors
Customization	Electoral considerations	Intrastate actors	Environmental interest groups
Enactment	Electoral considerations	Institutionally critical actors	N.J. Gov. Christine Todd Whitman

hope to convince voters to pay for protective environmental policies.[7] Thus, electoral considerations influence both the likelihood that officials will adopt a policy innovation and the content of the innovations that they endorse.

The impacts of limited time and reelection concerns vary throughout the four main policy-making stages of agenda setting, information generation, customization, and enactment. The early stages are most likely to be influenced by political forces that respond to time constraints, which affect both the models toward which officials are drawn and the ways in which they gather information about them. In contrast, electoral considerations are more likely to influence the later stages, affecting specific provisions of programs under consideration and the ultimate enactment of policy innovations. Table 5.1 displays the general contours of this analytical framework as well as some of the examples that are discussed in the following pages.

Agenda Setting: Focusing Events Grab Attention

When an existing social condition becomes a political issue, lawmakers can respond in virtually unlimited ways. The agenda-setting process narrows the possible alternatives to a subset that policy makers then focus on.[8] This crucial step in the diffusion process determines whether officials will even consider a policy innovation.

Time-constrained officials are most likely to be drawn to visible and politically salient policy innovations. Political forces that can raise the profile of a new policy idea are therefore likely to drive the agenda-setting process, sometimes across multiple states. Such forces do not necessarily have to invent or develop the innovation, merely to raise its political profile so that time-pressed officials will consider it. Once the policy innovation becomes a seriously considered option, it has already diffused to a certain extent.

A crisis, disaster, or other "focusing event" can increase the visibility of an issue and cause it to become an active agenda item.[9] Such events are commonplace in the context of environmental policy, ranging from the publication of such landmark works as Rachel Carson's *Silent Spring* in 1962 to such environmental disasters as the Three Mile Island accident of 1979. Focusing events have also raised the political profile of climate-change policy, such as when the Kyoto Protocol sparked substantial state activity in the late 1990s. Many states passed legislation or resolutions that were critical of the international agreement. Although most of these actions were purely advisory, West Virginia prohibited any unilateral steps to reduce greenhouse gases and prevented state agencies from entering into any agreement with federal agencies intended to reduce emissions.[10] The Kyoto Protocol and other events raise the political profile of a societal issue, and policy innovations that are viewed as responses to these developments typically become more prominent as a result.

Similarly, national government activity also influences state political agendas. National politics, whether political campaigns or policy debates, usually receive substantial attention from the mass media and rank among the most visible elements of American politics. Time-pressed officials seeking cues about salient or "hot" political issues consequently might be inclined to use federal developments as a measure of what is on the agenda, even though the national government rarely invents a policy innovation or imposes a mandate that requires state adoption. Nevertheless, state officials seem inclined to consider national controversies, even if unresolved, for their own jurisdictions.[11] Innovative programs that are debated at the national level provide a visible, salient example on which they can draw. This dynamic suggests that the recent congressional debate over climate-change policy may generate even greater interest at the state level. Although House passage of the American Clean Energy and Security Act in June 2009 was largely overshadowed by the ongoing congressional debate over health insurance reform and the Senate's later failure to endorse the bill, it nonetheless seemed to spur additional state-level interest in programs to promote renewable energy and energy efficiency.

Information Generation: Get Salient Facts Quickly

State officials typically have access to specialized reference centers whose main task is to collect and to distribute information that will be useful during the formulation of public policies. These libraries and centers often will compile state comparative data on a variety of issues. One could reasonably argue that an awareness of and interest in developments elsewhere are the essence of policy diffusion. Diffusion is not the mere fact of increasing incidence; it requires knowledge about existing programs and implies movement from the source of an innovation to its adopter.[12] The transmission of policy-relevant information can take on many different forms, from face-to-face interactions to media accounts, and diffusion implies that late adopters are at least aware of the developments that preceded their own decision to adopt an innovative policy.

When policy innovations emerge, officials ask two questions. First, how effective is the program? Officials want to duplicate the successes of their counterparts while avoiding the pitfalls faced by early adopters. Second, what will be its political impact? This answer can be just as important as knowing the program's substantive impact (see Albertson spotlight, p. 118). A policy innovation might prove beneficial to its primary sponsor, or it might

> What causes the public to care more or less about climate change and support or oppose new policies? See "Public Attitudes Toward Climate-Change Policy" on page 118.

spark an electoral backlash; either of these outcomes would be noteworthy from the perspective of an elected official. Policy advocates sometimes blur the distinction between substantive and political information by claiming that the mere existence of a policy innovation in another jurisdiction legitimates it as a reform alternative.

In an era of instantaneous communication, finding information is less likely to represent a challenge for officials than is sifting through a glut of it. A recent study examined five states and found that lawmakers in all of them met the requirements for "informed decision making."[13] These officials received information from federal agencies, the White House, twenty organizations, the press, academics and consultants, members of Congress, and contacts in other states. This wide range of information resources is striking because it implies that officials do learn about policy innovations that have been enacted elsewhere. In the current era, other policies seem equally likely to be characterized by a "superabundance" of policy-relevant information.[14]

In fact, many recent institutional, technological, and organizational changes facilitate the generation and collection of such data. A sharp increase in the number and quality of legislative and executive branch staff at the state level means that more qualified people are available to gather information for state officials. The emergence of information technologies, such as the Internet, increases the ease and the speed with which organizations can provide information. State officials can readily examine model legislation and statutory language online without even contacting an organization directly. Travel is less onerous than it used to be, facilitating attendance at regional and national professional meetings. Professional associations, policy research institutes, and think tanks have proliferated, becoming important additional information sources. All of these changes suggest that acquiring information is not nearly as difficult as sorting through everything that is available.

National organizations such as professional associations and think tanks host conferences that bring together state officials, publish reports on policy innovations, and often view the dissemination of policy-relevant information as a key component of their organizational missions. Many also have ties with intrastate actors who promote policy innovations within their states. Such organizations as the Council of State Governments, the National Conference of State Legislatures, and the National Governors Association tend to be active on a wide array of policy issues. National organizations produce documents that are distinguished by their level of technical detail and the frequency with which they refer to existing policy models from around the country, making them well suited to meet the information needs of time-pressed state officials.[15]

In a recent survey of state institutional officials, about 70 percent of respondents rated conferences "somewhat" or "very" important, while 63 percent characterized publications as either "somewhat" or "very" useful.[16] Lawmakers generally described these resources as more useful for policy formulation than for policy adoption. These results suggest that state lawmakers attach significance to the resources that professional associations offer; thus, they serve as key diffusion mechanisms during the information generation process.

Professional associations have had a significant impact on climate-change policy making. Such organizations as the Midwestern Governors Association have been driving forces in the development of administrative agreements, and similar groups have served as clearinghouses and repositories for policy-relevant information. Judith Resnik, Joshua Civin, and Joseph Frueh (chapter 6) describe how the US Conference of Mayors played such a role by convening a Climate Protection Summit in 2007 and publishing its *Climate Protection Strategies and Best Practices Guide*.[17] Modern communications technologies make the circulation of information easier, enabling organizations to post studies, meeting notes, and draft documents online. This type of knowledge sharing was crucial in the development of the Regional Greenhouse Gas Initiative and is described in more detail by Edella Schlager in chapter 7. Indeed, the leading entrepreneurs in climate-change policy are most commonly found in the upper tiers of state agencies with jurisdiction over a variety of related subjects.[18] They tend to have sufficient expertise and latitude to be a source of policy development, drawing heavily on the ideas and experience they have gained in different but highly relevant realms and establishing themselves as credible experts in designing new policies. These entrepreneurs generally operate out of the public eye but play a critical role in the formulation of climate-change policy, nurturing ideas and coalitions that sometimes lead to the adoption of innovative programs. Many of them maintain strong connections with the organizations described above. For example, Robert C. Shinn, Jr., who served for eight years as the commissioner of the Department of Environmental Protection in New Jersey and was one of the strongest advocates in the country for aggressive state action on climate change, also took on a leadership role in the Environmental Council of the States.[19]

Customization: Tailoring Policies to Local Conditions and Interests

Policy innovations take a variety of forms in the jurisdictions in which they are enacted because officials tailor programs to fit their states. Customization is the process through which officials adapt a proposal for technical or political reasons. Differences in policy content are especially important in the context of policy diffusion. Officials might adjust the specific provisions of a policy innovation based on early adopters' experiences. Alternatively, the same innovation may be adapted to account for particularities within a state. In either case, simply answering the yes-no question of *whether* lawmakers chose to adopt a policy innovation overlooks how they might have altered the existing template. Adopters are generally able to make changes to a policy innovation if they feel such changes are merited.[20] Policy diffusion takes place across time and space, and ignoring program content overlooks the important issue of variation across space. Such spatial variation is especially important in the context of climate-change policy where there is variation in program development across the states and in the stringency of state commitments.

The recent diffusion of renewable portfolio standards illustrates the significance of the customization process. These programs, described in more detail by David E. Adelman and Kirsten H. Engel in chapter 8, require a certain proportion of a utility's power plant capacity or generation to come from renewable energy sources by a specified date. According to the Pew Center on Global Climate Change, thirty-one states had established these standards by December 2009.[21] Focusing only on adoption patterns, however, hides considerable variation in the content of the state programs. The standards range from modest to ambitious. While Maine set a target of 10 percent by 2017, for example, neighboring New Hampshire set a more ambitious target of 23.8 percent by 2025. Some states also include "carve-outs" that require a certain percentage of the portfolio be generated from a specific energy source. The Illinois standard, for example, mandates that 75 percent of its target must be met with wind. A third dimension along which state standards vary is in the incentives offered. Maryland offered a 1.2 multiplier for wind-generated power installed before December 31, 2005, while Delaware offers a 3.5 multiplier for wind off the Delaware coast for projects sited before June 1, 2017. These examples illustrate considerable programmatic variation among the states that have adopted renewable portfolio standards.

Some politicians and commentators view the possibility of customization as one of the main benefits of devolution. In their view, customization is more democratic and efficient than imposing a national mandate. The devolution of policy-making authority means that state officials can adjust policy innovations to political conditions within their own jurisdictions, responding to the desires of local constituencies in a way that national officials presumably cannot. In addition to moving decision making "closer to the people," customization might be more efficient than a national mandate. In designing climate-change policy, for example, West Virginia and Ohio might gravitate toward the development of clean coal technology, whereas Texas might choose to focus on the development of power wind turbines. In short, devolution advocates argue that customization is desirable for reasons of democratic responsiveness and efficiency.

During the customization process, the impact of time constraints is likely to recede while the impact of electoral considerations becomes more pronounced, accounting for the inclusion or exclusion of specific provisions of policy innovations. Statutory language is developed during the customization process as general policy templates are amended. Officials are likely to gravitate to versions of policy innovations that have wide support and only modest opposition. Public opinion is taken into account through the efforts of activists and interest group leaders who are attentive to statutory minutiae. These individuals lobby officials, participate in hearings and task forces, and use other forums to voice their concerns. Threats to withhold support or actively oppose elected officials during future campaigns may trigger negotiations, during which statutory language can serve as a bargaining chip. The legislative process provides numerous settings in which interested parties can request that state officials support, reject, or amend a proposal. Organizations representing intrastate constituencies are especially likely to take advantage of these opportunities, either during committee hearings or through general lobbying campaigns. Elected officials have very strong incentives to respond to these requests because they rely quite heavily on in-state sources for campaign contributions and, of course, votes.[22]

The development of a carbon dioxide standard in Oregon illustrates the role of intrastate forces during the customization process. In the late 1990s, the state simultaneously streamlined its energy-facility–siting process and linked future siting initiatives with explicit commitments to reduce greenhouse gases.[23] The Oregon measure, which was signed into law in 1997, arose from an experiment linking energy development with carbon dioxide emission reductions. The success of the experiment spurred the governor and legislature to create a task force on the topic. Ultimately, the task force recommended the elimination of the state's existing facility site standard in exchange for carbon dioxide standards that would apply to all new or expanded natural-gas–based power plants in the state. This quid pro quo was endorsed by the key intrastate constituencies: environmental groups favored the carbon dioxide standards, while industry embraced the end of the facility site standard. The negotiation involved in creating the Oregon policy is emblematic of the political deal making that leads policy innovations to take on various forms in the states in which they are adopted. Entrepreneurs who formulate climate-change policy must design programs that "fit" the economic and political realities of their states and that can win the backing of key intrastate constituencies.

Enactment: When Leadership Becomes Crucial

In many ways, enactment is the culmination of policy diffusion; it is its most visible and easily recognizable aspect. An innovative program either gains enactment or is not adopted. Research on the diffusion of policy innovations among the American states generally emphasizes the adoption decision and focuses on such correlates of adoption as state wealth,[24] political ideology,[25] problem severity,[26] and the existence of the policy in neighboring states.[27] For example, a recent study of different state government approaches to the problem of abandoned and uncontrolled hazardous waste sites linked strong hazardous waste programs to state wealth, the severity of internal hazardous waste problems, and the influence of regional diffusion.[28] Identifying these correlates of adoption is useful but ignores the dynamism that characterizes the enactment process, which is often more complicated than a simple yes-no decision about the merits of a policy innovation. The passage of legislation frequently features multiple debates, shifting positions among key actors, and hurdles that must be cleared. To be enacted, policy innovations typically need to earn the endorsements of legislative committees, two full legislative chambers, and the governor. This process gives substantial power to institutionally critical actors whose positions allow them to serve as veto points during the enactment process.

In exercising their authority, institutionally critical actors in the legislative and executive branches are typically mindful of how their actions will affect the electoral interests of their fellow partisans. House speakers, senate leaders, and committee chairs have the responsibility and authority to help rank-and-file members of their party achieve reelection.[29] Similarly, governors possess institutional authority that enables them to play the role of party leaders. Governors who are particularly effective or ineffective can affect whether their fellow partisans are reelected. Thus, the influence of legislative leaders and governors grows, in part, out of electoral considerations, and these individuals have institutional perquisites that grant them considerable power over the enactment process.

Institutionally critical actors in the legislative and executive branches have played pivotal roles in the adoption of climate-change policy. In shepherding a carbon sequestration bill through the state legislature, for example, Nebraska State Senator Merton Dierks "used his role as chair of the Senate Agriculture Committee to address various concerns and secure an unusually rapid transition from bill development to enactment."[30] In New Jersey, in contrast, advocates of a stronger commitment to greenhouse-gas reduction circumvented the state legislature by issuing an administrative order with the approval of Governor Christine Todd Whitman. A working group then consulted with industry and environmental groups, leading to the release of the New Jersey Sustainability Greenhouse Gas Action Plan on April 17, 2000.[31] During the same period, Michigan moved in the opposite direction under the leadership of Governor John Engler, who presided over a series of major changes in environmental policy, including the abolition of nineteen state boards or commissions that oversaw various areas of environmental policy and the elimination of a series of programs promoting energy efficiency and conservation.[32] Legislative and executive branch leadership has been absolutely crucial to the development of state climate-change policy.

It is important to acknowledge, however, that climate-change policy is often stifled at the enactment stage of the diffusion process. Several of the renewable portfolio standards described in this chapter were adopted not through the conventional legislative process but instead through regulatory action or ballot initiatives.[33] Environmental policies typically associated with conservative causes have sometimes experienced difficulty in navigating the legislative process, such as when the Sierra Club lobbied against the adoption of voluntary remediation programs during the 1980s and 1990s.[34] Successful campaigns to address greenhouse-gas emissions in states such as Georgia and Texas have actually been stealth campaigns during which policy makers chose to refrain from referring to their policies as related in any way to greenhouse-gas reduction.[35]

Conclusion

As climate change continues to occupy a prominent place on the political agenda and as the states continue to take the lead in this policy arena, lawmakers and interested observers need to understand the political process through which innovative public ideas spread among multiple jurisdictions. To explain why some policy innovations diffuse widely and others do not, it is necessary to consider the constraints faced by the public officials who ultimately make the decisions. Time constraints affect the agenda-setting process, as time-pressed lawmakers are drawn to politically salient policy innovations that have achieved a degree of visibility or notoriety. As a result, political forces that can raise the profile of a policy innovation are likely to influence state political agendas. Time constraints also influence the dissemination of information. State officials receive policy-relevant information from a wide variety of sources but rely on those that consistently provide timely information without requiring significant time investment. National organizations, including professional associations and think tanks, are likely to play this role.

Electoral considerations also affect the diffusion of policy innovations. First, they can encourage lawmakers to endorse specific versions of a policy: state officials frequently modify a policy template in response to the support or opposition of a particular constituency. This customization can facilitate major changes. Reelection-minded officials are most likely to endorse innovations supported by their constituents or groups that can mobilize voters. Innovative programs are most likely to survive customization and enactment when they claim support from the intrastate constituencies to which elected officials must respond. Intrastate organizations and institutionally critical actors therefore represent important causal forces during the later stages of policy diffusion.

Recent developments in state climate-change policy provide insight on the general dynamics of the diffusion process. Developments in this policy arena highlight the importance of national and international focusing events at the agenda-setting stage, of professional associations as conduits of policy-relevant information, and of the ways in which innovations take on various forms in the jurisdictions in which they gain enactment. They also suggest that issue framing is a crucial component of the enactment process and that the same innovative program may be adopted for various reasons. Similar lessons are likely to emerge in the future because the "states are clearly moving into an accelerated phase of interstate policy diffusion concerning climate change."[36]

Notes

1. B. G. Rabe, "States on Steroids: The Intergovernmental Odyssey of American Climate Policy," *Review of Policy Research* 25 (2008):105–28.

2. B. G. Rabe, *Statehouse and Greenhouse: The Emerging Politics of American Climate Change Policy* (Washington, DC: Brookings Institution, 2004).

3. *New State Ice Co. v. Liebmann*, 285 U.S. 262 (1932).

4. C. Volden, "States as Policy Laboratories: Emulating Success in the Children's Health Insurance Program," *American Journal of Political Science* 50 (2006):294–312.

5. C. Z. Mooney, "Information Sources in Legislative Decision Making," *Legislative Studies Quarterly* 16 (1991):445–55.

6. R. Erikson, G. C. Wright, and J. P. McIver, *Statehouse Democracy: Public Opinion and Public Policy in the States* (Cambridge: Cambridge University Press, 1993).

7. D. L. Guber, "Environmental Voting in the American States: A Tale of Two Initiatives," *State and Local Government Review* 33 (2001):120–32. See also K. D. Dell, "The Grassroots Are Greener: Democratic Participation and Environmental Policies in State Politics," *Review of Policy Research* 26 (2009):699–727.

8. J. W. Kingdon, *Agendas, Alternatives, and Public Policies*, 2d ed. (New York: HarperCollins College, 1995), 3.

9. Kingdon, *Agendas, Alternatives, and Public Policies*, 94–100.

10. Rabe, *Statehouse and Greenhouse*, 20.

11. A. Karch, *Democratic Laboratories: Policy Diffusion among the American States* (Ann Arbor: University of Michigan Press, 2007).

12. D. Strang and S. A. Soule, "Diffusion in Organizations and Social Movements: From Hybrid Corn to Poison Pills," *Annual Review of Sociology* 24 (1998):265–90.

13. K. Mossberger, *The Politics of Ideas and the Spread of Enterprise Zones* (Washington, DC: Georgetown University Press, 2000), 193.

14. P. E. Converse, "Popular Representation and the Distribution of Information," in *Information and Democratic Processes*, ed. J. A. Ferejohn and J. H. Kuklinkski (Urbana: University of Illinois Press, 1990), 371.

15. Karch, *Democratic Laboratories*.

16. J. Clark and T. H. Little, "National Organizations as Sources of Information for State Legislative Leaders," *State and Local Government Review* 34 (2002):38–44.

17. US Conference of Mayors, *Climate Protection Strategies and Best Practices Guide* (2007), available at http://www.usmayors.org/climateprotection/documents/2007bestpractices-mcps.pdf, accessed February 28, 2011.

18. Rabe, *Statehouse and Greenhouse*.

19. Rabe, *Statehouse and Greenhouse*, 114.

20. R. E. Rice and E. M. Rogers, "Reinvention in the Innovation Process," *Knowledge* 1 (1980):499–514.

21. Pew Center on Global Climate Change, *Renewable and Alternative Energy Portfolio Standards* (2009), available at http://pewclimate.org/what_s_being_done/in_the_states/rps.cfm, accessed December 10, 2009.

22. Karch, *Democratic Laboratories*.

23. This description is based on the more comprehensive account in Rabe, *Statehouse and Greenhouse*.

24. J. Tweedie, "Resources Rather Than Needs: A State-Centered Model of Welfare Policymaking," *American Journal of Political Science* 38 (1994):651–72.

25. Erikson, Wright, and McIver, *Statehouse Democracy*.

26. D. C. Nice, *Policy Innovation in State Government* (Ames: Iowa State University Press, 1994).

27. F. S. Berry and W. D. Berry, "Tax Innovation in the States: Capitalizing on Political Opportunity," *American Journal of Political Science* 36 (1992):715–42.

28. D. M. Daley and J. C. Garand, "Horizontal Diffusion, Vertical Diffusion, and Internal Pressure in State Environmental Policymaking, 1989–1998," *American Politics Research* 33 (2005):615–44.

29. R. A. Clucas, "Principal-Agent Theory and the Power of State House Speakers," *Legislative Studies Quarterly* 26 (2001):319–38.

30. Rabe, *Statehouse and Greenhouse*, 72.

31. Rabe, *Statehouse and Greenhouse*, 115–19.

32. Rabe, *Statehouse and Greenhouse*, 41.

33. Pew Center on Global Climate Change, *Renewable and Alternative Energy Portfolio Standards*.

34. D. Daley, "Voluntary Approaches to Environmental Problems: Exploring the Rise of Nontraditional Public Policy," *Policy Studies Journal* 35 (2007):165–80.

35. Rabe, *Statehouse and Greenhouse*, 35–36.

36. Rabe, *Statehouse and Greenhouse*, 169.

Public Attitudes Toward Climate-Change Policy

Bethany Albertson

What causes the public to care more or less about climate change and support or oppose new policies? In surveys of Americans, the environment is considered less important than issues such as national security and the economy, but climate change is ranked as one of the most important environmental concerns. Advocates of climate-change policies must confront the challenges of a public that views the effects of climate change as physically and temporally remote. Also, according to a 2009 national survey by the Pew Research Center, the number of people who believe that climate change is occurring declined over previous years, particularly among Independents and Republicans.

A high-profile political event such as the Kyoto Protocol or a weather-related catastrophe such as Hurricane Katrina might catch people's attention and put climate change on the political agenda. However, attitudes about the causes of climate change and the appropriate level of government response are affected by political factors such as partisanship and one's sense of personal risk. People who believe they are more vulnerable to the effects of climate change (whether or not they are objectively at greater risk) are more likely to support proactive climate-change policies.

Other factors influencing the public's level of concern over climate change include their knowledge about climate change (its causes and impacts), their trust in scientists, and their belief in a scientific consensus on the causes of climate change.

Climate-change policy advocates can achieve greater public support when the immediate physical risk from climate change is low by shifting how the problem is framed. People who do not perceive risk might support environmental policies when they are framed as economic opportunities. Those not immediately vulnerable to the effects of climate change might pay more attention when they realize that economic and military resources are being (or may be) shifted to address weather-related catastrophes in other states and other countries.

Further Reading

Leiserowitz, A., E. Maibach, and C. Roser-Renouf, *Climate Change in the American Mind: Public Support for Climate and Energy Policies in January 2010*, Yale F&ES Project on Climate Change, George Mason University Center for Climate Change Communication, available at http://www.climatechangecommunication.org/images/files/PolicySupportJan2010%281%29.pdf.

Malka, A., J. A. Krosnick, and G. Langer, "The Association of Knowledge with Concern About Global Warming: Trusted Information Sources Shape Public Thinking," *Risk Analysis*, 29(5) (2009), 633–47.

Nisbit, M. C., and T. Myers, "Twenty Years of Public Opinion About Global Warming," *Public Opinion Quarterly*, 71(3)(2007), 444–70.

Pew Research Center, *Modest Support for "Cap and Trade" Policy: Fewer Americans See Solid Evidence of Global Warming*, October 22, 2009.

Chapter 6

Changing the Climate

The Role of Translocal Organizations of Government Actors
(TOGAs) in American Federalism(s)

Judith Resnik, Joshua Civin, and Joseph Frueh

In Brief ────────────────────────────────

- The dynamic policy and legal interactions among units within the US federation not only map the vertical relationship between the national government and states or the horizontal relationships among states but also cut across levels and layers of governmental structures.

- These dynamics are reflected in relatively understudied translocal organizations of government actors (TOGAs), which are private associations that are important sources of law and policy, and which gain political capital from the fact that their members are government officials and employees.

- One illustration is the US Conference of Mayors' Climate Protection Agreement, endorsed as of 2010 by some 1,000 localities, which effectively links the United States with the Kyoto Protocol even though the US Senate has not ratified the Protocol.

- Law can promote or hinder the impact of TOGAs; providing legal authority and responsibilities for them would be responsive to the developments within US federalism that they represent.

During the last decades, domestic policies in the United States on global warming have been shaped through interactions among transnational lawmakers, the national government, and hundreds of subnational entities. Exemplary are activities of the US Conference of Mayors, which developed a Climate Protection Agreement that has been endorsed (as of 2010) by more than 1,000 mayors. As a result, although the United States has not ratified the Kyoto Protocol on climate change, the principles that it represents have been embraced throughout the country.

This chapter, drawn from a longer article,[1] places the Climate Protection Agreement in the context of two more general phenomena: the impact of translocal organizations on American federalism and subnational importation of "foreign" law. Organizations such as the US Conference of Mayors resemble nongovernmental organizations (NGOs) but gain their political capital from the fact that their members are government officials or employees—such as mayors, attorneys general, governors, or legislators.

Political scientists write about public interest groups and special interest groups, using the unattractive acronyms "PIGS" and "SIGS." Lawyers study governmental bodies, corporations, class actions, and other forms of aggregation. To distinguish entities like the US Conference of Mayors from other groups that aggregate interests, we offer the term *translocal organizations of government actors*, and the acronym *TOGAs*, to capture their civic valence.

A small social science literature has begun to consider the function of such groups,[2] yet much of what TOGAs do is underexplored, both empirically and normatively. In the United States, TOGAs are expressive of American federalism because they mirror the layers of the federal system. Yet, by linking actors across jurisdictions, TOGAs also require a shift in focus from state-to-state or state–federal interaction to cooperative interjurisdictional activities, which are generally overlooked in standard federalism theory. Further, the political embeddedness of TOGAs—many of which are, like the US Conference of Mayors, constituted by elected leaders—undercuts criticism that importation of "foreign" law is necessarily counter-majoritarian. Moreover, the domestication of the Kyoto Protocol at the local level makes plain that the national government does not have exclusive dominion whenever "foreign" issues are implicated.

In this chapter, we provide examples of the roles that TOGAs play in policy making. We then analyze the significance of TOGAs for federalism and their relationship to social movements. Finally, we explore whether this form of aggregation ought to be specially enabled through public subsidies, recognized and accorded distinct and privileged status through doctrine and statutes, regulated to ensure accountability and participation of those presumed to be represented, or left mostly alone as are many other associations.

Porous Boundaries in International, National, and Local Lawmaking

In 1997, meetings in Kyoto, Japan, yielded an agreement to address global warming that posited the nation-state as central to international exchanges. The Kyoto Protocol created a framework of timetables for nations to reduce greenhouse-gas emissions.[3] In 1998, President William Jefferson Clinton signed the Protocol. Within the United States, however, opposition to the Protocol mounted. An entity that called itself the Committee to Preserve American Security and Sovereignty (COMPASS), which included many former government officials, issued a report that typified the objections to ratification.[4]

The group's acronym, COMPASS, captured its insistence on the relevance of geography to the many jurisdictional objections that it raised to the Protocol. COMPASS argued that the Protocol reflected a "new world order," shaped in large measure by "politically unaccountable NGOs." COMPASS further warned that the "Protocol may convert decisions usually classified as 'domestic' for purposes of US law and politics into 'foreign,' and thus move substantial power from the Congress, from state and local governments, and from private entities into the federal Executive Branch," which was presumed by COMPASS to be in charge of "foreign affairs."[5]

The COMPASS report is but one of many examples of *sovereigntism*, a posture stressing the importance of a nation's right to define its own lawmaking. The report adopted an *exclusivist* form of sovereigntism as it claimed that the legal regime in the United States ought to be made from within and protected from foreign influences. But a nation's effort to put its own stamp on its laws does not necessarily entail rebuffing ideas from abroad. South Africa's Constitution, for example, asserts an *inclusivist* form of sovereigntism, inviting cross-border dialogue.[6] It links the country to its counterparts in the "family of nations" in part through directives about the use of nondomestic law. South Africa's Constitution directs that, when interpreting that nation's bill of rights, jurists "must consider" international law and may consider comparable provisions in other countries' legal regimes.[7]

In the United States, proponents of exclusivist sovereigntism often ground their views in claims about the structure of US federalism. They argue that, under the US Constitution, the regulation of particular subject matters (in this context, climate policy) belongs to certain levels of government (in this instance, "domestic" decision making by localities and Congress). Further, they posit that US engagement with "foreign" law is problematic because "outsiders," rather than popularly elected officials, are "making" the law. The Climate Protection Agreement of the US Conference of Mayors, however, undercuts such arguments, for elected officials championed, at the local level, the importation of precepts from abroad.

The COMPASS report adopts a categorical approach that assigns a topic to a particular jurisdictional level as if it self-evidently and naturally inhered.[8] Critical theorists call this *essentialism*. That term is regularly used in discussions of race and gender. For example, essentialists argue that certain traits are intrinsically "female" or "male" because "nature" is the primary source of gender differences. But those views ignore how practices and ideas about the distinctions between women and men are shaped by expectations of and obligations imposed by gender roles and rules.[9] In the context of jurisdictional classifications about climate policy, essentialists make an analytically parallel claim—that certain kinds of problems are "domestic" in nature, while others are "foreign."

But how can one tell what problems are "domestic" or "foreign," and whether characterizing a problem as "domestic" necessarily precludes it from also being described as "foreign"? These questions have been posed in many legal contexts and, sometimes, end up in litigation. Examples include lawsuits about whether Massachusetts has the power not to use its taxpayers' dollars to buy goods made with forced labor in Burma,[10] and whether Illinois legislators and executive officials, who are appalled at genocide in Darfur, can divest their state's assets from Sudan.[11] Like questions of climate policy, these examples illustrate that problems are often both "domestic" *and* "foreign." Allocating a citizenry's tax dollars to control a state's or locality's treasury expenditures is a local political decision that can (depending on where dollars are spent) have national and global ramifications, just as how one consumes oil affects both domestic and foreign interactions.

At stake in these efforts to categorize are questions of power and process. For example, attacks on international global warming programs often come bundled with arguments about a "democratic deficit" in transnational lawmaking.[12] One claim is that conventions, treaties, and the like are not made through a sufficiently accountable process; another is that transnational lawmaking undercuts both the majoritarian procedures and the separation of powers embedded in the US Constitution. Thus, by positing transnational law as suspect, exclusivist sovereigntism equates itself with constitutionalism and popular will.

But compare those assumptions with what happened—on the "domestic" front—in the context of the Kyoto Protocol. A year after the 2000 election, President George W. Bush withdrew American support from the Kyoto Protocol. Some of his arguments echoed those made by COMPASS.[13] One could read the sequence of the election, in which control of the White House switched hands from the Democratic to the Republican Party, followed by the new president distancing the nation from the Protocol, as a majoritarian outcome. However, identifying exactly what views a majority of voters had about climate change is complicated, given that the Democratic candidate, Al Gore, who championed taking up the problems of global warming, won the popular vote.

When one turns from the national to the subnational level, the link between the COMPASS critique and majoritarianism weakens further. Localities within the United States affiliated with Kyoto's precepts by shaping a *de facto* transnational alliance through translocal action. Soon after President Bush withdrew support for the Protocol, cities as different as Seattle and Salt Lake City enacted ordinances aimed at conforming to the Protocol's targets for controlling local emissions of greenhouse gases. In March 2005, a group of nine mayors agreed to a Climate Protection Agreement and then garnered the support of many other mayors as well as the official approval of the US Conference of Mayors, which endorsed a modified version of the agreement in June 2005. The agreement aims for mayors to "meet or exceed the Kyoto Protocol targets . . . in their own operations and communities" through initiatives such as retrofitting city facilities, promoting mass transit, and maintaining healthy urban forests.[14] In addition, the mayors called upon federal and state governments to comply with Kyoto targets and urged Congress to pass bipartisan legislation to create an emission-trading system and "clear . . . emissions limits" for greenhouse gases.[15]

By November 2010, more than 1,000 mayors, representing towns and cities whose combined populations numbered more than 87.6 million people, had endorsed the Climate Protection Agreement.[16] Other forms of local action took place through coordinated initiatives within states. For example, in 2007, residents of 134 towns in New Hampshire approved resolutions supporting local and national efforts to combat climate change.[17]

Indeed, although the COMPASS report had argued that transnational lawmaking undercut domestic practices in the United States, the Bush administration's reluctance to participate in the Protocol at a national level helped to generate a sequence of subnational democratic debates about energy policy choices. Thus, while misunderstanding the potential for majoritarian processes presented by the Climate Protection Agreement, opponents of the Protocol were right to point out that lawmaking from abroad has domestic effects. The Protocol did influence mayors, who were persuaded by the mix of their own problems and the solutions proffered from outside the United States, to generate new policies. And that impact is not unique. One can find a repeating pattern of transnational influence in which localities function as ports of entry for non-US law and policy.[18]

The phenomenon of "law's migration" has a long history in the United States; the nineteenth-century abolition and women's suffrage movements are vivid examples. Ideas, norms, and practices do not stop at the lines that people draw across land, and subnational units provide an array of entry ports. Over time, the origins of rules blur.[19] Certain legal precepts are now seen as foundational to the United States, but one should not label them "made in the U.S.A." without an awareness that, like other "American" products, some parts and designs are produced abroad. In short, "local," "federal," and "international" interests are not fixed but emerge based on interactions among interdependent actors.

Conceptualizing TOGAs

Crisscrossing the Federalism Grid

TOGAs such as the US Conference of Mayors, which linked the country with the Kyoto Protocol, are legally and politically intriguing because they are national but are not part of the federal government. While TOGAs obtain their identity and some of their legitimacy from the fact that they are built on the federal structure of the United States, their activities require reconsideration of some stock precepts.

In discussions of federalism, states are typically conceived as individual and independent actors that must be placed on an "equal footing" by national law.[20] The environmental federalism literature is especially attentive to states as competitors; the metaphor is of races—to the bottom or the top—in which states tailor policies to attract industry and investment to their respective jurisdictions.[21] Less in view are the many joint actions undertaken by states. At the formal level of the Constitution's Compact Clause, some cross-jurisdictional state activities require congressional approval, obtained through statutes confirming specific compacts.[22] More common than compacts are coordinated initiatives through multistate executive orders, informal administrative agreements, or other joint ventures among similarly situated subnational actors.[23]

The term *horizontal federalism*—state-to-state interaction—has gathered some attention within the legal academy.[24] Scholars and policy makers use examples ranging from marriage laws to the treatment of criminal offenders after incarceration as they consider how regimes in one state must or can be used by another state when people or goods travel[25] and whether courts or Congress should impose national resolutions. Furthermore, concerns about *horizontal aggrandizement*—the possibility that some states will take advantage of their superior resources to obtain national legislation beneficial to their interests at the expense of other states—have been elaborated in support of arguments for judicial oversight of congressional decisions.[26]

Turning to the "vertical dimensions," one finds discussions of *cooperative federalism*—used to denote collaboration linking federal actors with either state or local actors, often in the context of city- or state-based implementation of national programs.[27] But the legal federalism literature does not pay much attention to federalist practices that cross both vertical and horizontal dimensions at the same time, which (at the conference from which this chapter emerged) Daniel Farber suggested we call *diagonal federalism*[28] and that we explore below as we examine the forms and functions of TOGAs. Translocal action requires, first, a reappraisal of the assumption that states act individually so as to appreciate their role as a collective national force. Second, questions emerge about what import this reconception should have for political theory and legal doctrine.

The Distinctive Attributes of TOGAs

A significant body of scholarly literature addresses social movements through a focus on "networks" of activists bringing parallel and coordinated initiatives across a spectrum of issues. These transnational advocacy networks (TANs) are often spawned by NGOs. Many commentators explore how "norm entrepreneurs," operating in NGOs and through TANs, affect society.

One could put organizations such as the US Conference of Mayors into the categories of both TANs and NGOs, as such nomenclature captures the idea that actors work (often transnationally) on issues because they share common values and a discourse through regular exchanges of information. But the term *NGO* generally refers to what its initials stand for—a *nongovernmental* organization—a group of persons in the private sector working in concert and playing a significant role in the public sphere in order to garner support for influencing government policies.

In contrast, the network that spawned the Climate Protection Agreement consisted of many individuals who knew each other because, as elected officials of cities with populations of 30,000 or more, they were eligible for membership in the US Conference of Mayors. That organization is one of several in the United States defined and populated by people holding positions in local or state government (see table 6.1). The US Conference of Mayors is *private* in the sense that it is not a part of local, state, or federal government. But the political capital of the US Conference of Mayors comes from the fact that its members are democratically elected, *public*-sector officials.

Yet the US Conference of Mayors is not a "GO"—a governmental organization. Rather, it is a voluntary association that is not bound by, nor does it bind, the government units of which its members are the mayors. The US

Table 6.1. Illustrative TOGAs

TOGA	Founding year
National Conference of Commissioners on Uniform State Laws	1892
National Association of Attorneys General	1907
National Governors Association	1908
International City/County Management Association	1914
Council of State Governments	1933
US Conference of Mayors	1933
National Association of Counties	1935
Conference of Chief Justices	1949
National League of Cities	1964
National Conference of State Legislatures	1975
National Association of Towns and Townships	1976

Conference of Mayors and its counterparts are also both public and private in terms of finances; their resources are generally a mix of grants, corporate sponsorships, and taxpayer funds.

These organizations could be captured by a clunky shorthand that, if fully descriptive (such as translocal private organizations of government officials and other actors), does not abbreviate well. We choose instead the phrase *translocal organizations of government actors* and therefore the acronym TOGA to hearken back to the ancient Roman garb that denoted dignity and marked citizenship.[29]

In the article on which this chapter is based, we detail the history and practices of eleven prominent TOGAs to illustrate the range of activities and distinctive (as well as overlapping) agendas. Table 6.1 provides a snapshot of some of these TOGAs, with founding dates for each; below we sketch the origins of four influential TOGAs and their roles in shaping climate-change policy.

US Conference of Mayors

We begin with mayors, as their Climate Protection Agreement provided our opening example of translocal and transnational policy making. The rules of the US Conference of Mayors provide that "each city is represented in the Conference by its chief elected official, the mayor."[30] The US Conference of Mayors was founded during the Great Depression "as a lobby group to represent the interests of large cities in the federal relief effort that the mayors knew would quickly follow the inauguration of Franklin D. Roosevelt."[31] By the 1970s, the group had come to serve as a fount of technical assistance to cities receiving federal funds to comply with and implement President Lyndon Johnson's city-focused Great Society.[32] While the US Conference of Mayors has always received support from dues, keyed to cities' populations and paid by members,[33] almost two-thirds of its budget came from federal contracts during the 1970s. Devolution under the administration of President Ronald Reagan cut those revenues and altered the fortunes of the US Conference of Mayors.[34] Yet as its current prominence in the global warming discussion makes plain, it has in recent times proved itself able to attract attention and to intervene in national policy debates. Reflected in the US Conference of Mayors' transnational activities is a general appreciation for the centrality of cities as part of what Saskia Sassen has called the "rescaling" of global economies.[35]

National Association of Counties

Moving to another level of government—counties—brings us to the National Association of Counties, which was founded in the 1930s.[36] Like other TOGAs, its definition of membership is based on a category of jurisdiction, in this case counties. As of 2010, it maintained twenty-four affiliated entities that provide support services aimed at specialists in particular areas of work. These include the National Association of County Civil Attorneys, the National Association of County Surveyors, and the National Association of County Parks and Recreational Officers.[37]

Representing three-fourths of all counties and more than 85 percent of the nation's population,[38] the National Association of Counties has come—like many TOGAs—to include climate policy among its priorities. In 2007, it adopted a resolution insisting that "climate disruption is a reality" and supported regulatory efforts at the national and subnational levels to combat global warming.[39] Also in 2007, the National Association of Counties convened what it called the "first-ever national forum for counties on the climate protection subject" in Washington, DC. Attendees learned about "best practices, tools and resources to assist them in developing and implementing a successful climate change program."[40]

National Governors Association

At the state level, one of the best-known TOGAs is the National Governors Association. Founded in 1908 as the "Governor's Conference," this group was assisted in its first efforts by President Theodore Roosevelt and one of his advisors, Gifford Pinchot, who also founded the US Forest Service.[41] Reflecting the long history of TOGA involvement in environmental issues, the agenda for the first meeting of the Governor's Conference was a favorite Roosevelt cause: conservation of natural resources.[42] The National Governors Association aims to be bipartisan and relies on that identity as a source of its authority and utility as a lobby. By the early 1960s, however, conflicts prompted the formation of the Republican Governors Association,[43] which at the time specified its distinct views on welfare policy.[44] A Democratic Governors Association emerged two decades later.[45] The founding of these party-identified subgroups did not prevent the umbrella group from continuing to operate, but some argue that they have limited the effectiveness of the national organization.[46]

As for climate change, the National Governors Association has repeatedly revised its policy positions on global climate change. The most recent revision in 2010 reflects efforts to bridge different points of view and reveals the constraints that come with bipartisanship. While acknowledging "the evidence and the risks of both overreaction and underreaction to climate change," the 2010 policy affirms that the National Governors Association is "committed to working in partnership with the federal government, businesses, environmental groups, and others to develop and implement programs that reduce greenhouse gas emissions in conjunction with conserving energy, protecting the environment, and strengthening the economy."[47] Going further than the National Governors Association, a few governors joined together in the spring of 2008 to press for more action on climate change at the national level.[48]

Council of State Governments

The Council of State Governments, founded in 1933,[49] is the current incarnation of an older association, the American Legislators' Association, which was launched in 1925.[50] Elected or appointed state government officials and staffers who serve in the legislative, judicial, and executive branches of state government are automatically eligible for membership.[51] The Council's 165-member governing board is composed of fifty-five governors and two legislators from each chamber in the fifty states and five territories.[52]

The Council of State Governments is centrally identified through its work on information gathering and dissemination. Since 1935, it has published annually *The Book of the States*, a compendium of tabulated data enabling comparisons of state services and resources.[53] The Council of State

Governments has also been a source of legislation: it began drafting model bills during World War II under a "Suggested War Legislation" program.[54] Further, like other TOGAs, it has "affiliated" organizations, including the National Association of State Treasurers, the National Lieutenant Governors Association, the National Association of State Facilities Administrators, the National Hispanic Caucus of State Legislators, and the American Probation and Parole Association.[55]

In terms of climate change, the position that the Council of State Governments adopted in 2007 resembles a pattern followed by many representative groups that aim to make statements that span sets of interests—resulting in generalizations that could be characterized as either moderate or vague. The Council of State Governments concluded that "the need for action on climate change is clear."[56] But, reflective of disagreements within, it also stated: "Devising the right program . . . is not as obvious. Thus it is important for legislators to carefully weigh the pros and cons of each proposal before making a decision. . . . A proactive approach to climate change by the states also may help spur federal action by making it easier to devise a national solution."[57]

TOGAs and Federalist Virtues

TOGAs could be viewed as improving deliberative democracy because they bring in not only more voices but a particularly interesting set of voices—those of officials structurally embedded in the problems of states and localities and cutting across both. Given the needs of TOGAs' constituents and the obligations of many of their members to administer state and local programs, these organizations may be especially attuned to practical concerns about developing and implementing innovative solutions.

But TOGAs ought also to give some pause to those who argue that federalism is a desirable political structure because it locates power at multiple levels and in theory produces variety and policy competition. TOGAs can generate uniformity, as exemplified by the National Conference of Commissioners on Uniform State Laws (which aims to do just that) and by hundreds of mayors signing on to a shared approach to climate change. On the other hand, for federalism skeptics, TOGAs may well provide evidence, from the "bottom up," that diversity is less useful in certain areas.[58]

This rapid overview underscores that TOGAs' agendas are themselves a product of interactions, rather than a set of interests produced at any one level and then promoted elsewhere. TOGAs represent the ongoing exchanges between local needs and state policies or between subnational needs and federal policies. Indeed, the federal government has been, on occasion, an important source of funding for some TOGAs and, in a few instances, has helped to create these translocal organizations in efforts to gain support for national policies and to diffuse criticism. Further, TOGAs are dynamic. Many have reconfigured over time or merged with other entities. Several have charters that result in sharing members with other TOGAs, such that a particular jurisdiction or government actor may be a member of more than one TOGA.

Moreover, identifying a TOGA by its jurisdictional level does not consistently predict whether that TOGA adopts views that can be styled "progressive" or "conservative." Similarly, issues such as environmentalism may not fit easily into those boxes; once seen as coming at the price of economic growth, efforts to be "green" are now promoted as the key to expanding development opportunities.[59] And, given that environmental regulation could affect differently situated subnational regimes in different ways, subnational organizations may adopt stances with which others disagree.

An example of this divergence comes from the controversy over the authority of the US Environmental Protection Agency (EPA) to regulate greenhouse-gas emissions by motor vehicles, an issue litigated in the Supreme Court in 2007.[60] In *Massachusetts v. EPA*, subnational participants took opposing positions. Massachusetts, the first named plaintiff, challenged the federal government's failure to regulate greenhouse-gas emissions. It was joined by eleven other states, three cities, and one US territory, as well as environmental organizations. Ten other states intervened in support of the federal government. In addition, an *amicus* or "friend-of-the-court" brief was filed in support of Massachusetts by the US Conference of Mayors, the National Association of Counties, and four cities, including Seattle, which introduced itself in its "statement of interest" as a pioneer of the Kyoto Protocol activism that helped to launch the US Conference of Mayors' Climate Protection Agreement.[61] In its filing with the Court, the US Conference of Mayors also underscored its translocal and transnational work.[62]

Massachusetts v. EPA is not idiosyncratic. In virtually all of the Supreme Court's major recent federalism cases, subnational actors representing their political units or through TOGAs have filed *amicus* briefs on both sides— arguing that a particular provision either exceeded or fell within congressional powers under the Constitution. Splits exist not only across TOGAs but also within them, as members debate whether to take a position and, if so, what it should be. In the national legislative arena, different levels of subnational government have frequently disagreed about policy initiatives and vied with one another for federal funds and targeted roles in statutes.[63]

In short, while counties, cities, states, and TOGAs bespeak their commitment to the "interests" of the jurisdictional levels of which they are a part, promoting something called state or municipal "interests" does not decide the question of what those interests are. Further, even if a TOGA has settled on a set of "interests," its posture can change depending on its leadership, membership, and particular problems at a given time. Indeed, several TOGAs have altered course dramatically over time, as their leaders and members develop new approaches.[64] For example, as women and men of all colors have become active participants, several TOGAs have taken up issues of gender and racial equality.

Law's Options: Regulation, Promotion, and Distance

Even if TOGAs are historically rooted and majoritarian in some of their workings, we need to consider whether their translocalism is a phenomenon that warrants lawmaking and, if so, what kind of legal or policy interventions could be appropriately undertaken by courts or legislatures in the federal or state systems.

Our responses require prefatory caveats. Others may probe whether the substantive policies that various TOGAs develop or promote are usefully designed to achieve their goals. For example, is the US Conference of Mayors' Climate Protection Agreement responsive to the problem of global warming? That type of metric, however, is not our focus, although the wisdom of TOGAs' interventions constitutes one factor relevant to whether they should be accorded special legal status. Another constraint comes from the limited empirical record about TOGAs. One's enthusiasm for using law to inscribe or circumscribe TOGAs' activities depends on more knowledge than is currently available about how they operate, their diversity, and their effects. Therefore, the examples below of ways for law to take TOGAs into account provide only a preliminary sketch of suggested contemporary interventions rather than universal or timeless prescriptions.

Engaging TOGAs through Doctrine and Statutes
Standing to Litigate

TOGAs could provide an important source of law enforcement through litigation about the meaning of federal statutory rights. This proposition could seem novel, but it finds its roots in two Supreme Court decisions regarding entities' standing to bring environmental litigation. The first decision, already noted, is *Massachusetts v. EPA*. The Supreme Court built on its own judicial doctrine of "sovereign immunity," which insulates states from defending their actions in federal lawsuits and shaped a parallel rule that states should have special status to bring cases as plaintiffs challenging federal regulations. The US Conference of Mayors filed an *amicus* brief making an additional argument, which the Court did not reach, that cities ought also to be empowered to serve as plaintiffs.[65]

The second case is the Court's 1972 decision in *Sierra Club v. Morton*. At issue was whether the Secretary of the Interior had violated federal statutes by issuing permits for the Disney Corporation to build a major hotel complex in the Sierra Madre Mountains, a federally protected area. The plaintiff, the Sierra Club, an NGO committed to environmentalism, sought to establish that organizations dedicated to the environment could be recognized under the Administrative Procedure Act as "aggrieved" by adverse decisions.[66] The Court's decision is important for its recognition that aesthetic and recreational interests are injuries protected by federal law. But the Court declined to permit either all public interest groups or just environmental groups to bring federal lawsuits as "private attorneys general."[67] Rather, the majority insisted that the Sierra Club had to show that the organization or its members had experienced an injury by alleging that its members had hiked in the woods or otherwise used the area in dispute.

Whether the Court properly imposed that limit, TOGAs present another option. They sit between governments and NGOs. In environmental litigation and elsewhere, law could accord them special status—or standing—as parties and especially in questions of state and federal law enforcement. Through case law or statute, TOGAs should be seen as appropriate plaintiffs or intervenors as of right, akin to the status accorded the US Attorney General, who is authorized to intervene when federal statutes are challenged.[68]

Opponents of proposals to enable litigation often raise concerns about how to deter frivolous claims. But TOGAs are jurisdictionally based institutions advancing a mélange of interests. Because they have intramember obligations of transparency and limited resources, they have to be selective about when to participate in litigation. Moreover, as illustrated by TOGAs' *amicus* filings, they can inform judges while also making plain that subnational institutions do not all agree on how to interpret the precepts of federalism.

Deferential Review of TOGA-Sponsored Policies

Federalism jurisprudence should take TOGAs' existence into account in another respect. Here we build on an idea put forth more than fifty years ago by Herbert Wechsler. He argued that because states were represented in Congress, the judiciary should be reluctant to step in at the behest of state and local actors to review congressional statutes affecting state powers.[69] Based on his famous formulation of the "political safeguards of federalism," Wechsler urged courts to leave questions about the proper degree of national regulation to political exchanges in the legislative arena. Wechsler's article was prompted by cases in which states went to the federal courts to obtain judicial protection from congressional legislation. Today, business organizations, often supported by the federal government, go to federal court to get protection from states and localities that have enacted emission controls, banned purchases from Burma, or mandated divestment from Sudan.[70] The claim is that local or state regulation should be preempted, or trumped, by federal action.

We join others in arguing that federal preemption is often neither required nor appropriate.[71] In our view, as a matter of constitutional law, many local and state actions with national, foreign, and transnational effects are permissible—and unavoidable. The text of the Constitution does not compel a contrary result. Rather, the idea of exclusive realms for executive or congressional action comes from judicial extrapolation that we think is wrong as matter of doctrine, and wrong as a matter of federalism.

Reformatting Wechsler's idea to entail "the political safeguards of trans-localism," we think the growing presumption in favor of federal preemption should be flipped. We suggest that, absent a clear statement from Congress directing federal preemption, the judiciary should be reluctant to preempt local majoritarian activities undertaken by TOGAs—such as the US Conference of Mayors' Climate Protection Agreement. Indeed, local actions could have a stronger claim to judicial deference than the congressional actions addressed in Wechsler's article. Critics have argued that Wechsler's approach fails to recognize that Congress is not a level playing field: the Senate gives equal votes to disparately situated states with widely varying populations, and some states can dominate others.[72] A presumption in favor of leaving state and local legislation and resolutions in place responds to those criticisms by permitting subnational variation to thrive through state and local political processes.

Turning to the national level, we propose that congressional legislation that has TOGAs' approval also deserves a presumption of protection from judicial review. Here we draw upon the Supreme Court's decision in *New York v. United States*,[73] finding unconstitutional a federal statutory provision that penalized any state that failed to cooperate with other states in disposing of low-level nuclear waste. At issue was whether the legislation sufficiently respected the boundaries of state authority. Yet the underlying statute had been proposed by the National Governors Association, one of the TOGAs discussed above. The Court substituted its judgment for that of both the Congress and the collective of governors speaking through a TOGA. The Court, instead, should have been particularly deferential to this TOGA-sponsored legislation. More generally, when federal statutes are supported by groups such as the National Governors Association, courts ought to be reluctant to find those statutes unlawful on federalism grounds and, instead, adopt a presumption that such statutes are appropriately state-regarding and thus constitutionally valid.

Providing Regulatory Rights for TOGAs

An argument for according TOGAs and TOGA-based work special recognition in litigation could also be a predicate for providing TOGAs specific roles in national policy-making processes. One example is the Advisory Commission on Intergovernmental Relations (ACIR), an organization chartered by the federal government, which existed from 1959 to 1996. ACIR's mission included "bring[ing] together representatives of the Federal, State, and local governments for consideration of common problems."[74] To do so, ACIR's governing board included members of Congress, federal officials, citizens, and four governors; in addition, relying on nominations by TOGAs, the president appointed three state legislators, four mayors, and three county officials to the ACIR board.

TOGAs were utilized in varying ways in the ACIR process to advance different presidential administrations' visions of how to allocate funds and authority in relationship to national or local control. For instance, President Johnson required federal agencies to consult with state and local officials in the development and implementation of major programs and regulations that affected states and localities. An executive circular specifically named the US Conference of Mayors, the National Governors Association, and other prominent TOGAs as official liaison groups.[75] Federal agencies channeled information on proposed regulations to ACIR, which forwarded it to the TOGAs, and the TOGAs consulted their members and sent comments back to the agencies via ACIR. According to some accounts, when TOGAs identified problems, federal agencies were required to negotiate with them.[76]

From a majoritarian standpoint, ACIR's efforts to encourage states and localities to channel their transnationalism through TOGAs could produce more policy-making consensus among diverse coalitions of subnational actors. But what could be lost are individual actions on the part of certain states or localities that spark innovation, even if those innovators also are outliers ahead of or behind any emergent national consensus. Crafting a contemporary version of ACIR would require a reevaluation of which TOGAs ought to be named participants, whether representation outside the channels of state and local organizations would be desirable, and how to structure individualized contacts between federal officials and specific localities and states.

ACIR represents a model of a statutory regime that brings various TOGAs together. Other kinds of regulatory rights are asymmetrical, favoring only particular subnational actors. For instance, certain federal statutes permit federal agencies to waive the applicability of rules for certain subnational units under specified circumstances.[77] The Clean Air Act provides an example of one such model. Although the Act generally does not allow states to "adopt or attempt to enforce" their own vehicle emission standards, it authorizes the US EPA to grant California, the only state that had adopted such standards prior to the Clean Air Act's enactment, a waiver for stricter enforcement standards than those imposed by the federal government.[78] Under the Act's "piggyback" provision, other states may adopt standards identical to those for which California receives a waiver.[79]

One could use these examples to craft federal statutes that provide similar recognition to states or localities that have been particularly innovative in other areas of policy development—for instance, Seattle as one of the progenitors of the translocal US Conference of Mayors' Climate Protection Agreement. Or Congress could impose a requirement that the federal government grant a waiver from application of federal law only if more than one—or five, or thirty—states signaled their intention to depart from the national standard. Congress could also encourage transnational networks of translocal actors, for instance, by permitting states or localities to enact heightened emission standards if they could provide evidence that one or more foreign nations or subnational governments outside the United States has already adopted such a law.

The caveat here is that waiver mechanisms, as currently formulated, give a great deal of power to federal agencies. California mounted a legal challenge to the refusal by President George W. Bush's administration to grant a waiver under the Clean Air Act for regulations adopted by the state to require new motor vehicles to reduce emission of greenhouse gases—a policy that was subsequently reversed by President Barack Obama's administration.[80] As further evidence of translocal coventuring, California was supported in the litigation by other states hoping to take advantage of the Act's piggyback provision and implement standards comparable to those imposed by California.

Aggregate Concerns: Regulating TOGAs by Structuring Representation and Forcing Disclosure

We turn now from ways to create policy and legal advocacy roles *for* TOGAs to questions about superintendence *of* them. A major vehicle for such oversight is the potential control imposed by the legal and political infrastructure in each individual jurisdiction that joins a TOGA. Our focus here, however, is on national—albeit not necessarily federal—law.

Political theories focusing on corporations, class actions, and other organizations have long explored problems of "bonding" representatives to those they represent to ensure loyalty and of organizing procedures to permit "monitoring" of named leaders, both to inform and to oversee them. In the TOGA context, the concern is that collective activities can undermine accountability. For example, the National League of Cities has 1,600 dues-payers—of which some are leagues of small cities—out of a total of 19,000 cities. Thus, the exact percentage of cities formally "represented" in the National League of Cities in the sense of paying dues is unclear, as is the import of decisions to affirmatively affiliate with the organization.

Regulatory responses can draw from experiences with class actions and corporations, in which disclosure, transparency, and accountability are mandated under the supervision of a federal judge or an agency. Given, however, that TOGAs are quasi-governmental and aim to serve as counterweights to federal authority, we would prefer to see such regulatory regimes developed by TOGAs themselves and the subnational entities from which they stem.

For example, TOGAs vary in their rules regarding when and how to use their voice or to advance policies on behalf of their membership. Regulatory regimes could make some of these practices mandatory by requiring that TOGAs develop mechanisms to clarify how they formulate positions and whether policies are the artifacts of their executive committees, fall within the purview of staff, or require affirmative assent from all members. (Overregulation is an unattractive risk, given that TOGAs ought to be seen as participants in the set of associational freedoms essential to democracy.) Regulatory regimes need not only be supervisory; another possible way to encourage particular structures would be to provide federal subsidies, such as tax credits or additional funding, for TOGAs. And a predicate to all such interventions would be a richer understanding of the political and economic valences of subnational actors' decisions to associate formally.

The Futures of Federalism(s)

As this chapter illustrates, TOGAs are exemplary of the multiplication of "national" players rooted in states and localities, yet reaching across them. We can certainly understand the need for national economic and energy policies and the potential costs of fragmentation,[81] but multiple and interacting legal regimes cannot be avoided. Indeed, this multiplicity is part of the federalist vision; competition about ideas and responses exists at the national level and enlivens debates about the shape of regulation. Legal interventions should further this engagement. TOGAs enrich the public sphere because they are identified through affiliations with jurisdictional levels and populated by actors choosing to work in the public sector.

Nevertheless, our enthusiasm about TOGAs generally does not suggest that specific positions taken by TOGAs are necessarily to be celebrated. In terms of democratic theory and concerns about fairness, transparency, and accountability, more evaluation and likely regulation should help to frame the representative roles of TOGAs engaged in policy making.

To return to where we began, the Climate Protection Agreement of the US Conference of Mayors illustrates that the notion of an exclusive, national authority to deal with issues deemed "foreign" cannot succeed. COMPASS and other opponents of the Kyoto Protocol may stand against transnational environmental ventures, and federal judges may find various local actions preempted. But, as all of these rule makers try to classify a set of problems— in this case, climate change—as categorically national or local, the world in which they are operating belies the boundaries imposed. The mayors' innovations not only affect climate policy through their interactions. The mayors' joint policy initiatives should also change our understanding of US federalism, as they exemplify the work of new entities, such as TOGAs, that federalism has helped to spawn.

Acknowledgments

All rights reserved, © 2011, Resnik, Civin, and Frueh. Our thanks to Adam Grogg, Yale Law School, 2010, and to Allison Tait, Yale Law School, 2011, who worked with us on the article "Ratifying Kyoto at the Local Level: Sovereigntism, Federalism, and Transnational Organizations of Government Actors (TOGAs)," from which this chapter developed.

Notes

1. J. Resnik, J. Civin, and J. Frueh, "Ratifying Kyoto at the Local Level: Sovereigntism, Federalism, and Translocal Organizations of Government Actors (TOGAs)," *Arizona Law Review* 50 (2008): 709; a condensed version has been published: Resnik, Civin, and Frueh, "Kyoto at the Local Level: Federalism and Translocal Organizations of Government Actors (TOGAs)," *Environmental Law and Policy Annual Review* 40 (2010): 10768.

2. A. M. Cammisa, *Governments as Interest Groups: Intergovernmental Lobbying and the Federal System* (New York: Praeger Publishers, 1995); C. C. Hicks, *Bringing the States Back In: The National Governors' Association and Transformations in U.S. Welfare Policy, 1986–1996* (PhD diss., Columbia University, 2007), available online at ProQuest, UMI No. 3249091; D. H. Haider, *When Governments Come to Washington: Governors, Mayors, and Intergovernmental Lobbying* (New York: Free Press, 1974); D. S. Arnold and J. F. Plant, *Public Official Associations and State and Local Government: A Bridge Across One Hundred Years* (Fairfax, VA: George Mason University Press, 1994).

3. *Kyoto Protocol to the United Nations Framework Convention on Climate Change*, International Legal Materials 37 (1997): 22, available at http://unfccc.int/essential_background/ kyoto_protocol/items/1678.php.

4. Committee to Preserve American Security and Sovereignty, *Treaties, National Sovereignty, and Executive Power: A Report on the Kyoto Protocol* (1998), available at http://jamesvdelong.com/articles/environmental/kyoto.html.

5. Committee to Preserve American Security and Sovereignty, *Treaties, National Sovereignty, and Executive Power.*

6. V. C. Jackson, *Constitutional Engagement in a Transnational Era* (New York: Oxford University Press, 2009).

7. South African Constitution, pmbl. and ch. 2, § 39 (1996).

8. J. Resnik, "Categorical Federalism: Jurisdiction, Gender, and the Globe," *Yale Law Journal* 111 (2001): 619.

9. E. V. Spelman, *Inessential Woman: Problems of Exclusion in Feminist Thought* (Boston: Beacon Press, 1988).

10. *Crosby v. National Foreign Trade Council*, 530 U.S. 363 (2000).

11. *National Foreign Trade Council, Inc. v. Giannoulias*, 523 F. Supp. 2d 731 (N.D. Ill. 2007).

12. Committee to Preserve American Security and Sovereignty, *Treaties, National Sovereignty, and Executive Power.*

13. President George W. Bush, "Remarks on Global Climate Change," *Public Papers* 1 (2001): 634.

14. US Conference of Mayors, Mayors Climate Protection Center, *The U.S. Mayors Climate Protection Agreement (as endorsed by the 73rd Annual U.S. Conference of Mayors meeting, Chicago, 2005)*, available at http://www.usmayors.org/climateprotection/documents/mcpAgreement.pdf.

15. US Conference of Mayors, *U.S. Mayors Climate Protection Agreement.*

16. US Conference of Mayors, Mayors Climate Protection Center, *List of Participating Mayors*, available at http://www.usmayors.org/climateprotection/list.asp (last visited November 28, 2010).

17. K. Zezima, "In New Hampshire, Towns Put Climate on the Agenda," *New York Times* (March 19, 2007).

18. J. Resnik, "The Internationalism of American Federalism: Missouri and Holland," *Missouri Law Review* 73 (2009): 1105.

19. J. Resnik, "Law's Migration: American Exceptionalism, Silent Dialogues, and Federalism's Multiple Ports of Entry," *Yale Law Journal* 115 (2006): 1564.

20. *Coyle v. Smith*, 221 U.S. 559, 567 (1911).

21. R. L. Revesz, "Rehabilitating Interstate Competition: Rethinking the 'Race-to-the-Bottom' Rationale for Federal Environmental Regulation," *New York University Law Review* 67 (1992): 1210; K. H. Engel, "State Environmental Standard-Setting: Is There a 'Race' and Is It 'to the Bottom'?" *Hastings Law Journal* 48 (1997): 271, 274.

22. U.S. Const., art. I, § 10, cl. 3.

23. A. O'M. Bowman, "Horizontal Federalism: Exploring Interstate Interactions," *Journal of Public Administration Research and Theory* 14 (2004): 535, 544.

24. G. E. Metzger, "Congress, Article IV, and Interstate Relations," *Harvard Law Review* 120 (2007): 1468; A. Erbsen, "Horizontal Federalism," *Minnesota Law Review* 93 (2008): 493.

25. W. A. Logan, "Horizontal Federalism in an Age of Criminal Justice Interconnectedness," *University of Pennsylvania Law Review* 154 (2005): 257.

26. L. A. Baker, "Putting the Safeguards Back into the Political Safeguards of Federalism," *Villanova Law Review* 46 (2001): 951, 955–56, 966–67.

27. N. M. Davidson, "Cooperative Localism: Federal-Local Collaboration in an Era of State Sovereignty," *Virginia Law Review* 93 (2007): 959, 968–69; R. C. Schragger, "Can Strong Mayors Empower Weak Cities? On the Power of Local Executives in a Federal System," *Yale Law Journal* 115 (2006): 2542.

28. D. Farber, *Federalism and Climate Change: The Role of the States in a Future Federal Regime*, Remarks at the William H. Rehnquist Center Conference (February 11, 2008), available at http://www.law.arizona.edu/FrontPage/Events/Gallery/fedconference/index.htm; L. Kramer, "Understanding Federalism," *Vanderbilt Law Review* 47 (1994): 1485, 1551–59.

29. C. Vout, "The Myth of the Toga: Understanding the History of Roman Dress," *Greece and Rome* 43 (1996): 204, 214–16.

30. US Conference of Mayors, *About the U.S. Conference of Mayors*, available at http://usmayors.org/about/overview.asp (last visited November 28, 2010).

31. Arnold and Plant, *Public Official Associations*, 77; R. M. Flanagan, "Roosevelt, Mayors, and the New Deal Regime: The Origins of Intergovernmental Lobbying and Administration," *Polity* 31 (1999): 415, 415–16.

32. R. M. Flanagan, "Lyndon Johnson, Community Action, and Management of the Administrative State," *Presidential Studies Quarterly* 31 (2001): 585, 595–96.

33. US Conference of Mayors, *2010 Dues for the U.S. Conference of Mayors*, available at http://usmayors.org/about/dues.asp (last visited November 28, 2010).

34. J. Walters, "Lobbying for the Good Old Days," *Governing* 4 (1991): 35; C. H. Levine and J. A. Thurber, "Reagan and the Intergovernmental Lobby: Iron Triangles, Cozy Subsystems, and Political Conflict," in *Interest Group Politics*, 2d ed., edited by A. J. Cigler and B. A. Loomis (Washington, DC: CQ Press, 1986), 202, 212.

35. S. Sassen, "Globalization or Denationalization?" *Review of International Political Economy* 10 (2003): 1, 6, 14–15.

36. National Association of Counties, *About NACo—the Voice of America's Counties*, available at http://www.naco.org/about/Pages/default.aspx (last visited November 28, 2010).

37. National Association of Counties, *NACo Affiliates*, available at http://www .naco.org/ABOUT/PARTNERS/Pages/Affiliates.aspx (last visited November 28, 2010); Arnold and Plant, *Public Official Associations*, 100.

38. National Association of Counties, *County Membership*, available at http:// www.naco.org/about/join/Pages/CountyMembership.aspx (last visited November 28, 2010).

39. National Association of Counties, *Resolution Urging Congress and the Administration to Take Practical Actions to Reduce the Risks of Global Warming* (2007), previously available at http://www.naco.org/Template.cfm?Section=Media_ Center&template=/ContentManagement/ContentDisplay.cfm&ContentID=22852 (last visited July 17, 2008).

40. National Association of Counties, *County Climate Protection Forum* (2007), previously available at http://www.naco.org/Template.cfm?Section=New_Technical_ Assistance&template=/ ContentManagement/ContentDisplay.cfm&ContentID= 25222 (last visited July 17, 2008).

41. J. D. Nugent, *Federalism Attained: Gubernatorial Lobbying in Washington as a Constitutional Function* (PhD diss., University of Texas, 1998), available online at ProQuest, UMI No. 9838067I, 143.

42. Arnold and Plant, *Public Official Associations*, 50.

43. Republican Governors Association, *About*, available at http://www.rga.org/ homepage/about/ (last visited November 28, 2010).

44. Hicks, *Bringing the States Back In*, 128–34.

45. Democratic Governors Association, *About the DGA*, available at http://www.democraticgovernors.org/about?id=0001 (last visited November 28, 2010).

46. Hicks, *Bringing the States Back In*, 138, 144, 148–53.

47. National Governors Association, *Policy Position NR-11, Global Climate Change* (2010), available at http://www.nga.org/portal/site/nga/menuitem.8358ec 82f5b198d18a2781105010100a0/?vgnextoid=220b9e2f1b091010VgnVCM10000 01a01010aRCRD (last visited November 28, 2010).

48. D. Funkhouser, "Yale Plans a Warming Summit: Schwarzenegger to Join Rell, Others to Urge U.S. Action on Problem," *Hartford Courant* (March 28, 2008).

49. Council of State Governments, *About CSG*, available at http://www.csg.org/about/default.aspx (last visited November 28, 2010).

50. H. W. Toll, "The Work of the American Legislators' Association," *American Political Science Review* 22 (1928): 127.

51. Council of State Governments, Midwestern Office, *Member Services*, available at http://www.csgmidwest.org/memberservices/Services.htm (last visited November 28, 2010).

52. Council of State Governments, *CSG Committees and Task Forces*, available at http://www.csg.org/about/committees.aspx (last visited November 28, 2010).

53. Council of State Governments, *Book of the States*, available at http://www.csg.org/policy/publications/bookofthestates.aspx (last visited November 28, 2010).

54. E. N. Sims, "The Council of State Governments: A National Information Provider," *Government Information Quarterly* 3 (1986): 407, 410.

55. Council of State Governments, *CSG Affiliates*, available at http://www.csg.org/about/affiliates.aspx (last visited November 28, 2010).

56. D. Myers, "Not Too Hot to Handle," *State News* (September 31, 2007), available at http://www.csg.org/pubs/Documents/sn0709NotTooHotToHandle.pdf.

57. Myers, "Not Too Hot to Handle."

58. E. L. Rubin and M. Feeley, "Federalism: Some Notes on a National Neurosis," *UCLA Law Review* 41 (1994): 903.

59. K. Schneider, "Salt Lake City Is Finding a Payoff in Conservation," *New York Times* (November 7, 2007).

60. *Massachusetts v. EPA*, 549 U.S. 497, 531–35 (2007).

61. Brief of Amici Curiae U.S. Conference of Mayors et al., *Massachusetts v. EPA*, 549 U.S. 497 (2007) (No. 05-1120), 2006 WL 2569574, *3.

62. Brief of Amici Curiae US Conference of Mayors et al., *Massachusetts v. EPA*, *23–29.

63. Arnold and Plant, *Public Official Associations*, 5, 77–83, 122–23.

64. Arnold and Plant, *Public Official Associations*, 105–6.

65. Brief of Amici Curiae US Conference of Mayors et al., *Massachusetts v. EPA*.

66. 405 U.S. 727, 741, 732–35 (1972).

67. 405 U.S. at 741, 737–41.

68. Fed. R. Civ. P. 24(a).

69. H. Wechsler, "The Political Safeguards of Federalism: The Role of the States in the Composition and Selection of the National Government," *Columbia Law Review* 54 (1954): 543, 546, 559–60.

70. *Crosby v. National Foreign Trade Council*, 530 U.S. 363 (2000); *Green Mountain Chrysler Plymouth Dodge Jeep v. Crombie*, 508 F. Supp. 2d 295 (D. Vt. 2007); *National Foreign Trade Council, Inc. v. Giannoulias*, 523 F. Supp. 2d 731 (N.D. Ill. 2007).

71. D. A. Farber, "Climate Change, Federalism, and the Constitution," *Arizona Law Review* 50 (2008): 879, 881; J. Resnik, "Foreign as Domestic Affairs: Rethinking Horizontal Federalism and Foreign Affairs Preemption in Light of Translocal

Internationalism," *Emory Law Journal* 57 (2007): 31, 41–42; N. Robinson, "Citizens Not Subjects: U.S. Foreign Relations and the Decentralization of Foreign Policy," *Akron Law Review* 40 (2007): 647, 713–15.

72. Baker, "Putting the Safeguards Back," 955–56, 966–67.

73. 505 U.S. 144 (1992).

74. Pub. L. No. 86-380, § 2(1), (4), 73 Stat. 703, 703–4 (1959).

75. Bureau of the Budget, Circular No. A-85 (June 28, 1967).

76. Haider, *When Governments Come to Washington*, 114–43; J. J. Gunther, *Federal-City Relations: The Role of the Mayors in Federal Aid to Cities* (Cranbury, NJ: Associated University Presses, 1990), 230–33; Arnold and Plant, *Public Official Associations*, 111.

77. 20 U.S.C. § 5891b(b) (2006).

78. 42 U.S.C. § 7543 (2006).

79. 42 U.S.C. § 7507 (2006).

80. F. Barringer, "EPA Grants California the Right to Enforce Emissions," *New York Times* (June 30, 2009); F. Barringer, "California Sues EPA over Denial of Waiver," *New York Times* (January 3, 2008).

81. D. J. Bederman, "Diversity and Permeability in Transnational Governance," *Emory Law Journal* 57 (2007): 201; P. B. Stephan, "What Story Got Wrong—Federalism, Localism Opportunism and International Law," *Missouri Law Review* 50 (2008): 64; T. W. Hazlett, "Federal Preemption in Cellular Phone Regulation," in *Federal Preemption: States' Powers, National Interests*, edited by R. A. Epstein and M. S. Greve (Washington, DC: AEI Press, 2007), 113–33.

Chapter 7

Acting in Concert

State Efforts to Regionally Address Climate Change

Edella Schlager

In Brief ───

- States have begun using administrative agreements to collectively address regional climate-change issues. Such agreements are more flexible than compacts, requiring the endorsement of fewer branches of government and imposing no limits on state autonomy. However, they are nonbinding—states are free to back out regardless of repercussions to the remaining parties.

- Interstate administrative agreements have been formed in the US Northeast, West, and Midwest to create regional cap-and-trade systems and other regional climate policies.

- Interstate administrative agreements gain traction when state legislatures pass laws or regulation to pursue the goals of the agreement; they lose traction when state legislatures decline to cooperate with provisions of an agreement signed by its governor.

- Administrative agreements are supported by a polyphonic federalist system in which states and regions can pursue climate-change policy appropriate to the characteristics of the area while also anticipating and influencing federal interests and policies.

As the other chapters in this section make clear, in the realm of environmental policy, states interact with, influence, and affect one another in a variety of ways, from policy innovation and diffusion (Karch, chapter 5), to information sharing, lobbying, and position taking through professional associations (Resnik, Civin, and Frueh, chapter 6), to technology development and diffusion (Adelman and Engel, chapter 8). In addition, states—particularly governors and state agencies—have begun to coordinate regional responses to climate change using a relatively unfamiliar but useful arrangement known as an administrative agreement. This chapter explores states' use of administrative agreements to act in concert to address shared environmental problems and take advantage of opportunities that may be realized only through joint action. Administrative agreements are the primary tool that states have used to pursue regional goals, such as upgrading regional electric grids to incorporate green forms of electricity generation and to form regional greenhouse-gas (GHG) cap-and-trade systems.

This chapter begins by comparing administrative agreements to their more common relative, compacts. To date, states have used only administrative agreements to collectively address regional climate-change issues. Nonetheless, very little scholarly or popular attention has been devoted to their role in policy making to address climate change or other issues. Next, the chapter examines three interstate administrative agreements in the Northeast, West, and Midwest to create regional carbon cap-and-trade systems and other regional climate policies and points out the challenges and obstacles to implementation of such agreements. It then examines why these regional efforts have emerged and what their purpose is before concluding with an assessment of their strengths and limitations and how they fit within a federal form of governance.

Comparing Compacts and Administrative Agreements

Compacts and administrative agreements identify goals and objectives as well as actions to be taken by states to realize those goals. For instance, the South Platte River Compact's goal is to divide and apportion the waters of the river to Colorado and Nebraska. Colorado, the upstream state, attains this goal by allowing a specified amount of water to pass to Nebraska, the downstream state, during certain times of the year.[1] Similarly, the Regional Greenhouse Gas Initiative (RGGI), an administrative agreement, has the goal of stabilizing and reducing carbon dioxide emissions from its member states. In turn, member states achieve their goals by creating and participating in a regional carbon dioxide cap-and-trade system.

In practice, states have used only administrative agreements—not compacts—to pursue shared climate-change goals and objectives. The reasons for this primarily concern the processes of creation, implementation, and dissolution of agreements and compacts. Administrative agreements are more flexible than compacts, requiring the participation and buy-in of fewer public officials and levels and branches of government. They also do not require limiting state autonomy like compacts may. Such flexibility comes with a limitation: administrative agreements, unlike compacts, are nonbinding among states. States cannot enforce administrative agreements against one another. To appreciate the strengths and weaknesses of administrative agreements requires an examination of how they are formed, implemented, and dissolved in comparison to compacts.

Formation

The US Constitution, under Article 1, Section 10, allows states to enter into compacts with the consent of the US Congress. The purpose of compacts is to allow states to address subnational issues in a way that is crafted for the particular issue at hand while also accounting for national issues and values. The impetus to form a compact may come from either the states or Congress. For instance, in 1980, Congress passed legislation encouraging states to form interstate compacts to oversee regional low-level radioactive waste-disposal facilities. In contrast, most of the western interstate river compacts in place today resulted from states petitioning Congress for permission to devise compacts for governing shared rivers.[2] In either case, Congress must approve the effort to form a compact. Once a compact has been negotiated, it must also be approved by the legislatures and governors of the member states and by the US Congress and president. Compacts are part of the statutory law of each of the member states and of the national government.[3]

In contrast, administrative agreements are not directly or explicitly provided for in the US Constitution. As Joseph Zimmerman notes, "The Constitution contains many silences and one of the most important silences relates to *ad hoc* and permanent interstate joint and reciprocal administrative agreements."[4] Their process of creation is also distinct. Rather than involving the legislative and executive branches of government at the state and federal levels, administrative agreements simply require the consent of state governors. Unlike compacts that, once approved, become part of state and federal law, the extent to which administrative agreements become codified into law depends on governors and legislators.

Upon engaging in an administrative agreement, governors act by issuing executive orders to guide the actions of state agencies, such as creating inventories of GHG emissions, or task forces to construct state climate-change mitigation plans. Administrative agreements that only require the action of governors and/or planning and consultation among states agencies are quite common and are used extensively in addressing climate-change issues. For instance, state members of the Western Climate Initiative (WCI) have developed climate-change plans that include developing GHG inventories and assessing mitigation measures for meeting GHG emission-reduction goals.[5]

Administrative agreements gain additional traction when states devise administrative regulations and/or statutory laws to pursue the goals of the agreement. Governors may direct state agencies to engage in administrative rule making at their discretion. For instance, many states of the WCI and all member states of the northeastern RGGI (both discussed below) have adopted California's stricter auto emission standards through the administrative rule-making authority of their air quality agencies. The states may also monitor and enforce compliance via administrative rules.

In some cases, legislation is necessary in order to realize some of the objectives of an administrative agreement. For instance, the Platte River Recovery Implementation Program is an administrative agreement entered into by Colorado, Nebraska, Wyoming, the US Fish and Wildlife Service, and the Bureau of Reclamation with the purpose of collectively managing the Platte for the recovery of endangered species. One of the commitments made by the three states was to increase the amount of water that remains in the river as a means of supporting habitat for endangered species. To carry out its duties under the agreement, Nebraska required a major revision of its groundwater law. This took almost a decade to accomplish due to resistance by agricultural water users to the imposition of restrictions on their access and use of groundwater.

Governors have been much more active and engaged than have legislatures in supporting climate-change administrative agreements. Challenges occur when legislative action is required to implement the terms of an agreement. In such cases, action depends not only on a single actor, the governor, but on the governor gaining the consent of dozens of legislators to move forward. In turn, just as governors may have difficulty securing the consent of legislatures, legislatures cannot prevent the signing of such agreements or the withdrawal of states from them without passing legislation to that effect. But such legislation would require the signature of the governor, who presumably supports the administrative agreement and would not sign such legislation. Consequently, administrative agreements are as grounded in law as governors and legislatures allow them to be.

Revision and Dissolution

The differences in revising or dissolving compacts and administrative agreements illustrate the differences in a state's autonomy in relation to each arrangement. A compact limits the autonomy of a state to act unilaterally in relation to the issue covered by a compact; an administrative agreement does not.

Compacts, particularly those around highly salient issues such as water allocation, have very strict revision and dissolution clauses. For a compact to be revised, all members must agree to reopen it, revise it, and adopt the revisions through regular legislative processes. Likewise, all members must unanimously agree to dissolve it.

In contrast, administrative agreements are more like contracts than constitutions in that a member may unilaterally withdraw from an agreement, although the agreement may make it costly to do so. Often, a governor may withdraw his or her state from an administrative agreement without obtaining the consent of the legislature. An administrative agreement also may protect the interests of those remaining in the agreement. For instance, the administrative agreement creating a regional carbon cap-and-trade system among northeastern states provides a means by which the agreement will be adjusted if a state withdraws—the regional carbon emission cap is adjusted to reflect the withdrawal.[6]

Implementation and Administration

While the origins, constitutional foundations, and dissolution of compacts and administrative agreements are distinct, their administration and implementation are much less so. In practice, the only way to know whether an interstate effort is based on a compact or an administrative agreement is to uncover its origins. The administration of compacts and administrative agreements runs the gamut from individual state agencies administering the requirements of the agreement or compact with very little contact or communication among member states, to formal boards and agencies with representatives from each member state.

States have used administrative agreements, not compacts, to engage in regional efforts to reduce GHG emissions and to realize low-carbon economies. They have probably done this for a variety of reasons. Administrative agreements are more easily entered into and allow for quick action, whereas compacts may take a decade or more to create. In addition, administrative agreements are more flexible, governors may readily enter into and withdraw from agreements, and they may be at least partly implemented through executive orders. In contrast, compacts are more fixed, requiring the consent of executive and legislative branches of government of all compact members and of the federal government to revise or dissolve.

Another reason states may be using administrative agreements and not compacts in pursuing climate-change mitigation policies is the inaction and at times hostility of the federal government to such policies at the national level. Federal government inaction has left a policy vacuum that the states have rushed to fill using administrative agreements.

The Regional Pursuit of Common Policies

States in the Northeast, the West, and the Midwest have been particularly active in pursuing regional climate-change policies. In the Northeast and Midwest, the regional governors associations, which are types of translocal organizations of government actors (TOGAs), have provided the venues for governors to meet, discuss, and develop administrative agreements. For instance, in 2001, the Northeastern Governors/Eastern Canadian Premiers Association adopted a climate-change action plan from which a number of administrative agreements, including the one that created the RGGI, have sprung. Likewise, in 2007, the Midwestern Governors Association (MGA) sponsored a midwestern energy, security, and climate summit, which included the participation of most of the association's membership, a Canadian province (Manitoba), and many different interest groups and industries interested in and affected by energy and climate change. A number of declarations, promises of cooperation, and administrative agreements emerged from the summit, including an agreement to devise a carbon cap-and-trade system.[7]

The administrative agreements between the states have centered on energy: promoting energy efficiency, developing and distributing "green" forms of energy, and reducing and/or capturing GHG emissions from burning fossil fuels. Among these activities, the regional cap-and-trade systems being developed and implemented by states receive the most media attention; however, the agreements have encompassed a wide variety of energy-based activities, from investing in biofuel technologies to designing infrastructure to transport captured carbon emissions and developing deep underground repositories. As Barry G. Rabe notes in chapter 11, these policies are being touted as means for addressing a very serious environmental problem and embraced across the country as an engine of economic development.

Regional Cap-and-Trade Systems

The three groups of states have either implemented or are planning to implement regional GHG cap-and-trade systems. The RGGI in the Northeast was devised in 2005, became fully operational in 2009, and is the model upon which other systems have been organized, with modifications. The WCI and the Midwestern Greenhouse Gas Reduction Accord are scheduled to begin operation in 2012.

The Northeast's RGGI is based on a memorandum of understanding—an example of an administrative agreement. It spells out the design of a sophisticated cap-and-trade system that captures many of the features that climate-change economists and policy scholars had been debating for several years, such as setting a regionwide cap, allocating shares of the cap to the individual states, incorporating carbon offsets, and auctioning off allowances.[8] Furthermore, the states created a regional, nonprofit organization and governing board to implement and monitor the system, while enforcement remains the responsibility of individual states.

The states devised a model rule detailing the cap-and-trade system. Each state's legislature or appropriate regulatory agency then adopted legislation or rules in accord with the model rule. States' legislation varies primarily around how detailed the cap-and-trade system is defined. For instance, some states direct that allowances not purchased in an auction be retired, whereas other states did not address the issue legislatively.[9]

Overall, the RGGI is a highly coordinated regional system. The cap establishes regionwide carbon dioxide emission levels for all large electricity-generating plants to achieve a 10 percent reduction in carbon dioxide emissions. Each participating state is allocated a portion of the regionwide cap; each state's portion is denominated in one-ton allowances, and the allowances are auctioned to the utilities required to participate in the program.[10]

The RGGI appears to be performing well, although the end of the first compliance period is not until 2011, at which time compliance for each regulated utility will be determined. Seven auctions have been conducted, raising almost $600 million, almost three-quarters of which has been devoted to energy efficiency programs and renewable energy projects by the RGGI states.[11] In addition, carbon emissions are well below the cap. From 2005, when the cap was initially adopted, through 2009, carbon emissions declined by 33 percent.[12] The sharp decline has been attributed to a variety of factors: lower demand for electricity because of energy efficiency investments and a weak economy, utilities switching from fossil fuels to lower cost natural gas, and increased use of nuclear, wind, and solar capacity.[13] Finally, the cap-and-trade system has had minimal effect on consumer electricity prices.[14]

The members of the WCI and the Midwestern Greenhouse Gas Reduction Accord are still in the process of devising cap-and-trade systems, both of which will be broader in scope than the RGGI system. First, six GHGs and not just carbon dioxide will be covered. Second, in addition to electricity generation, the cap-and-trade systems also will include emissions from combustion at commercial and industrial facilities, industrial process emissions, and residential, commercial, and transportation fuels. As in the RGGI, each state will be allocated a portion of the regional cap, most allowances will be auctioned, and states will devote a substantial portion of auction revenues to energy efficiency programs and renewable energy projects.[15]

The WCI system is scheduled to go into effect January 1, 2012. Currently, it appears that only California and Manitoba will have cap-and-trade systems in place by 2012. California adopted comprehensive climate-change legislation that mandates a cap-and-trade system be in place by 2012, and the state appears to be on course for accomplishing this. Whether the Midwest system will be implemented is less clear. Members of the accord have stated their very strong preference for a national cap-and-trade system; to date, no state has considered or adopted legislation necessary to create its own cap-and-trade system.

Non–Cap-and-Trade Policies and Initiatives

The states involved in the regional initiatives recognize that they must pursue policies that complement a cap-and-trade system in order to reduce their GHG emissions and transition to low-carbon economies. The Northeast and the West established regional GHG emission reduction targets that they will in fact be unable to meet without complementary policies. These policies center on goals and projects that are regional in scope, such as the siting and development of transmission lines that tie alternative energy sources such as wind or solar power into a regional power grid. As the midwestern governors, via the MGA, noted in 2009, "The diversity of the region means that there is no single path that all jurisdictions can or should follow in their effort to transform their energy sectors."[16]

The complementary policies and initiatives engaged in by the states of the three regions are either directly or indirectly grounded in additional administrative agreements. The midwestern states have tended to use administrative agreements to realize specific goals, whereas the western and northeastern states have tended to support regional coordination through resolutions and task forces originating in their governors' associations. In other words, the RGGI and WCI, both administrative agreements, commit their members to pursuing complementary policies, but have not yet developed additional administrative agreements for doing so.

The complementary policies engaged in by the states may be classified into three categories: energy production, energy efficiency and conservation, and transportation. These categories target GHG-emitting activities and sources not covered by the cap-and-trade systems. At the same time, each set of poli-cies reflects regional circumstances and context. For instance, the midwestern states emphasize carbon capture and storage and biofuels, reflecting their reliance on coal-fired utility plants and large agricultural economies.

Energy Production

Each of the overarching regional initiatives has pursued a variety of green-energy production goals. For instance, the midwestern states have set a goal that 30 percent of electricity consumed in the region will be from renewable sources. In comparison, the WCI is developing policies that would encour-age the widespread adoption of small-scale renewable energy resources, also known as distributed power, such as residential and commercial investment in solar or wind power.[17] The northeastern states, through their governors association, have developed a renewable energy blueprint that identifies specific means by which states may coordinate contracting for renewable sources of power to encourage private-sector investment. As the governors note, "Interstate coordination to aggregate the states' supply needs and contracting authority would strengthen the region's ability to support those renewable generation projects most able to serve New England consumers cost effectively."[18]

Given the push to invest in renewable energy sources, each of the regional efforts is increasingly focusing on developing additional transmission lines. Regional planning and investment is necessary because high–wind-power–generating areas are typically located far from high-use areas and are not currently linked through transmission systems.[19] At the 2009 MGA sum-mit, a regional initiative was formed to develop a cost-share formula for state investments in a regionwide transmission system for wind energy and construction of new transmission capacity.

In addition to "green" sources of energy, the midwestern states, more than any other region, are investing in and encouraging the widespread adoption of advanced coal and carbon capture and storage (CC&S) technologies, including commercial-scale, advanced-technology, coal-fired plants equipped with CC&S technology and a multijurisdictional pipeline to transport captured carbon. These states are also considering creating geo-logic carbon sequestration utilities that would manage cross-jurisdictional storage sites that accept carbon from multiple projects and sources.[20] They are pursuing clean coal technologies because not only are some states major producers of coal but also most of the region's utilities and industries rely on coal to generate electricity.

Each of the regions is aggressively pursuing renewable energy generation and the infrastructure to support it. These regional efforts in turn ease the ability of each state's utilities to realize their renewable portfolio requirements and increase the likelihood that the northeastern and western regions will meet their emission reduction goals.

Energy Efficiency and Conservation

Energy efficiency and conservation are viewed by the three associations of states as a cost-effective means of realizing GHG emission goals and transitioning to low-carbon economies. Energy efficiency not only allows utilities to avoid power plant construction but also benefits consumers through lower utility bills. Each region is adopting different policy approaches due to their different circumstances. For instance, the New England states have devoted almost three-quarters of the revenues from auctioning carbon allowances in the RGGI to energy efficiency and conservation programs, such as home weatherization programs, rebates, and low-interest loans for energy-efficient appliances, windows, and heating and cooling systems.[21]

The midwestern governors, however, have been most aggressive in setting and pursuing energy efficiency targets. Midwestern states have adopted the aggressive goals of requiring utilities to realize energy efficiency savings equal to 2 percent of annual retail sales of natural gas and electricity beginning in 2015. Iowa, Minnesota, and Wisconsin have already adopted such goals and are encouraging all member states to do likewise.[22]

Furthermore, to support energy efficiency efforts, states and provinces in each of the three regional associations have agreed to have their government agencies and employees lead by example through building energy-efficient government offices and providing alternative transportation programs for employees.[23] In general, the states, through their governors' associations, are encouraged to adopt energy efficiency policies. These efforts center more on policy diffusion than on explicit forms of coordination across state lines.

Transportation

Emissions from automobiles and trucks constitute 25 percent of all US GHG emissions;[24] thus, transportation is an important sector to target for emission reductions. Again, the three regional groups of states are taking varying approaches. Midwestern states are targeting the production and use of biofuels and other low-carbon fuels through two administrative agreements. One is centered on developing a regional system of signage for biofuels, designating biofuel travel corridors, and educating fuel retailers on converting to E85 (85 percent ethanol) fuel pumps. The other encourages collaboration on research into advanced biofuel production, sharing information about the location of advanced biofuel production plants, and coordinating siting and permitting guidelines for such plants.[25]

The WCI and RGGI have focused on developing low-carbon fuel standards, which do not mandate that a certain percentage of transportation fuels be bio-based, as does the MGA approach. Rather, a low-carbon fuel standard provides a method of calculating the carbon intensity of fuels and requires fuel sellers to reduce over time the carbon intensity of the mix of fuels they sell.[26]

The regional coalitions of states are engaged in developing and implementing a diverse portfolio of climate-change policies centered on clean energy. Underlying each regional effort is the recognition that realizing public benefits and goods requires regional cooperation; individual state action cannot accomplish the desired goals. For instance, sufficient demand to encourage investment in low-carbon fuels requires a regional market. Likewise, infrastructure investment in carbon capture and storage is beyond the means of a single state, but a regional effort could muster the resources for such an undertaking. Thus, these regional efforts do not consist just of states adopting similar policies, but of states creating regional markets and infrastructure to support low-carbon economies.

Who Develops and Implements Administrative Agreements?

As noted above, administrative agreements, unlike compacts, do not require the participation of the legislative branches of state governments to be adopted and implemented. Rather, governors and executive branch agencies may engage and implement such agreements. Variation in which branches of government form and administer climate-change administrative agreements is clearly present among the three regions. The northeastern states stand out for the active participation of their states' legislatures; the western states are known for the open hostility of some legislatures to the notion of climate change. The western and midwestern governors rely heavily on summits, task forces, and advisory committees to further their goals; the northeastern governors rely on executive agency staff.

For instance, shortly after the northeastern governors and Canadian premiers unanimously adopted a climate-change plan, in 2001, the northeastern governors pursued the many policy goals they committed themselves to, often with the support of their legislatures. Each of the states' governors adopted vehicle GHG emission standards, with the governors of Connecticut, Rhode Island, New Jersey, and Maryland signing laws passed by their state's legislatures.[27] In the other northeastern states, emission standards were adopted by air quality boards and agencies. Furthermore, each of the northeastern states' legislatures passed laws creating the necessary administrative authorization for their states to participate in the RGGI cap-and-trade system, as well as specifying how revenues from the auctions would be used.[28]

In contrast to the cooperation exhibited by the executive and legislative branches of the northeastern states, the experience of the members of the WCI and Midwest Energy Security and Climate Stewardship administrative agreements is decidedly more mixed around legislative action. Only California's legislature has adopted the necessary laws to realize a cap-and-trade system. However, on other climate-change policies, legislatures of a few states have consistently acted in concert with their governors to adopt laws and policies promoted by the WCI and midwestern administrative agreements.

In the Midwest, the Minnesota legislature passed legislation establishing statewide GHG emission reduction goals, whereas the Illinois legislature adopted emission caps for electric utilities. In the West, the Washington, Oregon, and California legislatures have adopted laws establishing GHG emission reduction goals, as well as emission performance standards for electric utilities. Each of these actions complements the operation of regional cap-and-trade systems. Statewide GHG emission goals act like statewide caps, both supporting the formation of a regional cap-and-trade system and ensuring that the burden of reducing emissions does not fall only on the industries and businesses required to participate in a system.

In the West, two legislatures are actively opposed to engaging with climate-change initiatives or policies. The Arizona and Utah legislatures have both adopted resolutions questioning climate-change science and urging their state governors to withdraw from WCI. In February 2010, the Utah legislature adopted a resolution questioning the validity of climate-change science and urged the federal government to cease all efforts to reduce carbon emissions. But the conservative Republican governors of the two states, although sympathetic to the concerns of their legislatures, have refused to withdraw. Both argue that participation in the WCI allows their states' interests to be considered in regional and national discussions of climate-change policy.[29]

The governors and executive branch agencies, even without the participation of legislatures, have not acted alone. In the Midwest and West, the regional initiatives have repeatedly drawn on task forces and advisory committees to assist in devising administrative agreements, engage in research and analysis of policy alternatives, participate in planning activities, and provide input and feedback on the design of cap-and-trade systems and complementary policies. For instance, the WCI, in developing its cap-and-trade system, established committees that focused on different aspects of the system, including emissions tracking and reporting, allocating allowances among partners, and incorporating offsets. Each committee included and consulted with a variety of interested stakeholders. Drawing on a variety of stakeholders allowed governors to tailor the outcome to the characteristics of their specific regions. In addition, the committees and task forces, in order to make consensus recommendations, had to work out their varying interests and values around particular policies, ideally resulting in policies with broader popular appeal. Tapping into stakeholders allows governors to build support for climate-change policies, projects, and actions, which is particularly important if legislatures are not initially supportive.

The various patterns of participation reveal the flexibility of administrative agreements. They may be initiated solely by governors, who with the assistance of state executive branch agencies actively engage with climate-change activities and policies. In addition, governors and executive branch agencies may tap into the support of energy companies, environmental groups, agricultural associations, and local and federal officials. However, in many instances, like the development of cap-and-trade programs, full implementation of regional policies will ultimately require the active participation of legislatures.

The Roles of Climate-Change Administrative Agreements in State and National Climate-Change Policies

When states act around a policy issue that has clear national or international implications, such as climate change, they may do so for a variety of reasons, many of which concern their relation to the federal government. For instance, states may wish to lobby and position themselves to influence federal action. They may try to anticipate and prepare themselves to act quickly once federal legislation on an issue is adopted. States also may try to act as policy laboratories, demonstrating to the federal government what works and what does not when it comes time for the federal government to act.[30] While these federal-government–centered explanations partly account for the administrative agreements reviewed above, the regional climate policy actions taken by states also reflect the autonomy of states, their ability to move into the policy breach when the federal government fails to act, and their ability to pursue goals important to them regardless of national or federal interests. In other words, the administrative agreements reflect polyphonic federalism as associations of states pursue state and regional interests while also anticipating and influencing federal interests and policies.

States are currently positioning themselves to influence, guide, and constrain federal climate-change policies. This is certainly the case with the regional GHG cap-and-trade systems. The administrative agreements forming each system explicitly request that any federal action to create a national market take into account the regional system. In addition, representatives of the three regional systems have met twice. The most recent meeting was in Washington, DC, at the end of 2009 to collaborate on harmonizing their policies on using offsets and identify issues that would have to be addressed if the three plans were to be linked. They also met with the US Environmental Protection Agency and testified before the Senate Energy and Energy Resources Committee on the role of states in implementing federal initiatives. Furthermore, the three regions have actively engaged federal agencies on different policies, from planning and siting transmission lines to investing in biofuels research and carbon capture and storage technologies.

It is also clear that states are preparing to participate in a national cap-and-trade system. The RGGI states have agreed to review any national cap-and-trade program that Congress adopts. If it meets their standards, they intend to dissolve their program and incorporate within the national system. Of course, federal legislation could preempt regional cap-and-trade systems, settling the issue for the states. Furthermore, states are developing the administrative infrastructure necessary to engage in regional and national cap-and-trade systems. The WCI and MGA states have developed emission tracking and reporting systems. And, if federal efforts fail, these states plan to move into the breach.

Also, state governors and public officials view a number of their efforts as experiments, designed to show that even controversial policies, such as cap-and-trade, can be adopted and implemented effectively. The simple design of the RGGI cap-and-trade system is often justified in terms of an experiment. That system was intentionally kept simple—with a not-too-constraining cap and a single GHG (carbon) regulated from a single industry (electric utilities) using an auction—to demonstrate that a GHG cap-and-trade system in the United States is feasible.[31]

Finally, and most important, regional energy initiatives are viewed by members of the administrative agreements as vital mechanisms for spurring much-needed economic development while ensuring stability and security of energy supplies. That is, in their pursuit of climate-change policy development, states are also pursuing their own interests in economic development. The states are coordinating regional efforts to develop low-carbon economies in ways that match their circumstances. This is most clearly illustrated through the various midwestern administrative agreements. Unlike other regions, the midwestern agreements do not emphasize cap-and-trade. Instead, they focus on two other policy areas—biofuels and carbon capture and storage—that relate to three key midwestern economic sectors: agriculture, manufacturing industries, and coal-fired electric utilities. Agriculture, according to the midwestern governors, provides the production base for biofuels research and development. In addition, the region's manufacturing base and utilities rely on coal to power their plants. Carbon capture and storage is important for maintaining and growing both sectors while reducing GHG emissions.

While the states of each of the three regions share the goal to transform regional and state economies into low-carbon economies, each region has a distinctive approach for realizing that goal. It is thus difficult to pigeonhole regional climate-change initiatives in defining their role within the broader climate-change policy landscape, and it is a mistake to dismiss them simply as experiments to be set aside once the federal government acts. They simultaneously reflect national, regional, and state interests, and they anticipate a future in which the federal government is a more active partner to the states in the pursuit of a clean energy economy.

Conclusion

State officials and elected leaders have a variety of institutional mechanisms at their disposal to coordinate state actions to address regional issues. Administrative agreements and compacts have each been utilized effectively around different issues at different points in time. Each institutional mechanism serves a different purpose: administrative agreements are used for coordinating, implementing, and administering common but independent programs, and compacts, for forming special purpose governments to create a single common program across jurisdictions. Resolutions, a third tool, are used for lobbying and position taking.

Administrative agreements allow states to coordinate and cooperate around regional issues in ways tailored to a region. They also allow states to maintain their autonomy in a federal system while influencing and pressing the Congress and president to act in certain ways. Administrative agreements are flexible. They can readily be entered into and can take advantage of the discretionary authority of governors and state agencies to act and pursue policy goals within their legal mandates. States have embraced administrative agreements as the predominant mechanism for addressing climate change, from reducing emissions to encouraging the development and deployment of low-carbon technologies.

The strengths of administrative agreements are also closely related to their limitations. Administrative agreements are voluntary. They are not enforceable agreements among and between states; thus, they work only as well as their members want them to work. To date, the three regional initiatives appear to be relatively vibrant, moving their climate-change agendas forward through regular meetings, active use of advisory committees and task forces, governors issuing executive orders, state agencies engaging in rule making, and, occasionally, legislatures adopting complementary legislation.

But, because administrative agreements are voluntary, states may unilaterally withdraw from them, or they may unilaterally change the terms of their participation, and such actions may trigger responses on the part of other states that may lead to the weakening of such agreements. For instance, in 2009, after the RGGI cap-and-trade system was operational, New York governor David Paterson publicly proposed to increase the number of allowances that New York utilities would be granted for free, as opposed to purchasing at auction. Such a move could have been viewed as granting New York utilities unfair advantage over competing utilities in other RGGI states that have to pay for most of their allowances. Carbon trading firms and environmental groups strongly criticized the governor, arguing that changing market rules just when the market appears to be developing and performing well undermines trust in regulators and, ultimately, trust in the markets. In the end, governors of other RGGI states announced that New York's actions would not affect their commitment to the program, and Paterson took no such action.[32]

Given the limitations of administrative agreements, do they make a difference in mitigating climate-change impacts? The answer depends on what is used as a measure of difference. Regional administrative agreements are no substitute for federal government action. Not all states participate in the regional agreements; consequently, they are unlikely to realize substantial nationwide GHG emission reductions of the sort that will be required to avoid runaway climate change. Also, while Resnik et al. (chapter 6) and others note that state and local officials engage with international issues, such as mitigation efforts, their engagement is not viewed by foreign governments as replacing national commitments.

If making a difference means that administrative agreements meet some or all of their goals, then they do represent valuable initiatives. The administrative agreements have targeted actions and policies that states are well suited to address, and they have pushed the boundaries of state action, particularly in their formation of cap-and-trade systems. The agreements have begun to create the administrative, regulatory, and technical foundations that will support and enhance federal climate-change policies. For instance, cap-and-trade, biofuel distribution systems, and the development of competitively priced biofuels ease the ability of fuel producers, auto manufacturers, and consumers to meet low-carbon emission fuel standards, and the planning, siting, and funding of new transmission lines encourages investment in wind and solar power.

The regional administrative agreements that states have entered into illustrate the notion of polyphonic federalism that Robert A. Schapiro identified in chapter 2. Climate-change policy in a federal system is not an either/or proposition—for either states or the federal government to enact. It is an "and" issue—the states acting individually *and* collaboratively with each other *and* the federal government. The states, as the early—and primary—climate-change policy actors, have staked out and acted on a variety of climate-change policy initiatives that will shape and form the terms of the national debate and federal government action.

Notes

1. Colorado Statutes, Title 37, Water and Irrigation/Water Conservation Board and Compacts/Interstate Compacts, Article 65, South Platte River Compact.

2. C. Weissert and J. Hill, "Low Level Radioactive Waste Compacts: Lessons Learned from Theory and Practice," *Publius* 24 (1994):27–43; E. Schlager and T. Heikkila, "Resolving Water Conflicts: A Comparative Analysis of Interstate River Compacts," *Policy Studies Journal* 37(3) (2009):367–92.

3. J. F. Zimmerman, *Interstate Cooperation: Compacts and Administrative Agreements* (Westport, CT: Praeger, 2002).

4. Zimmerman, *Interstate Cooperation*, 163.

5. Western Climate Initiative, *Partner Climate Action Plans*, available at http://www.westernclimateinitiative.org/climate-action-plans (last accessed May 17, 2010).

6. Regional Greenhouse Gas Initiative (RGGI), *Regional Greenhouse Gas Initiative, Memorandum of Understanding* (2005), available at http://rggi.org/docs/mou_final_12_20_05.pdf.

7. Midwest Governors Association, *Energy Security and Climate Stewardship Platform for the Midwest* (2008), available at http://www.midwesterngovernors.org/Publications/EnergyPlatform.pdf; and *Energy Security and Climate Stewardship Roadmap* (2009), available at http://www.midwesterngovernors.org/Publications/Roadmap.pdf.

8. RGGI, *Regional Greenhouse Gas Initiative Model Rule* (2007), available at http://www.rggi.org/docs/model_rule_corrected_1_5_07.pdf.

9. Environment Northeast, *RGGI at One Year: An Evaluation of the Design and Implementation of the Regional Greenhouse Gas Initiative* (February 2010), 4, available at http://www.env-ne.org/public/resources/pdf/ENE_2009_RGGI_Evaluation_20100223_FINAL.pdf (accessed December 2, 2010)

10. RGGI, *Model Rule.*

11. RGGI, *RGGI CO$_2$ Auction Yields Millions for Investment in Clean Energy and Job Creation*, press release (March 12, 2010), available at http://www.rggi.org/docs/Auction_7_Release_MM_Report_2010_03_12.pdf.

12. RGGI, *Relative Effects of Various Factors on RGGI Electricity Sector CO$_2$ Emissions: 2009 Compared to 2005*, draft white paper, prepared by New York State Energy Research and Development Authority (November 2010), 3, available at http://www.rggi.org/docs/Retrospective_Analysis_Draft_White_Paper.pdf.

13. RGGI, *Relative Effects*, 3.

14. Environment Northeast, *RGGI at One Year*, 2.

15. Western Climate Initiative, *Design Recommendations for the WCI Regional Cap-and-Trade Program* (2009), available at http://www.westernclimateinitiative.org/component/remository/func-startdown/14/; *Midwestern Greenhouse Gas Reduction Accord, Final Draft of the Recommendations of the Advisory Group* (2009), available at http://www.ef.org/documents/Accord_Draft_Final.pdf.

16. Midwestern Governors Association (MGA), *Energy Security and Climate Stewardship Roadmap*, i.

17. Western Governors Association, *Clean Energy, a Strong Economy, and a Healthy Environment, Report of the Clean and Diversified Energy Advisory Committee to the Western Governors* (June 2006), available at http://www.westgov.org/wga/publicat/CDEAC06.pdf; Western Climate Initiative, *Final Complementary Policies White Paper* (May 20, 2010), available at http://www.westernclimateinitiative.org/component/remository/Complementary-Policies-Committee-Documents/Final-Complementary-Policies-Whte-Paper/.

18. New England Governors' Conference, Inc., *New England Governors' Renewable Energy Blueprint* (September 15, 2009), 16, available at http://www.nescoe.com/uploads/September_Blueprint_9.14.09_for_release.pdf.

19. MGA, *Energy Security and Climate Stewardship Roadmap*.

20. MGA, *Energy Security and Climate Stewardship Roadmap*, and *Energy Security and Climate Stewardship Platform for the Midwest*.

21. Conference of New England Governors and Eastern Canadian Premiers, *Resolution 33-4, Resolution Concerning Energy Efficiency* (September 2009), available at http://www.cap-cpma.ca/images/pdf/eng/2009%20NEGECP%20Conference/Resolution%2033-4%20Energy%20Efficiency%20E.pdf; RGGI, *RGGI Investment Programs*, available at http://www.rggi.org/states/program_investments (accessed May 17, 2010).

22. MGA, *Energy Security and Climate Stewardship Roadmap*, and *Energy Security and Climate Stewardship Platform for the Midwest*.

23. MGA, *Energy Security and Climate Stewardship Roadmap*.

24. US Environmental Protection Agency, *Draft Inventory of U.S. Greenhouse Gas Emissions and Sinks 1990–2009* (2010), available at http://www.epa.gov/climatechange/emissions/usinventoryreport.html.

25. MGA, *Energy Security and Climate Stewardship Platform for the Midwest*.

26. Northeast/Mid-Atlantic States, *Low Carbon Fuel Standard Program, Memorandum of Understanding* (December 2009), available at http://files.dep.state.pa.us/Energy/Office%20of%20Energy%20and%20Technology/OETDPortalFiles/Climate%20Change%20Advisory%20Committee/011210%20CCAC%20meeting/LCFS%20MOU%20Govs%20Final.pdf.

27. Pew Center on Global Climate Change, *Vehicle Greenhouse Gas Emissions Standards* (2010), available at http://www.pewclimate.org/what_s_being_done/in_the_states/vehicle_ghg_standard.cfm.

28. Pew Center on Global Climate Change, *Regional Greenhouse Gas Initiative (RGGI)*, available at http://www.pewclimate.org/what_s_being_done/in_the_states/rggi/.

29. S. McKinnon, "Arizona Quits Climate Endeavor," *Arizona Republic* (February 10, 2010); J. Fahys, "Utah Sticking with Climate Pact but Not Its Cap-and-Trade Plan," *Salt Lake Tribune* (April 21, 2010); R. Gerhke, "House OKs Resolution Doubting Climate Change," *Salt Lake Tribune* (February 9, 2010).

30. K. Schneider, "Regional Climate Pact's Lesson: Avoid Big Giveaways to Industry," *Yale Environment* (2008):360.

31. Schneider, "Regional Climate Pact's Lesson."

32. Kate Galbraith. "Little Impact Is Foreseen over New York's Proposed Change for Emissions Allowances," *New York Times, Section A* (March 7, 2009):13.

Chapter 8

Reorienting State Climate-Change Policies to Induce Technological Change

David E. Adelman and Kirsten H. Engel

In Brief

- Inducing technological change is a justification for state action on climate change independent from federal action that may or may not occur.

- States may be better suited to promote adoption of existing technologies, which requires consideration of capital and operating costs, product characteristics, and environmental benefits, rather than development of new technologies, which must focus on potential market size and may respond more favorably to federal incentives.

- Governments can induce technological change directly, through subsidies that affect adoption decisions of new technology consumers, or indirectly, through increasing potential market payoffs, which induce research and development in new technologies.

- State and regional cap-and-trade programs should be retained but the focus of state climate efforts should be on the promotion of clean technologies using state public benefits funds and tax credits that subsidize the adoption of technologies; or state renewable portfolio standards, state-level production standards, and green building codes and certification systems that expand markets.

The prospect of federal action on climate change follows a period of rapid policy development by state and local governments. In the absence of strong federal leadership, a growing number of states have filled the void in climate policy with a broad array of programs, including regulation of greenhouse-gas emissions from vehicles and power plants, renewable energy mandates, greenhouse-gas emission registries, and energy efficiency initiatives. This diversity in policies is matched by the variation in program development across the states and the stringency of state commitments.[1]

The question addressed in this chapter is whether state climate-change initiatives can be justified independently of their capacity to influence federal policy. We argue that it can and that such an independent justification can be found for state policies that induce technological change—one can think globally and still act locally. According to this view, innovation is a distinct regulatory end that provides its own rewards. Many states, for example, are motivated by the direct economic advantages (e.g., new jobs, energy security) of fostering green innovation[2] and the prospect of gaining a "first-mover" advantage by cultivating a critical mass of green industries in their jurisdictions.[3] Furthermore, state action can distribute the uncertainties associated with technological innovation, as a diverse range of independent strategies is more likely to succeed over a monolithic approach by the federal government.

Our approach complements and goes beyond existing justifications for state action. Anticipating the current groundswell of industry interest in federal legislation, a prominent theory holds that costly state policies can trigger federal action by motivating powerful multistate firms to seek uniform national standards.[4] A notable qualification of this and the other rationale is that they treat state programs as derivative of federal action (see Rabe, chapter 11). The first part of this chapter explores several avenues for states to induce technological change, whether through new innovations or adoption of existing technologies. The second part identifies promising opportunities for state action in the federal system. These insights suggest a two-tiered strategy: regulation of aggregate greenhouse-gas emissions at the federal level, complemented by state (as well as federal) policies designed to promote innovation and adoption of greenhouse-gas mitigating technologies. The chapter concludes with policy recommendations for reorienting state climate-change programs, paying particular attention to when, and the degree to which, federal preemption can be justified. We focus particular attention on identifying strategies for state programs in the event that the federal government enacts significant legislation to reduce greenhouse-gas emissions.

Inducing Technological Change through State Policies

According to standard economic theory, environmental regulation is justified when businesses and consumers fail to internalize the negative environmental impacts (or "negative externalities") of their actions.[5] Environmental policy is not limited, however, to deterring or restricting behavior with bad environmental consequences, such as excessive levels of pollution; it also seeks to promote development of new technologies that reduce abatement costs and enable more aggressive action. State regulation has significant potential to complement federal policies that promote technological change and even has certain advantages over them.

In spite of the fact that innovation will be an essential element of efforts to mitigate climate change and critical to controlling the costs of climate-change policies,[6] technological change continues to be overshadowed by the interest of policy makers and public interest advocates in achieving more direct greenhouse-gas emission reductions. This bias is clearly evident in debates over the merits of state programs for mitigating climate change. To date, the focus has been on measures to reduce greenhouse-gas emissions, such as cap-and-trade programs and environmental taxes, with little consideration of the potential for state- or national-level policies to induce technological change.[7]

For our purposes, technological change encompasses research and development that produces *new* technologies and adoption (or diffusion) of *existing* technologies. The latter produces innovation as experience is gained with the use and production of a technology—a process known as "learning by doing." Both forms of technological change are critical to the success of climate-change policies. One of the most prominent studies on climate-change mitigation identifies a collection of fifteen technology-specific means of stabilizing carbon emissions over the next fifty years.[8] While acknowledging the importance of new, groundbreaking technologies, the authors show that *existing* technologies—assuming efficient technology adoption—are more than adequate to meet standard emission stabilization goals through about 2050. These findings provide a strong basis for the importance of technology adoption to climate-change mitigation. They also demonstrate that calls for technological change are not based on mere speculation and technological optimism; many of the technologies already exist.

The Capacity of State Policies to Complement Federal Policies Intended to Induce Technological Change

Economists have long recognized that technological innovation is subject to market failure stemming from inventors' inability to capture the full social value of their work.[9] This lost value leads to underinvestment in research and development. Technology adoption and the innovation from learning by doing that it promotes are impeded for similar reasons. Early adopters of new technologies, for example, absorb the costs of working through the kinks in early versions of a technology. This learning process produces valuable knowledge and refinements, which firms adopting the technology later benefit from without having to incur any of the costs.

Government regulation has the potential to correct technology market failures because "the rate and direction of innovation are likely to respond to changes in relative prices."[10] Under this theory, governments can induce technological change either directly, through subsidies, or indirectly, through increasing an investor's return on his or her investment in a particular technology. Accordingly, government policies that increase the costs of polluting activities or improve the economics of innovative work can potentially stimulate innovation that lowers pollution abatement costs and, in doing so, enhance collective capacities to reduce greenhouse-gas emissions.

Policies will differ, however, according to whether they are designed to promote development of new technologies or adoption of existing ones. For companies considering investing in new technologies, the key factors will be research and development costs, expected revenues, projected market share, and any likely royalties. The potential market size for a technology is often of particular importance in such investment decisions.[11] By contrast, adopters of existing technologies will typically focus on factors such as capital and operating costs, product characteristics, and the environmental benefits of a product.[12] Because none of these factors is sensitive to market size, adoption of existing technologies ought to occur at any level of government and state incentives, for technology adoption can be equally effective at the state and federal levels.

State-level policies encouraging technology adoption also have certain advantages over their federal counterparts. While a federal standard can reach a much greater number of potential technology adopters, multiple state-level measures can mitigate problems with tunnel vision, pork barrel politics, and picking the wrong technology that can compromise technology programs.[13] For instance, the rise in federal support for biofuels, particularly ethanol produced from corn, is the most glaring example of interest-group politics overtaking sound policy.[14] Despite the enthusiasm among legislators, the benefits of biofuels are shockingly small.[15] Sharing responsibility for technology adoption between federal and state governments will provide a counter to the broad-scale adoption of unwise policies.

State programs can generate a diversity of approaches by virtue of their multiplicity and differing mixes of socioeconomic, environmental, and political factors. For example, within the field of renewable energy, some states require that solar power constitute a specific share of an electricity provider's portfolio, while others emphasize wind or geothermal resources.

Similarly, states such as West Virginia and Ohio, both of which have large supplies of coal, are supporting innovation directed at clean coal technology, whereas Texas, with its abundant wind resources, has focused on developing power wind turbines. Other states, such as New Jersey, have been driven by a mix of the potential threats and adopted a more integrated strategy. The constellation of state-level programs thus reflects the diversity of conditions present in the states.

The case for state action on climate is bolstered further by the scale at which technological change occurs most efficiently. In particular, whereas meaningful reductions in greenhouse-gas emissions require coordinated large-scale action, technological change occurs most readily at small geographic scales. Broad consensus exists that innovation is enhanced in geographic clusters (e.g., the Silicon Valley phenomenon) because spatial concentrations allow inventors to readily access knowledge that reduces the costs of research, development, and commercialization.[16] These knowledge externalities are dominated by "tacit knowledge," which is "vague, difficult to codify and often only serendipitously recognized," and thus by definition cannot be formalized or written down.[17] These characteristics, the Internet notwithstanding, limit the spread of tacit knowledge to the kinds of frequent face-to-face interactions that occur most efficiently in small geographic areas.

States clearly have a role to play in promoting technological change. To the extent that market size matters, state programs will be inferior to federal regulation. However, while state-level regulation may provide weaker overall incentives, its compensating virtue is the diversity of approaches and experimentation that are a hallmark of state policies. Moreover, where innovation is subject to substantial uncertainties, diversity is often more important than the coordination and large scale found in federal programs. These competing factors reveal important trade-offs between federal and state programs, particularly as they apply to research and development. By contrast, technology adoption, which is insensitive to the size of the market being regulated, is less constrained by these trade-offs. Finally, states are arguably in a better position to establish geographically concentrated centers of innovation that can boost development of new technologies.

Inducing Technological Change through Environmental Regulations

Significant empirical support exists for the benefits of using environmental regulations to induce technology adoption. Examples include studies of prominent regulations under the Clean Air Act and the Clean Water Act.[18]

Positive correlations have also been found between energy prices and adoption rates of energy-efficient products.[19] The most compelling evidence is associated with Corporate Average Fuel Economy (CAFE) standards, which have been found to be substantially more effective than increases in fuel prices.[20] One potential reason for these robust results is the absence of a temporal schism between the timing of regulation and investments in technology adoption. Both technology adoption and learning by doing are responsive to incentives created by *current* environmental policies. This dramatically reduces the uncertainties that undermine regulatory incentives for technology innovation.

The Merits of a Portfolio Approach

A portfolio approach to climate-change policy, which includes a combination of environmental regulations (e.g., a carbon tax) and policies designed to induce technological change (e.g., direct innovation subsidies), may be the most effective and efficient approach. The efficiencies gained by combining environmental regulatory measures and technology policies are borne out by a recent comparative study of environmental taxes in Europe targeted at reducing carbon dioxide emissions. The author, Monica Prasad, found that environmental taxes in several Scandinavian countries dating back to the early 1990s have had little discernable effect, except in the case of Denmark.[21] Prasad identified several reasons for Denmark's success, including, most important for our purposes, that "Danish policy makers made huge investments in renewable energy and subsidized environmental innovation."[22] By ensuring that substitute technologies were readily available, the Danish government overcame the risk aversion of firms, countervailing sunk costs, and network effects that often limit technology adoption. Denmark encouraged technology adoption through direct subsidies, differentially high taxes on coal, and tax benefits to industries that voluntarily agreed to reduce emissions. Prasad concluded that this mix of environmental taxes and technology policies was essential to Denmark's success and ultimately distinguished its system from the failed policies of other European countries.

The existing econometric analyses and the Prasad study reveal the benefits of combining traditional environmental regulations with technology policies to address climate change. They also highlight the importance of remaining attentive to the two distinct but related objectives of climate policy: reducing greenhouse-gas emissions and promoting the technological changes that will be essential to meeting long-term greenhouse-gas emission targets.

Particular State Climate Policies and Their Potential to Induce Technological Change

Some critics disparage subglobal climate-change regulation as ineffective if not outright counterproductive.[23] While we agree that state-level policies to reduce direct emissions of greenhouse gases will have a limited impact upon global greenhouse-gas concentrations, we disagree with the inference that states have no role in addressing climate change outside influencing federal policy. States *can* play a meaningful role in addressing inadequate investment in technological change, and there *can* be a "federalist" response to climate change: both the individual states and the central government have meaningful roles to play.

States have enacted a panoply of climate programs over the past decade. The earliest focused on constructing greenhouse-gas inventories and using state procurement policies to provide initial markets for energy efficient products. A diverse range of state programs now exist: more than twenty states have created public benefits funds (PBFs) to support technology adoption and innovation;[24] hundreds of entities across North America have joined the Climate Registry, which provides a common system for measuring, tracking, verifying, and reporting greenhouse-gas emissions;[25] more than half of the US states have established renewable portfolio standards (RPSs) for electrical power generation;[26] and more than forty states have adopted building codes for energy efficiency.[27] We analyze only the most prominent types of state programs, as a comprehensive review is prohibitive given the number and variety that exist.

Carbon Emission Caps

The most publicized state climate initiatives are directed primarily at reducing greenhouse-gas emissions. Two of the most prominent cap-and-trade programs are the Regional Greenhouse Gas Initiative (RGGI), which encompasses New York and nine New England and Mid-Atlantic states, and California's cap-and-trade program established under the state's 2006 Global Warming Solutions Act (Assembly Bill 32; see Thompson spotlight, p.180). The RGGI currently applies only to large electrical generating units. The RGGI states have agreed to cap carbon dioxide emissions at current levels through 2015 and subsequently to reduce them by 10 percent by 2018. Under AB 32, California has mandated that statewide greenhouse-gas emissions be reduced to 1990 levels by 2020, but unlike the RGGI, the law is not limited to the electric-power–generating sector and allows a one-year extension of the target

What does California's example illustrate about the benefits of state-level innovation? See "State Leadership in Energy Innovation: California's Example" on page 180.

emission level under extraordinary circumstances.[28] Two other regional programs, the Western Climate Initiative and the regional Midwestern Greenhouse Gas Reduction Accord, have also been established but lag the RGGI and California in their development (see Schlager, chapter 7).

The effect of these programs in terms of inducing technological change is weak. Emission caps and taxes do not effectively compel new investments in research and development because the standards adopted are usually too weak and the compliance period too short. The RGGI and AB 32 exhibit both of these shortcomings because they focus on the short term and neither program requires dramatic emission reductions. The RGGI compounds these weaknesses by allowing for many avenues of compliance that do not involve new technologies. AB 32's and RGGI's weak caps also limit their capacities to promote technology adoption, such that their influence will depend on the specific barriers to adoption and the existence of complementary programs that might mitigate them. On their own, these state and regional cap-and-trade programs are not structured to achieve significant reductions in greenhouse-gas emissions or technological change.

Renewable Portfolio Standards

Renewable portfolio standards (RPSs) are arguably the most popular program for promoting low–greenhouse-gas–producing electrical generation capacity. Under an RPS, electricity suppliers are required to have a minimum percentage of renewable energy in their portfolio of electricity generators. An RPS is a type of subsidy insofar as the guaranteed renewable share of the electricity market is subsidized by nonrenewable generators. It differs from most subsidies, however, by encompassing many types of renewable technologies, thereby avoiding the pitfalls of direct subsidies to specific technologies. The most important of these arises when a less-than-optimal technology, such as corn-based ethanol, is selected for political or other nonenvironmental reasons. RPSs avoid this problem by fostering competition among multiple qualifying technologies for the market share that is guaranteed to them as a group.

RPSs are highly effective means of inducing technological change.[29] For most state programs, this will center on technology adoption and learning by doing, given the low targets for renewable capacity and short compliance timelines. In particular, by operating as mandatory technology phase-in policies, RPS programs circumvent the many potential barriers to adoption that would otherwise impede the diffusion of renewable technologies. Consistent with these predictions, roughly half of the renewable capacity created in the United States from the late 1990s through 2006 occurred in states with RPS policies.[30] Thus, while other factors may contribute to the diffusion of renewable technologies, a strong correlation exists between the growth in renewable capacity and state RPS programs. The raw percentages for RPSs in the most aggressive states—more than 20 percent of generating capacity—are impressive in their own right, and this is particularly true relative to the corresponding percentages of global greenhouse-gas emission reductions that these programs can achieve.

Public Benefits Funds and Tax Credits

State climate-change initiatives that provide direct subsidies or tax incentives are now common. One reason for their popularity is that they often are the most effective means for state or local governments to promote innovation and technology adoption.[31] Further, while tax breaks and subsidies suffer from the problems associated with selecting specific technologies, they have important countervailing virtues. Direct subsidies avoid the time lag that undermines regulatory efforts to induce investments in research and development. Subsidies also neutralize common barriers to technology adoption, such as limited access to capital, transaction costs, and technological or market risks, and have proven more effective than regulatory penalties.

State subsidy programs have had many notable successes, particularly in promoting wind and solar energy.[32] Public benefits funds (PBFs) are currently found in almost half of the states and are the most popular form of direct subsidy program.[33] PBFs are usually collected through a small charge on the bill of every electric customer and are dedicated to supporting energy efficiency and renewable energy projects. Complementing these programs, eighteen states have organized to establish the Clean Energy States Alliance, which will enable them to leverage and coordinate their investments in renewable energy projects.

California is notable for its leadership (it established the first PBF in 1996) and for the size of its programs. The recently created $3.3 billion California Solar Initiative has become a model program for promoting adoption of solar technology through installation subsidies for solar power systems in homes and businesses.[34] The initiative also spurs investments in and growth of solar industries in California, including firms conducting research and development on new solar technologies. Moreover, there are signs that the growth in solar research is beginning to generate knowledge feedbacks that are characteristic of innovation clusters and may reward California for being a "first mover" in this area.

California is not alone in the scale and ambition of its programs. New York has collected about $2.8 billion in public- and private-sector resources for efficiency-related projects,[35] and Texas and Wisconsin are investing hundreds of millions of dollars annually in energy efficiency and renewable energy.[36] The scale of these programs, and state PBFs collectively, now rivals federal expenditures in these areas, and the states are making substantial contributions to promoting technological change and cultivating centers of innovation for green technologies.

Product Standards

Product standards for energy efficiency exist for more than seventy-five products ranging from vehicles to air conditioners.[37] Under federal laws such as the Energy Policy Act of 2005, product standards (many of which are based on earlier state standards) have been set for more than forty products. The preemptive federal standards are augmented by standards in ten states that cover more than thirty-five types of products.

Despite their limited capacity to achieve significant reductions in global greenhouse-gas emissions, product standards do have the power to promote technological change. Product standards operate, in effect, as phased-in bans on products that fail to meet specified criteria for energy efficiency or greenhouse-gas emissions. Similar to RPS programs, product standards do not single out particular technologies, mitigating problems with the inherent uncertainties and potential errors in technology selection. For instance, evidence exists in the motor vehicle context that aggressive standards (e.g., zero-emission vehicles) can stimulate investment in research and development.[38] The primary weakness of product standards is their limited ability to address products already in use, which can encourage inefficiently prolonged use of older technologies. However, mitigation of this problem can be achieved with a portfolio approach in which product standards are used in conjunction with subsidy programs or emission regulations.

Green Building Codes and Certification Systems

Green building codes are among the most important measures that states can implement. Yet current programs, while widespread in the United States, are very modest in their goals. Forty-three states have adopted energy efficiency codes for residential buildings, and forty-one for commercial buildings.[39] These measures have great potential, as simple cost-effective measures are available that could reduce energy use in buildings by 30 percent or more.

While past savings have been modest, particularly for individual consumers and businesses, the aggregate numbers are significant and will grow dramatically in the coming years.

State building codes have been supplemented by much more elaborate voluntary green-building rating systems. Two rating systems have dominated the market: Leadership in Energy and Environmental Design (LEED) and Green Globe. Under LEED, developers receive points for adopting environmentally friendly design features, such as energy-efficient heating systems and water conservation features. Buildings with a sufficient number of points receive a "certification," and their builders gain the bragging rights (and potential economic premium) associated with green buildings.

Government policies and private certification also operate in concert. Increasingly, many state and local governments are promoting construction of green buildings by mandating that public buildings receive green building certification or by offering various subsidies for builders to meet green building certification standards. Local governments, for example, will cut permit fees or grant property-tax exemptions to owners that build LEED-certified green buildings. This innovative hybrid of public incentives and private certification reduces oversight burdens on local governments, although with the potential cost of misplaced reliance on the effective implementation of private programs.

Much more ambitious green building policies are beginning to emerge at the local level. The BuildSmart program, recently adopted in such locales as Boulder County, Colorado, is exemplary of a new wave of building codes that integrate renewable energy requirements and greenhouse-gas emission limits.[40] The BuildSmart code applies only to residential buildings, and it becomes progressively more stringent with the size of the home.[41]

Establishing rigorous building codes for energy efficiency is among the most effective contributions to mitigating climate change that states can make. The greenhouse-gas emissions from the building sector are a significant fraction of US emissions, and the opportunities for reducing emissions in this sector are among the most cost-efficient. The policy tools available to state and local governments are also well established. Performance-based codes are clearly appropriate given the barriers to technology adoption that exist (e.g., investor/user splits), but incentive programs will also be needed to address existing structures. Indeed, the failure of consumers and businesses to exploit cost-saving measures only serves to highlight the barriers to energy-efficient technologies in the building sector and the value of government action. Moreover, the federal system reinforces this delegation of responsibility to the states because, as a quintessential state function, building codes lie outside the province of federal authority.

Recommendations for Reorienting State Climate Policies to Induce Technological Change

A central premise of this chapter is that federal and state climate-change policies should be complementary. Federal action is essential to achieving the dramatic greenhouse-gas emission reductions that scientists predict will be necessary, and it will play a critical role in promoting technological change as well. A critical role of the states should be fostering technological change, particularly technology adoption and innovation through learning by doing. Federal laws should therefore enhance the ability of states to contribute to climate-change mitigation in these ways. With this objective in mind, we propose four key recommendations for federal and state climate-change legislation.

Federal and State Climate-Change Programs Should Adopt a Portfolio of Greenhouse-Gas Emission-Reducing and Technology-Forcing Measures. The importance of technological development to climate-change policy and the distinct advantages of pursuing multiple policies to induce technological change provide a strong basis for a continuing state role in climate policy making, even after the enactment of federal climate legislation. By adopting a portfolio approach, states and the federal government leverage synergistic benefits that are greater than either can achieve alone. Under this approach, emission reductions should be left primarily to federal policy (i.e., cap-and-trade regimes), while states focus on technology change in parallel with the federal government.

A portfolio approach is consistent with standard principles of federalism. It reflects the understanding that some policies are more effectively pursued by the federal government, while others are better addressed by the states.[42] Beyond its focus on reducing greenhouse-gas emissions, federal policies can make valuable contributions by establishing minimum technology portfolio standards, regulating sectors that transcend state boundaries (e.g., transportation), and offering subsidies for research and development and technology adoption. The states can play a complementary role by supporting innovations in policy development, particularly strategies for inducing technological change such as technology portfolio standards, product and appliance standards, building codes, and subsidy programs for stimulating energy efficiency and renewable sources of energy.

State and Regional Cap-and-Trade Programs Should Be Retained but Should Not Be the Focus of State Climate Efforts. Once a federal program enacts a legitimate cap-and-trade program, investment of substantial resources in parallel state or regional cap-and-trade programs is unwarranted if the only objective is reducing greenhouse-gas emissions, as opposed to promoting new policy development. These programs, particularly if focused on the short term, generate little in the way of technology development or adoption, and they achieve only nominal reductions in greenhouse-gas emissions relative to even a modest federal program.

Federal legislation nonetheless should not entirely preempt state and regional cap-and-trade programs. State and regional greenhouse-gas emission reduction programs have the potential to augment emission reductions over and above those of any federal program that is ultimately adopted. While the amount will be small, any federal program is unlikely to be optimally stringent, and any additional reductions should not be needlessly precluded.

State Technology Portfolio Standards Should Not Be Preempted Expressly, Impliedly, or Structurally by Federal Regulations. State technology portfolio standards, most prominently RPSs, can and should coexist with parallel federal regulations. In most cases, federal and state portfolio standards will complement each other. A federal minimum can jump-start the adoption of new technologies in states that lack such portfolio standards; those states will benefit from the technology spillovers from states with more stringent standards, and the preferences and opportunities of individual states to adopt more stringent standards will be preserved.

Congress Should Enhance Technology-Forcing Product Regulation by Allowing Limited Exceptions for State Standards. Parallel state regulatory authority can enhance the technology-forcing potential of federal product standards, as evidenced by the nation's experience with California's vehicle emission standards. California, which has a unique authority to regulate motor vehicle emissions under the Clean Air Act, has led the way in promulgating rigorous vehicle emission standards and promoting new technologies. The success of the California experiment owes a great deal to the severity of air pollution in California cities that prompted aggressive state action, as well as the decision by Congress to leverage the California program by permitting other states to adopt its standards. Nevertheless, the California program remains an exception to Congress's general policy of preempting state product standards.[43]

Congress should strengthen and extend this model. Above all, the model of partial preemption established under the Clean Air Act should be duplicated with respect to other product standards, although this need not privilege a single state. A number of potential variants could be considered, such as allowing a consortium of states to depart from a federal standard when they have demonstrated leadership and expertise in developing standards for a particular area of commerce. Experimentation with a variety of regimes, perhaps allowing for more than one alternative standard, is warranted given the success of the California program.

Conclusion

From the narrow perspective of reducing excess greenhouse-gas emissions, the grounds for state climate regulation are modest. Among other limitations, state regulation encompasses only a small fraction of global greenhouse-gas emissions. But focusing on greenhouse-gas emission reductions presents an incomplete picture, as it addresses just one aspect of the climate-change policies needed. The other needed aspect, sufficient investment in technological change, is amenable to state policies. States can make important contributions to mitigating climate change by enhancing the variety of new or existing technologies being developed and adopted.

Reorienting state climate-change policies to induce technological change necessarily implicates federal programs. Federal policies should preserve and enhance the degree to which states can contribute to technological change. Specifically, an approach that integrates federal and state programs can reduce the costs of emission reductions and provide an overarching framework for allocating responsibilities for climate-change programs between the states and the federal government. As a general rule, the federal government should have primary responsibility for implementing programs that directly regulate greenhouse-gas emissions, while an important aspect of states' climate strategy—in parallel with the federal government—should be upon developing programs for inducing technological change.

Notes

1. See K. H. Engel and B. Y. Orbach, "Micro-motives and State and Local Climate Change Initiatives," 2 *Harv. L. & Pol'y Rev.* 119 (2008): 122–27, available at http://hlpronline.com/law/wp-content/uploads/2009/12/Engel_Orbach_HLPR.pdf.

2. B. G. Rabe, *Statehouse and Greenhouse: The Emerging Politics of American Climate Change Policy* (Washington, DC: Brookings Institution Press, 2004): 29, 424–25.

3. See, for example, M. Richtel and J. Markoff, "A Green Energy Industry Takes Root in California," *New York Times* (February 1, 2008): C1; M. Feldman and R. Martin, "Constructing Jurisdictional Advantage," 34 *Res. Pol'y* 1235 (2005): 1236–37.

4. See E. D. Elliott et al., "Toward a Theory of Statutory Evolution: The Federalization of Environmental Law," 1 *J. L. Econ. & Org.* 313 (1985): 332–33.

5. A. Jaffe et al., "A Tale of Two Market Failures: Technology and Environmental Policy," 54 *Ecol. Econ.* 164 (2005): 168–69.

6. A. B. Jaffe et al., "Technological Change and the Environment," in *Handbook of Environmental Economics*, vol. 1, edited by K.-G. Maler and J. R. Vincent (Boston: North-Holland/Elsevier, 2003): 463; R. G. Newell et al., "The Effects of Economic and Policy Incentives on Carbon Mitigation Technologies," 28 *Energy Econ.* 563 (2006): 564.

7. But see J. B. Wiener, "Think Globally, Act Globally: The Limits of Local Climate Policies," 155 *U. Pa. L. Rev.* 1961 (2007): 1973.

8. S. Pacala and R. Socolow, "Stabilization Wedges: Solving the Climate Problem for the Next 50 Years with Current Technologies," 305 *Science* 968 (2004).

9. Jaffe et al., "Technological Change," 471.

10. Jaffe et al., "Technological Change," 469–70.

11. Jaffe et al., "Technological Change."

12. Newell et al., "The Effects," 566.

13. J. Bushnell et al., "Local Solutions to Global Problems: Climate Change Policies and Regulatory Jurisdiction," 2 *Rev. Envtl. Econ. & Pol'y* 175 (2008): 191, available at http://reep.oxfordjournals.org/cgi/reprint/ren007v1.

14. A. Barrionuevo, "Boom in Ethanol Reshapes Economy of Heartland," *New York Times* (June 25, 2006): A1; L. L. Geyer, "Ethanol, Biomass, Biofuels and Energy: A Profile and Overview," 12 *Drake J. Agric. L.* 61 (2007): 64–69.

15. For example, corn-based ethanol provides a meager 12 percent reduction in greenhouse-gas emissions over oil-based gasoline and has a marginal capacity to meet gasoline demand in the United States (i.e., less than 10 percent). J. Hill et al., "Environmental, Economic, and Energetic Costs and Benefits of Biodiesel and Ethanol Biofuels," 103 *Proc. Nat'l Acad. Sci. U.S.A.* 11206 (2006).

16. Feldman and Martin, "Constructing Jurisdictional Advantage."

17. D. B. Audretsch and M. P. Feldman, "Knowledge Spillovers and the Geography of Innovation," chap. 61 in *The Handbook of Regional and Urban Economics*, vol. 4, edited by J. V. Henderson and J.-F. Thisse (New York: North-Holland, 2004), 2718.

18. Jaffe et al., "Technological Change," 502; S. Kerr and R. G. Newell, "Policy-Induced Technology Adoption: Evidence from the U.S. Lead Phasedown," 51 *J. Ind. Econ.* 317 (2003): 340–41.

19. R. G. Newell et al., "The Induced Innovation Hypothesis and Energy-Saving Technological Change," 114 *Q. J. Econ.* 941 (1999): 967–70; Newell et al., "The Effects," 567.

20. P. K. Goldberg, "The Effects of the Corporate Average Fuel Economy Standards in the U.S.," 46 *J. Ind. Econ.* 1 (1998): 2–3; D. L. Greene, "CAFE or Price? An Analysis of the Effects of Federal Fuel Economy Regulations and Gasoline Price on New Car MPG, 1978–89," 11 *Energy J.* 37 (1990): 55–57.

21. M. Prasad, "Taxation as a Regulatory Tool: Lessons from Environmental Taxes in Europe," chap. 11 in *Government and Markets: Toward a New Theory of Regulation*, edited by J. J. Balleisen and D. A. Moss (Cambridge: Cambridge University Press, 2009); M. Prasad, "On Carbon, Tax and Don't Spend," *New York Times* (March 25, 2008): A27.

22. Prasad, "On Carbon," A27.

23. Wiener, "Think Globally," 102; see also Bushnell et al., "Local Solutions"; L. H. Goulder, "California's Bold New Climate Policy," *Econ. Voice* (September 2007): 1.

24. Pew Center on Global Climate Change, *Public Benefit Funds*, available at http:// www.pewclimate.org/what_s_being_done/in_the_states/public_benefit_funds.cfm.

25. Climate Registry, available at http://www.theclimateregistry.org/.

26. Pew Center, *Public Benefit Funds*.

27. Rabe, *Statehouse and Greenhouse*, 19. Other policies have included adopting nonbinding greenhouse-gas emission targets (often in the range of 10–20 percent below 1990s levels by 2020 and 70–80 percent by 2050), decoupling utility profits from sales volumes, and providing public information on greenhouse-gas emissions and consumers with the ability to purchase green energy. Pew Center, *Public Benefit Funds*, 12–13.

28. California Health and Safety Code (Deering's California Codes Annotated, 2008): §§ 38560, 38599.

29. J. A. Alic et al., *U.S. Technology and Innovation Policies: Lessons for Climate Change* (Pew Center for Global Climate Change, 2003), available at http:// www.climate-tech-policy.org/resources/technology/us-technology-and-innovation -policies-lessons-for-climate-change.

30. R. Wiser et al., *Renewables Portfolio Standards: A Factual Introduction to Experience from the United States*, LBNL-62569 (Lawrence Berkeley Nat'l Lab., April 2007), available at http://eetd.lbl.gov/ea/ems/reports/62569.pdf, at 8–9.

31. Bushnell et al., "Local Solutions," 17; see also M. L. Hymel et al., "Trading Greenbacks for Green Behavior: Oregon and the City of Portland's Environmental Incentives," in *Critical Issues in Environmental Taxation*, vol. 5, edited by N. J. Chalifour et al. (New York: Oxford University Press, 2008); US Department of Energy, *DSIRE, Database of State Incentives for Renewables and Energy Efficiency*, available at http://www.dsireusa.org (last visited September 6, 2008).

32. Alic et al., *U.S. Technology and Innovation Policies*, 28.

33. Pew Center, *Public Benefit Funds*.

34. See California Solar Initiative, *Getting Started*, available at http://www .gosolarcalifornia.ca.gov/csi/index.html. Not surprisingly, the California Solar Initiative has been criticized by economists. Bushnell et al., "Local Solutions," 13–14.

35. US Environmental Protection Agency (EPA), *Clean Energy-Environment Guide to Action: Policies, Best Practices, and Action Steps for States* (2006), ES-14, available at http://www.epa.gov/cleanenergy/documents/gta/executivesummary.pdf.

36. US EPA, *Clean Energy-Environment Guide*, ES-14, ES-16.

37. US EPA, *Clean Energy-Environment Guide*, ES-15.

38. National Research Council, Committee on State Practices in Setting Mobile Source Emissions Standards, *State and Federal Standards for Mobile-Source Emissions* (Washington, DC: National Academies Press, 2006): 173.

39. US EPA, *Clean Energy-Environment Guide*, ES-4–ES-20. For residential buildings, states have adopted either the Model Energy Code or International Energy Conservation Code (IECC), while for commercial buildings, states have adopted building codes from either the American Association of Heating, Refrigerating, and Air-Conditioning Engineers or IECC.

40. Boulder County, Colorado, International Residential Code. Chap. 11: Energy Efficiency Resolution 2010-30, available at http://www.bouldercounty.org/find/library/build/2011buildsmartcode.pdf; see also B. J. Feder, "The Showhouse That Sustainability Built," *New York Times* (March 26, 2008): H6.

41. Boulder County Ordinance, at 4, table 1.

42. See also T. D. Peterson et al., "Developing a Comprehensive Approach to Climate Policy in the United States That Fully Integrates Levels of Government and Economic Sectors," 26 *Va. Envtl. L. J.* 227 (2008).

43. National Appliance Energy Conservation Act of 1987, Pub. L. No. 100-12, 101 Stat. 103 (1987) (codified as amended at 42 U.S.C. §§ 6291–93, 6295–97, 6305–6, 6308 (1987)).

State Leadership in Energy Innovation

California's Example

Barton H. Thompson, Jr.

In the early 2000s, an advertisement showing a Hummer in an icy locale hung in a New York subway station. While the original text proclaimed, "Does well at the poles," someone had defaced the ad to caution, "Does well *melting* the poles." As the vandal wished to highlight, technology has significantly contributed to climate change. Technology, however, is also central to solving the challenge of climate change.

To effectively mitigate climate change, the world will need to develop new energy and energy efficiency technologies and also ensure that existing and future technologies are commercialized and broadly adopted. That will require a sizable investment of talent and funds. Experts estimate that the United States needs to invest anywhere from about $15 billion to $30 billion annually in energy research and development to ensure the technological change needed to stabilize atmospheric concentrations of carbon dioxide equivalents at 550 parts per million. Unfortunately, the United States in recent years has invested less than $6 billion annually. Indeed, both public and private investment in energy research and development is down significantly from thirty years ago—even fifteen years ago. Recent scientific assessments, moreover, suggest that the world may need to stabilize carbon concentrations at significantly lower levels to avoid serious climate impacts.[1]

The federal government inevitably must play a leading role in driving and supporting energy-related research and development, but as David E. Adelman and Kirsten H. Engel emphasize in chapter 8, states also can and should help advance the technological innovation needed to mitigate climate change. California provides an illustration of the role that states can play in promoting energy innovation and the resulting benefits that innovation accrues. In the early 1980s, for example, the California Public Utility Commission helped ensure a stable local market for wind by requiring the state's two largest utilities to offer long-term wind contracts at favorable energy rates. The state also provided a 25 percent tax credit for new wind installation and provided scientific support to wind investors. As a consequence, California enjoyed more than 90 percent of the nation's installed wind capacity at the turn of the twenty-first century.[2]

California also has encouraged the development and deployment of a broader set of energy and energy efficiency technologies both by promoting demand for new technologies and by providing financial support for research and development. For more than three decades, California has promoted new energy efficiency technologies by mandating appliance and building standards and encouraging utilities to promote efficiency. In 2002, California increased demand for renewable energy technology by adopting a standard requiring 20 percent of the state's energy to come from renewable sources by 2010 (and Governor Arnold Schwarzenegger subsequently established a renewables target of 33 percent by 2020). On the climate front, Assembly Bill 32 imposed the nation's first mandatory statewide program for reducing greenhouse gases, and Governor Schwarzenegger set a state goal of reducing greenhouse-gas emissions 80 percent by 2050. The California Energy Commission also administers research and development grant programs totaling approximately $85 million per year.

Such policies have provided significant benefits to the state. California's energy efficiency measures have helped reduce per capita energy use 40 percent below the national average, producing household energy savings of $56 billion from 1972 to 2006, with concomitant economic benefits to the entire state. Appliance efficiency standards have also spurred job growth and technological innovation. One recent study concludes that AB 32, by creating new incentives for innovation and increasing state energy efficiency by an additional percentage point per year, will increase California's gross state product by approximately $76 billion and create "as many as 403,000 new efficiency and climate action driven jobs."[3]

Such benefits already appear to be leading California and other states to pursue a "race to the top." Given the national benefits of active state involvement, however, the federal government can and should support and promote state efforts. To start, the federal government should ensure greater coordination between state and federal programs promoting new energy technology; today, the programs are too often isolated. In addition, the federal government should consider encouraging greater state efforts by offering matching funds to any support provided by states. In these regards, the federal government should consider establishing a network of joint federal–state programs that draw on the expertise of local universities and laboratories across the nation to pursue both transformational energy technologies and technology deployment.

As California's history illustrates, states have already made progress through established policies. The federal government can and should further such state involvement through programs to coordinate with and help fund such state efforts.

Notes

1. G. F. Nemet and D. M. Kammen, "U.S. Energy Research and Development: Declining Investment, Increasing Need, and the Feasibility of Expansion," 35 *Energy Policy* 746 (2007); J. Duderstadt, G. Was, R. McGrath, et al., *Energy Discovery-Innovation Institute: A Step Toward American's Energy Sustainability,* Brookings Policy Brief (February 2009); Intergovernmental Panel on Climate Change, *Climate Change 2007: Synthesis Report— Summary for Policy Makers* (2007), available at http://www.ipcc.ch/pdf/assessment-report/ar4/syr/ar4_syr_spm.pdf.

2. J. M. Loiter and V. Norberg-Bohm, "Technology Policy and Renewable Energy: Public Roles in the Development of New Technologies," 27 *Energy Policy* 85 (1999).

3. D. Roland-Holst, *Energy Efficiency, Innovation, and Job Creation in California* (Berkeley: Center for Energy, Resources, and Economic Sustainability, University of California, Berkeley, October 2008): 11–20.

State and Federal Dynamics

State and Federal Dynamics

The $64,000 question is, when will the federal government enter the climate-change policy arena, and to what effect? As amply demonstrated in the preceding section, state and local governments have actively engaged climate-change issues by experimenting with and implementing a wide variety of measures. While such state and local policy activity is crucial if the United States is to substantially reduce its greenhouse-gas (GHG) emissions, significant reductions cannot be made without an active and engaged federal government. For instance, the federal government can do things that states cannot, such as set national GHG emission targets, or that states have not been allowed to do under other environmental laws, such as regulate automobile emissions. Furthermore, the federal government can leverage resources, both money and expertise, that may be directed at activities that states alone cannot adequately support, such as research and development of clean technologies. The chapters in this section examine the types of climate-change mitigation policies the federal government should adopt, and the interaction of state policies with federal policies.

Thus far, federal-level congressional debates and action have largely been limited to cap-and-trade systems. In June 2009, the US House of Representatives passed the American Clean Energy and Security Act, also known as the Waxman-Markey bill, which would create a national cap-and-trade system if the Senate were able to pass similar legislation (which to date it has not). As Holly Doremus and W. Michael Hanemann argue in chapter 9, however, cap-and-trade systems are limited in their ability to accomplish substantial GHG emission reductions of the sort required to avoid catastrophic climate change. Consequently, the federal government should consider additional policies that, combined with state activities, are more likely to achieve the necessary emission reductions.

They propose that the federal government adopt a GHG regulatory system modeled on the Clean Air Act. Such a regulatory system would reach across all GHG emission sources and treat states as critical and active partners in accomplishing substantial emission reductions in ways suited to the circumstances of each state.

If the federal government were to adopt a cap-and-trade system, what would be the effect on state and local government activity? Would federal action preempt some forms of state and local climate policies? How would the role of state and local governments be affected? Daniel A. Farber (chapter 10) addresses these issues in relation to the legal concept of preemption, according to which state lawmaking is bound by the US Constitution, regardless of what is contained in state constitutions. Federal and state governments regularly legislate and regulate on the same issues, such as protecting and recovering endangered species or limiting the disposal of toxic pollutants. Federal action per se does not preempt state action but instead limits, shapes, and guides it. As Farber points out, except in cases where preemption issues are clearly addressed, such as when Congress expressly preempts state action, the courts are often called upon to determine whether state action is allowed.

Farber also explains how preemption considerations are likely to affect states once the federal government begins to adopt climate-change policies. According to Farber, unless the federal government expressly preempts state action, or unless state laws conflict with federal laws, states will continue to exercise considerable latitude around climate-change policies. Ultimately, Farber believes, most state action around climate change will continue unless states choose to bow out and allow the federal government to take over and dominate the field.

The federal government, when it chooses to act, will thus do so in a policy area whose basic contours have been developed by state and local actors. In chapter 11, Barry G. Rabe outlines more than a decade of state climate-change policy activity to show how state action will likely affect federal government climate-change action. As Rabe notes, twenty-six states containing more than half of the US population have adopted twelve or more climate-change–related policies. All fifty states have adopted at least one such policy, a fact that reveals continued and sustained support for climate-change policies among the states, with the anticipated effect of supporting federal action.

Nonetheless, while state activity may suggest support for federal climate-change policies, what states believe those policies should be is diverse, making it difficult to determine the types of policies the federal government is likely to adopt. As Rabe argues, low-emitting policy-active states "will be keen to ensure that any future federal policy follows their example, both to ease transition costs and to maximize credit-claiming opportunities for political leaders." In contrast, high-emitting limited-policy states are very concerned over the costs of achieving significant GHG emissions. According to Rabe, these states, primarily located in the Southeast, are likely to oppose aggressive federal climate-change legislation, although as they experience increasingly severe climate-change effects, they may become more open to climate-change legislation. While deep partisan divisions and severe economic problems may pose roadblocks to federal passage of climate-change legislation, so too do the very different experiences of the states, both in their emission profiles and in their taste for climate-change policies.

Though the path forward for federal climate-change policy is impossible to predict, and state diversity may pose challenges for finding common ground on national policies, Rabe's analysis of the types of policies that states have both adopted and failed to adopt so far may suggest the types of policies that the federal government may build upon.

Examining federal–state relations in a policy area in which the federal government is largely absent leaves the authors of this section to engage in reasoned argument over what the federal government should do, how courts should police the relations among governments, and how states' climate-change policies are likely to shape eventual federal action. As this set of chapters makes clear, what is not open to argument or speculation, however, is the necessity of federal action.

Chapter 9

Clean Air Act Federalism as a Template for Climate-Change Legislation

Holly Doremus and W. Michael Hanemann

In Brief

- Achieving sufficient greenhouse-gas (GHG) emission reductions to avoid drastic climate change will require more than a cap-and-trade system.

- Even if it eventually adopts a national cap-and-trade system for GHG emissions, Congress should also include provisions modeled on the Clean Air Act, making the federal government responsible for setting national GHG standards but leaving the states responsible for achieving them.

- Like the Clean Air Act, an act that reduces GHG emissions should allow states to make many key policy choices regarding their own implementation plans.

- The federal government can use such an act to prevent a "race to the bottom" by setting a federal floor that compels a minimum of climate-change actions from all states.

In the political debates over addressing climate change, cap-and-trade has been the primary policy tool proposed at the international, national, regional, and state levels. Although a 2009 cap-and-trade bill that passed the US House of Representatives failed in the Senate, we do not believe this indicates that politicians have turned away from the cap-and-trade concept entirely. Instead, for now, no regulation seems more attractive to US politicians than a cap-and-trade program. Cap-and-trade remains the dominant approach in the states—the northeastern states have created a carbon market, and California is in the process of doing so—and internationally.

We have no quarrel with the idea that cap-and-trade strategies should play a role in addressing greenhouse-gas (GHG) emissions. Trading is a politically palatable (or at least more palatable than command-and-control regulation) and cost-effective way to address some of the "low-hanging fruit" of GHG emissions. But the focus on emission trading has been so narrow that it threatens to drive out interest in other policy instruments. We do have a quarrel with that.

Trading is useful for addressing some, but by no means all, aspects of the GHG problem (see Doremus and Hanemann spotlight, p. 209). Although trading has worked well for some air pollution problems, global climate change presents a much bigger challenge. Achieving emission reductions on a large enough scale and rapidly enough to prevent the most extreme manifestations of climate change will require substantial changes in behavior by a wide swath of actors—consumers as well as producers—in all economic sectors in high-emission nations such as the United States. It will also require notable technological advances.[1]

How does cap-and-trade work, and what are its limitations? See "The Limits of Cap-and-Trade Systems in Addressing Global Warming" on page 209.

The changes needed are qualitatively different and more profound than those attained by past emission-trading programs. Experience with those earlier programs suggests that emission trading alone is not likely to be sufficient to motivate those changes.

In the wake of the climate bill's failure and the Supreme Court's ruling in *Massachusetts v. EPA*, the Clean Air Act is the single national regulatory authority that limits GHG emissions. The US Environmental Protection Agency (EPA) is moving ahead with regulation of GHG emissions from cars and new or modified stationary sources, while dragging its heels on developing and implementing air quality standards. The current situation is highly unstable. The Obama administration and legislators on both sides of the aisle agree that the Clean Air Act is not the best fit for the climate-change problem. Before too long, Congress will have to address the GHG issue again.

When it does so, we urge it not to throw the baby out with the bathwater. In the current political climate, it is entirely possible that Congress will simply choose to leave GHG emissions unregulated, exempting them from the Clean Air Act without adopting GHG-specific legislation. If, however, the president is willing to wield his veto power, that approach may be infeasible. If legislators choose or are forced to address GHG emissions directly, we hope they will recognize that the Clean Air Act framework has much to offer a nation committed to reducing its carbon footprint. In particular, applying the Clean Air Act's state planning requirements to the climate-change problem can encourage behavioral change and technological innovation in a way that emission trading alone cannot, while also offering significant political advantages.

In this chapter, we first briefly explain how the Clean Air Act works, with special attention to the role of federal and state authorities. We then examine in more detail how a similar framework could be used to address GHG emissions. We conclude that climate-change legislation should set carbon emission reduction targets rather than asking the US EPA to set air quality standards for GHGs, but should leave to the states the primary role in determining how to meet those targets. GHG emissions should be exempted from the Clean Air Act's air quality standards provisions, but climate legislation should leave two other parts of the Clean Air Act (the two on which the US EPA is making regulatory progress) intact. The Act's requirements that mobile sources (cars and trucks) meet federal technology-based standards should be applied to GHG emissions, allowing California to regulate more stringently just as it currently does for other pollutants. The mandate that stationary sources meet federal technology-based standards should also be preserved, allowing states to impose additional restrictions on sources within their borders if they choose to do so.

Cooperative Federalism in the Clean Air Act

The Clean Air Act is perhaps the most complex of the federal environmental laws, occupying nearly 300 pages of the US Code. Nonetheless, its basic structure is relatively simple. For our purposes, we need only consider three major focal points of the Act: (1) air quality standards, (2) technology-based standards for mobile sources, and (3) technology-based standards for stationary pollution sources. Moreover, it is not the details of those statutory elements that concern us here, but rather the different roles they assign to federal and state actors. The Clean Air Act's version of cooperative federalism, we assert, is not only sensible for the "conventional" air pollution problems Congress had before it in 1970, but also surprisingly well suited to the somewhat different problem of global warming.

Air Quality: Federal Standards, State Implementation

The National Ambient Air Quality Standards (NAAQS) are the heart of the Clean Air Act. Section 108 directs the US EPA to create a list of "criteria pollutants," defined as those air pollutants that are emitted from numerous or diverse sources and cause or contribute to air pollution that may reasonably be anticipated to endanger the public health or welfare.[2] For each pollutant in this category, the US EPA must set primary and secondary NAAQS, that is, air quality levels that must be achieved nationwide. Primary NAAQS are set at a level "requisite to protect the public health with an adequate margin of safety,"[3] while secondary NAAQS are set at a level sufficient to protect public welfare. Costs may not be considered in setting the NAAQS.

Once the US EPA sets the NAAQS, states draft state implementation plans (SIPs) to achieve them.[4] The SIP program leaves many key policy choices to the states but also provides considerable federal oversight. In formulating their implementation plans, states first conduct a statewide inventory of emission sources, including both mobile and stationary sources. If NAAQS levels are exceeded in any part of the state, the state must determine the level of emission reduction necessary to reach the NAAQS, a process that requires complex modeling for localized pollutants. Next, the state decides how to make the needed reductions and chooses a suite of control measures to deliver them, which may include a mix of regulations and incentives for voluntary measures. To ensure that the state plans will actually be carried out, the Clean Air Act requires that they include monitoring and enforcement programs and that the states demonstrate that they have adequate personnel, funding, and legal authority. The completed SIP is submitted to the US EPA for approval. Once approved, it becomes enforceable as a matter of federal, as well as state, law.

The US EPA must disapprove the SIP if it finds that the plan as written will not achieve the NAAQS. If the state fails to correct the problem, it becomes subject to sanctions in the form of withdrawal of federal highway funding and the imposition of a two-for-one offset requirement as a condition of permitting any new stationary sources, although in practice the imposition of sanctions is rare.[5] If the state still fails to produce an adequate SIP, the US EPA is required to impose a federal implementation plan.

Once the US EPA approves a SIP, federal agencies may not take, approve, or fund any activity that does not conform to the SIP. In the area of transportation planning, the US EPA has issued detailed rules governing conformity analysis for federally funded or approved highway projects in nonattainment areas. The conformity requirement can force local transportation authorities to shift funding from highway expansion to transit, bicycle, and pedestrian facilities.[6]

Mobile Sources: Federal Standards with a State Prod

The Clean Air Act directs the US EPA to prescribe standards for the emission from new motor vehicles of pollutants that "cause, or contribute to, air pollution which may reasonably be anticipated to endanger public health or welfare."[7] The standards are intended to push the development of new pollution control technologies; they can be adopted before the technology needed to achieve them is available, but they must provide adequate lead time to allow for its development. In general, state regulation of tailpipe emissions is preempted. The Act provides a limited exemption, however, for any state that had automobile emission standards in place prior to 1966, a category that includes only California. The US EPA must waive federal preemption of California standards if the state's standards are at least as protective of public health and welfare as the federal ones, the state needs its standards to address compelling and extraordinary conditions, and they provide enough lead time for development of the required technology. Once a waiver is granted, allowing California to adopt its own standards, other states with nonattainment areas may choose to opt in to California's mobile source regulations.

Stationary Sources: Federal Technology-Based Emission Limits

For the most part, the Clean Air Act leaves the states free to choose what regulations to apply to stationary sources, but new and modified sources are subject to minimum federal emission standards. The US EPA sets New Source Performance Standards for categories of sources, requiring that they achieve a level of emission control equal to that achievable by the best-demonstrated available technology.[8] In addition, new or modified sources exceeding certain emission thresholds must undergo New Source Review. States with approved SIPs conduct that review, which requires, among other things, that they impose technology-based emission control requirements, subject to oversight by the US EPA.[9] The states remain free to adopt tougher air quality standards, to impose more stringent emission limitations on federally regulated sources, and to regulate sources that do not fall within the federal net.[10]

Applying Cooperative Federalism to Global Warming

The US EPA's general counsel opined in 1998 that the agency had authority to regulate GHG emissions as air pollutants under the Clean Air Act,[11] but the agency took no steps to do so. Five years later, a different general counsel working for a different administration offered a different interpretation, asserting that the Clean Air Act did not allow the US EPA to regulate GHGs.[12] That conclusion rested on the view that the Clean Air Act's regulatory framework was ill-suited to the problem of global climate change. Some important politicians agree. Congressman John Dingell (Michigan) said that regulation of GHGs under the Clean Air Act would produce "a glorious mess,"[13] and President George W. Bush worried that applying the Clean Air Act (or the Endangered Species Act or National Environmental Policy Act, for that matter) to global warming would cripple the economy.[14] Those concerns featured prominently in an Advance Notice of Proposed Rulemaking that the US EPA issued in July 2008,[15] belatedly responding to *Massachusetts v. EPA*. In an unusual personal preface, then–US EPA Administrator Stephen Johnson described the Clean Air Act as "ill-suited for the task of regulating global greenhouse gases."[16] The administration of President Barack Obama, which has more interest than its predecessor in addressing global warming, has been more willing to invoke some parts of the Clean Air Act.

In December 2009, US EPA Administrator Lisa Jackson issued formal findings that GHG emissions endanger public health and welfare and that mobile source emissions cause or contribute to that endangerment.[17] Based on those findings, the US EPA and the National Highway Transportation Safety Administration have issued joint regulations limiting GHG emissions from light-duty vehicles. Because the Clean Air Act requires that state permitting agencies impose technology-based limits on the emission of any "regulated pollutant" from new or modified stationary sources, the tailpipe standards also have consequences for stationary sources. The US EPA has tried to blunt those consequences by issuing a "tailoring rule" purporting to exempt many sources from that requirement or at least delay its applicability. All of the US EPA's GHG regulatory initiatives have been challenged; the litigation has yet to be resolved.

We applaud the US EPA's regulatory efforts, but we note that the US EPA has so far resisted calls to issue GHG NAAQS, which would invoke the SIP requirement. We agree that the NAAQS provision is difficult to apply directly to GHG emissions. Nonetheless, we believe that something very much like it, together with the regulatory efforts the US EPA is undertaking, would serve the nation well in tackling global warming. The combination of federal minimum standards for both stationary and mobile sources with state obligations to meet emission targets could address many of the gaps that emission trading will inevitably leave.

The Air Quality Standards Problem

The one conspicuous misfit between the present Clean Air Act and the global warming problem is the Act's reliance on national air quality standards. The US EPA's 2003 determination that it lacked the authority to regulate carbon dioxide (CO_2) emissions rested in large part on its conclusion that the NAAQS were not a useful way to address global warming. The general counsel wrote:

> Unique and basic aspects of the presence of key GHGs in the atmosphere make the NAAQS system fundamentally ill-suited to addressing global climate change . . .
> . . . [A]ny CO_2 standard that might be established would in effect be a worldwide ambient air quality standard, not a national standard—the entire world would be either in compliance or out of compliance.
> Such a situation would be inconsistent with a basic underlying premise of the [Clean Air Act] regime for implementation of a NAAQS—that actions taken by individual states and by EPA can generally bring all areas of the US into attainment of a NAAQS.[18]

It is true that no state on its own could ensure compliance with an air quality standard for CO_2. In that sense, the NAAQS approach is a poor fit for any global, or even regional, problem. Furthermore, the impacts of GHGs on health and welfare are significantly different than those of the current criteria pollutants. Instead of direct effects on human life and ecosystems, impacts of CO_2 are largely indirect, mediated through changes in air and water temperatures due to increased retention of solar energy.

Not surprisingly, many people have looked to the Clean Air Act's acid rain program as a model for dealing with GHGs. The effects of CO_2 in the atmosphere are even less direct and more independent of the geographic location of emission than the acid rain effects of sulfur dioxide (SO_2). Surely the sense that the Clean Air Act cannot deal with such a delocalized pollution problem, together with the desire to solve the problem as painlessly as possible, has contributed significantly to the marked preference for cap-and-trade approaches over command-and-control regulation.

National Emission Targets Instead

We believe that Congress should identify the goals of GHG regulation outside the strictures of the air quality provisions of the Clean Air Act. Those provisions require that the US EPA set NAAQS at levels requisite to protect public health and welfare, without regard to costs. Given the difficulty of deciding what level of global warming is acceptable, the likelihood that we are already committed to a level of warming that will significantly affect public health and welfare,[19] and the potentially high costs of reaching our GHG goals, it is probably essential that Congress take the lead in setting those goals.

We also believe that an emission target makes more sense in this case than an atmospheric concentration target. The level of CO_2 in the atmosphere is essentially independent of the decisions of any individual state; indeed, because other nations are important emitters, it is at least somewhat independent of the decisions of all the US states together. States should not face sanctions, as they might under the NAAQS framework, for atmospheric CO_2 levels that are beyond their control. Nonetheless, the fact that domestic emission reductions cannot ensure attainment of the atmospheric goal need not be a barrier to regulation. The fight against global warming must proceed on a number of fronts. The 1970 Clean Air Act set emission limits for automobiles based on back-of-the-envelope calculations of the level of reduction in automobile emissions necessary to achieve desired air quality levels.[20] In much the same way, targets could be set for domestic emission reductions with the understanding that vigorous pursuit of an international successor to the Kyoto Protocol will also be necessary to ensure that climate goals are realized.

The Clean Air Act, then, is not quite the right tool for setting regulatory goals and determining acceptable emission levels for GHGs. But the fact that the initial step under the NAAQS provisions does not seem to work for CO_2 should not blind us to the many benefits that could come from applying the SIP framework used to achieve the NAAQS to GHG emissions. That framework would engage the states as full partners in addressing the problem, leverage the work they are already doing, provide information needed to tackle aspects of the problem that are not well suited to markets, recognize local variation in challenges and opportunities, take advantage of the special political and practical abilities of the states to deal with behavioral emissions, and help states learn from one another's successes and failures. Given all these benefits, any federal climate legislation should retain the SIP implementation model even as it throws out the idea of a national GHG air quality standard.

We acknowledge that setting emission targets for individual states will be a daunting political problem. A national emission budget could be divided among the states in any number of ways—on a per capita basis, on a historic emission basis, or on the basis of fuel availability, for example. That allocation problem need not be any more daunting than the equivalent problem associated with any cap-and-trade program, however. We also acknowledge that decisions will have to be made about cross-boundary transactions, such as the production of electricity in one state for consumption in another. Our goal in this article is not to address all the complications of any strategy, but rather to point out that a state-by-state planning strategy, which has not been seriously addressed in any of the political debates to date, has much to recommend it.

The Need for a Federal Mandate

Global warming is a daunting problem, one that will be far more difficult to solve than the pollution problems that gave rise to the Clean Air Act. Stabilizing the climate at an acceptable CO_2 level will take the concerted efforts of many nations, all levels of domestic government, and a committed citizenry. Others have argued—quite correctly—that federal GHG legislation should protect the ability of states to engage in their own climate-change efforts.[21]

We would go further. For this problem, it is not enough to allow states to participate to the extent they choose. Because global warming provides textbook temptations for a "race to the bottom," in which states compete for industry by lowering their environmental standards, emission goals should be set at the national level. States should have a strong voice in the goal-setting process because they have much at stake. Ultimately, however, there must be a federal floor that compels action by all states, so that states do not face an unpalatable choice between protecting the atmosphere and protecting their economy. Beyond that floor, states should be free to adopt more stringent goals, should they choose to do so, just as they are currently free to impose on themselves air quality standards tougher than the federal NAAQS.

Once the federal government sets minimum emission reduction goals, the states should be required to play a primary role in implementing those goals. Federal legislation can and should affirmatively confer upon states the authority and responsibility to play that role. Surprisingly, none of the early crop of GHG bills has dealt with the role of the states in any depth. None would have assigned the states an important role, or even provided them with incentives to voluntarily assume such a role. The Waxman-Markey bill, which passed the House of Representatives in 2009, said only that states could not operate a cap-and-trade program for GHG emissions between 2012 and 2017. It did not require, or even encourage, the states to partner with the federal government in addressing the GHG problem.

That is an unfortunate omission. Global warming cries out for recognition of a strong state role in part because the states are well ahead of the federal government. By 2008, every state in the country had some kind of climate-change policy or law.[22] At least thirty-three states, and a large number of cities and counties, have drafted climate action plans for reducing GHG emissions.[23] Forty-two states have some form of GHG emission inventory.[24] Seventeen states, and 284 cities outside those states, have set emission reduction targets.[25] They are using a wide variety of approaches to try to reach those targets. According to one study, "states have undertaken well over 250 different types of policy actions" to mitigate climate change.[26]

Not only are the states already addressing this problem; they are also indispensable to any solution. John Dwyer pointed out in 1995 that the federal government needs the states' resources and political capital to address the problem of conventional air pollution.[27] That remains true today for conventional pollution, and even more so for climate change. Furthermore, with nearly forty years of environmental federalism under their belts, many states are sophisticated environmental players, with as much or (particularly for this problem) more expertise than the US EPA. Federal GHG legislation should use existing state efforts and the energy behind them as the foundation for an essential state role in addressing the climate-change problem. There may be other models that would work, but the Clean Air Act's SIP program provides a useful and readily available starting model for an appropriate state role. Through a SIP-like state climate planning requirement, federal law could recognize the importance of state action, offer standard models without unduly restricting creativity, and provide seed funding to help build state and local capacity.

The Role of Federal Oversight

We are not arguing that the states should be free to do what they will about the climate-change problem. The states must be key players, but their efforts should be coordinated and overseen by federal authorities, in the same way that the US EPA currently oversees SIP development and implementation. Federal oversight will ensure that every state does its part to deal with the climate problem.

Federal oversight also can provide needed consistency and standardization. Although state climate action is independent, it is increasingly systematized. States are communicating with one another about climate-change measures, and a fairly standard set of procedures has emerged: states are generally inventorying emissions, establishing registries, and using "consistent methods to prioritize similar [GHG] mitigation actions."[28] Still, state climate plans could be standardized in ways that would generate information needed to tackle aspects of the climate-change problem that are not well suited to markets. State climate inventories could highlight the possibilities and challenges of reducing indirect and behavioral emissions. At the moment, we have little reliable data at a local planning scale connecting GHG emissions to land uses, development patterns, and infrastructure choices.[29] A carefully framed planning mandate, supported by adequate guidance and federal funding, could address that need. Standardized state GHG inventories could also tie into SIP development for other criteria pollutants, because GHGs are frequently coemitted with criteria pollutants. Finally, state planning obligations could be framed in such a way that they would include evaluation of the impacts of unavoidable warming, helping deal with the need to adapt to a warmer world.

Federal oversight could also maximize the opportunity for states to learn from each other's successes and failures. The much-touted idea that devolving regulatory authority to the states allows them to play the role of laboratories of experimentation works only if someone is paying attention to and evaluating the various forays. Those states that are already active in climate change are making efforts to coordinate with one another.[30] Coordination would be easier, however, if state plans were standardized by federal guidelines and made available through a federal climate clearinghouse. Applying the Clean Air Act's requirements for emission monitoring, and adding requirements for regular updating of the state emission inventory and climate implementation plan, would put the US EPA in a good position to undertake or commission comparative evaluation of the effectiveness of disparate state strategies.

The Need for State and Local Efforts

Engaging the states could plug some key gaps that a cap-and-trade system will inevitably leave. The states are in a better position than either the federal government or the market to address the individual behaviors responsible for a large proportion of the nation's GHG emissions; indeed, many states are already taking steps to do so. Federal climate-change legislation should acknowledge the states' legal and political advantages and leverage their enthusiasm.

Mandatory state planning not only takes advantage of state resources and energies but also allows policy choices to respond to local variation in challenges and opportunities. There is considerable variation in the ways that states contribute to climate change, as well as in the relative economic costs and social disruption that would be associated with various emission reduction measures. For example, a higher proportion of emissions in California are attributable to transportation than in many other states,[31] because vehicle miles traveled per capita are high while winter heating needs are low. Even where emissions are traceable to a single general sector, such as electricity generation, the uses of electricity, and consequently the costs associated with reducing generation, can be very different. In California, the water use cycle, including conveyance, treatment, storage, and wastewater treatment and disposal, is the largest energy user, responsible for 19 percent of the state's electricity consumption, 30 percent of its non-power-generation natural gas use, and the burning of 88 billion gallons of diesel fuel every year.[32] Water conveyance from the wet northern portion of the state to the dry but populous south accounts for the largest proportion of that energy use.[33] Politically responsive decision makers in California, rather than utility company officers or federal bureaucrats, should decide whether those numbers suggest that promoting water conservation in Southern California offers a prime opportunity to reduce GHG emissions, or instead that electricity conservation should be sought in other sectors in order to protect the state's ability to move water to communities that need it. There is no objectively right or wrong answer to that question, or its counterparts in other states. The point is that, just as for criteria pollutants, the details of how to reach a given level of GHG emission reduction can be enormously important to states and localities. Those decisions, therefore, should be made locally to the extent feasible.

There is yet another reason to keep a substantial share of the responsibility for reducing GHG emissions at the state and local level: those governments have greater political and practical abilities than the federal government to deal with a substantial share of emissions, particularly those connected to individual behaviors. Allowing any level of government to directly regulate the sorts of individual behaviors responsible for GHG emissions is awkward at best, not to mention politically challenging. Most behavioral changes will have to be voluntary, triggered by education, norm activation, or other catalysts. Nonetheless, there is a clear role for government, and that role is best served at the state or local level.

State and local governments have authority over key infrastructure choices that mediate behavioral decisions and the emission consequences of those decisions. They determine, among other things, patterns of development, building codes, and the availability of public transit. They can regulate farming practices, wetland draining, and the extraction of fossil fuels, although so far they have largely chosen not to do so. The choices available to state and local governments can have large effects on GHG emissions. Building codes and development patterns strongly affect carbon emissions and are subject primarily to state control. States can set appliance efficiency requirements where the federal government has not done so, or with a federal waiver.[34] Development impact fees assessed on a sliding scale tied to the level of carbon emissions offer another potentially promising approach.[35] The key point is that states have open to them a wide variety of measures that could reduce GHG emissions; a state inventory and planning requirement would force them to confront the challenge of GHG emissions while encouraging experimentation and allowing adjustment to local social and economic conditions.

Improving on the SIP Program

While we are convinced that the SIP framework provides a useful model for addressing climate change, we are not blind to its limits. Noting that more than 130 million people in the United States live in areas that are not yet in compliance with the NAAQS, Arnold Reitze has proclaimed the SIP approach to control of criteria pollutants a "failure."[36] Nonetheless, we view reforming and reinforcing existing state and local planning and implementation roles as a more promising strategy than beginning from the ground up with an entirely new framework or leaving everything to an emission market.

The SIP program has suffered from three major flaws. First, the US EPA has consistently been late with needed regulations and guidance and slow to review state submissions. Second, states have been able to manipulate the models used to demonstrate attainment. Third, states have never been forced to confront the problem of increasing vehicle miles traveled. The first of these flaws will be a problem for a GHG program unless the president and Congress make the program a priority. The second will not pose the same problems as for criteria pollutants, because evaluating compliance with GHG emission reduction goals would be much less sensitive to the kinds of highly uncertain modeling assumptions that plague assessment of compliance with the NAAQS for localized pollutants. However, there may be difficult questions about how to oversee the use of offsets or cross-boundary emissions. The third will certainly be a significant problem for a state-centric approach to climate-change mitigation. That does not mean that a program modeled on the SIP approach cannot work, but it does mean that such a program must be carefully designed. If Congress is serious about dealing with climate change, it must mandate that state plans explicitly address the effect of development and other decisions on vehicle miles traveled and force states that are unwilling to cut back on driving to compensate with other emission reductions. It should also direct the US EPA to refine estimates of the effect of development patterns on GHG emissions and to develop "best practices" recommendations for low-carbon land use planning. If the states are serious about dealing with climate change, as many of them now appear to be, they will pressure Congress to include such requirements in climate-change legislation and pressure the US EPA to enforce them. The ability to change American driving habits will be a key test of any strategy for reducing carbon emissions.

Mobile Source Emission Controls

As explained above, the federal government and California share authority to regulate tailpipe emissions of conventional pollutants under the Clean Air Act. Applying the same framework to GHG emissions makes good policy sense, because it is well suited to the GHG problem. In fact, the US EPA is currently moving ahead with applying the Clean Air Act to emissions of GHGs from cars and trucks. *Massachusetts v. EPA*[37] strongly suggested that such regulation was mandated. After a protracted period of resistance in the G. W. Bush administration, the US EPA under the Obama administration has moved forward, authorizing California to regulate GHG emissions from cars and issuing combined federal GHG emission and fuel efficiency regulations.

In 2003, the US EPA rejected a petition seeking federal regulation of GHG emissions under Title II of the Clean Air Act.[38] The US EPA relied principally on its conclusion that GHGs could not be considered "air pollutants" subject to regulation under the Clean Air Act. That position, subsequently rejected by the US Supreme Court in *Massachusetts v. EPA*, appears to have been driven by the agency's discomfort with the idea of setting a NAAQS for CO_2. The US EPA also argued that the Clean Air Act's provisions for limiting tailpipe emissions from mobile sources should not be applied to CO_2 because "at present, the only practical way to reduce tailpipe emissions of CO_2 is to improve fuel economy,"[39] a task supposedly delegated by Congress exclusively to the US Department of Transportation, which sets corporate average fuel economy standards under the Energy Policy and Conservation Act of 1975. That position, too, was rejected by the Supreme Court, which noted that the US EPA's obligation to protect public health and welfare could overlap with the Department of Transportation's mandate to promote energy efficiency without any inconsistency.

Following *Massachusetts v. EPA*, it appeared inevitable that the US EPA must regulate CO_2 emissions from mobile sources. Nonetheless, the US EPA dragged its heels, waiting more than a year to issue a call for public comment on potential approaches, prefaced by a statement of the agency's unwillingness to use the Clean Air Act against GHG emissions in any way. While avoiding action itself, the US EPA under the Bush administration also sought to prevent California from acting, denying the state's request for a waiver allowing it to regulate tailpipe GHG emissions. The US EPA's attitude shifted with the change of administration, however. Under the Obama administration, it has now granted California's waiver,[40] found that GHG emissions from tailpipes do endanger public health and welfare and therefore must be regulated,[41] and issued joint regulations with the Department of Transportation to address GHG emissions and fuel efficiency together.[42]

In fact, there is no good reason not to regulate tailpipe emissions of GHGs under the Clean Air Act.[43] Conceptually, it makes no difference whether emissions are controlled by improving fuel efficiency or by removing pollutants from the emission stream. In either case, regulation may be necessary to ensure that lower-polluting vehicles make it to the market. And in either case, regulation under the Clean Air Act, with its requirement for sufficient lead time to allow compliance, can push technological advancement without threatening the automobile industry.

Through a creative combination of federal and state authority, the Clean Air Act's mobile source provisions encourage technology forcing without threatening the chaos of fifty different sets of standards. Only California may regulate more stringently than the US EPA, although other states with attainment problems may choose to adopt California's standards. Ann Carlson concludes that by singling out California for special regulatory authority, the mobile source provisions of the Clean Air Act "may have enhanced environmental innovation."[44] California's unique air pollution problems and massive market power, perhaps coupled with the relative unimportance of the conventional automobile industry to its economy, have encouraged the state to adopt emission controls more stringent than the US EPA's. Those controls, in turn, have acted as a kind of one-way ratchet. When California adopts and implements its regulations, the automobile industry must choose between withdrawing from the large California market or conceding that it can meet California's standards. In practice, California's standards have often led to tightening of the national standards or persuaded manufacturers to make all their cars to California standards.[45] That ratchet effect would be just as useful for GHG pollution as it has been for conventional pollution.

Technology-Based Emission Limits for Stationary Sources

Like tailpipe regulation, technology-based regulation of emissions from stationary sources is well suited to the GHG problem. The fact that no effective technologies for removing CO_2 at the smokestack currently exist need not deter technology-based regulation. Regulators could concentrate on processes and practices that reduce fuel use, and/or could seek to aggressively force the development of carbon sequestration technology. Under the G. W. Bush administration, the US EPA disclaimed any authority to regulate GHG emissions from stationary sources. It has now changed that view and is preparing to require permits for some new or modified sources, although it is trying to minimize the number of sources that will be covered by federal technology-based standards.[46]

For much the same reasons that California should be free to regulate GHG emissions from mobile sources more strictly than the US EPA, all states should be permitted to adopt more stringent limits on stationary sources. Those limits could help the states meet their emission targets or free up emissions for other sectors. The concerns about uniformity that have limited the Clean Air Act to one state alternative for mobile sources do not apply to stationary sources. Nor is there any inconsistency in allowing states to impose additional regulations on stationary sources on top of a federal market strategy. The acid rain trading program—the poster child for market efforts—has been successfully layered on top of the SIP foundation. Federal SO_2 allowances are necessary but not sufficient to authorize emissions; sources subject to the trading program must also comply with all applicable state requirements.[47]

Federal Enforceability

Finally, one other aspect of the Clean Air Act's approach to cooperative federalism merits inclusion in federal GHG legislation. As we mentioned above, once approved by the US EPA, state SIPs become enforceable as a matter of federal law. That means that the US EPA can step in if a state drafts a strong plan but then ignores it. Because the Clean Air Act contains a broad citizen suit provision, citizens can enforce the plan if the US EPA does not. The possibility of outside enforcement action will likely be crucial to the success of any climate regulation scheme, because state and federal politicians and bureaucrats will face strong temptations to endorse plans that seem to aggressively tackle the problem but allow powerful economic players to escape full implementation of such plans.

Conclusion

We understand both the appeal of carbon markets and the reluctance of the US EPA to turn to the Clean Air Act's regulatory mechanisms to control GHG emissions. Markets promise painless (or nearly painless) environmental improvement, and carbon emissions seem particularly well suited to a market approach. Regulations have a reputation for being both economically painful and politically bruising, and their implementation has often been distressingly slow. In addition, the Clean Air Act looks, at first glance, like an uncomfortable fit for the global climate-change problem.

Unfortunately, there is good reason to believe that carbon markets alone will not be adequate to the task of preventing disastrous global warming. Although we believe that carbon markets will and should be part of any national climate mitigation strategy, those markets should be combined with regulatory approaches. Once it is acknowledged that regulation must be part of the solution, the Clean Air Act begins to look better. Although in its current form the Clean Air Act is by no means a perfect fit for the global warming problem, several elements of the Act's cooperative federalism structure could be adapted to the GHG context. Global warming is a problem that calls for national goals, implemented by local authorities in ways that are responsive to local economic and social conditions. It requires individual behavioral change to a far greater extent than historic air pollution problems; state and local governments have better access than the federal government to policy levers connected to GHG-generating behaviors. Mitigating carbon emissions will also require faster and more innovative technological change than past air pollution problems; technology-forcing regulation with a state ratchet offers more promise than do markets for catalyzing that sort of rapid technological evolution.

As the US EPA moves to regulate some GHG emissions under the Clean Air Act, the pressures on legislators to directly address the GHG problem will increase. Policy makers should look for ways to maintain and even strengthen those aspects of the Act that are well suited to addressing global warming while they throw out those that are not. The price of legislatively exempting CO_2 emissions from the NAAQS requirement should be the adoption of a robust federal mandate for development and implementation of state GHG emission reduction plans, federal tailpipe emission standards that encourage California to adopt its own more stringent standards, and federal technology-based minimum standards for stationary source emissions, appropriately tailored to the types of sources and amounts of emissions typical for CO_2.

Notes

1. M. I. Hoffert et al., "Advanced Technology Paths to Global Climate Stability: Energy for a Greenhouse Planet," 298 *Science* 981 (2002).

2. 42 U.S.C. § 7408(a) (2006).

3. 42 U.S.C. § 7410(a) (2006).

4. D. R. Williams, "Cooperative Federalism and the Clean Air Act: A Defense of Minimum Federal Standards," 20 *St. Louis U. Pub. L. Rev.* 67 (2001): 91–95.

5. J. E. McCarthy, *Transportation Conformity Under the Clean Air Act: In Need of Reform?* (Washington, DC: Congressional Research Service, April 23, 2004), 2.

6. *See* McCarthy, *Transportation Conformity*, 6; Michael R. Yarne, "*Conformity as Catalyst: Environmental Defense Fund v. Environmental Protection Agency*," 27 Ecol. L. Q. 841 (2000): 844–45.

7. 42 U.S.C. § 7521(a)(1) (2006).

8. 42 U.S.C. § 7411(a)(1).

9. 42 U.S.C. § 7503(c); 42 U.S.C. § 7479(3).

10. 42 U.S.C. § 7416.

11. US Environmental Protection Agency (EPA), Memorandum from Jonathan Z. Cannon, US EPA General Counsel, to Carol Browner, US EPA Administrator, *U.S. EPA's Authority to Regulate Pollutants Emitted by Electric Power Generation Sources* (April 10, 1998).

12. US EPA, Memorandum from Robert E. Fabricant, US EPA General Counsel, to Marianne L. Horinko, Acting Administrator, *U.S. EPA's Authority to Impose Mandatory Controls to Address Global Climate Change Under the Clean Air Act* (August 28, 2003).

13. *Strengths and Weaknesses of Regulating Greenhouse Gas Emissions Using Existing Clean Air Act Authorities: Hearing on Climate Change Before the H. Comm. on Energy and Commerce, Subcomm. on Energy and Air Quality*, 110th Cong. (April 10, 2008).

14. G. W. Bush Administration, *President Bush Discusses Climate Change* (White House, April 16, 2008), available at http://georgewbush-whitehouse.archives.gov/news/releases/2008/04/images/20080416-6_p041608nr-0553-597v.html.

15. US EPA, *Regulating Greenhouse Gas Emissions Under the Clean Air Act*, 73 Fed. Reg. 44,354 (July 30, 2008).

16. US EPA, *Regulating Greenhouse Gas Emissions*, 44,355.

17. 74 *Fed. Reg.* 66496 (December 15, 2009).

18. US EPA, Memorandum from Robert E. Fabricant, 7–8.

19. Intergovernmental Panel on Climate Change, *Climate Change 2007: Synthesis Report—Summary for Policy Makers* (2007), available at http://www.ipcc.ch/pdf/assessment-report/ar4/syr/ar4_syr_spm.pdf.

20. F. P. Grad et al., *The Automobile and the Regulation of Its Impact on the Environment: A Study* (Norman: University of Oklahoma, 1975), 33–36.

21. W. Andreen et al., *Cooperative Federalism and Climate Change: Why Federal, State, and Local Governments Must Continue to Partner*, White Paper (Washington, DC: Center for Progressive Reform, May 29, 2008).

22. Andreen et al., *Cooperative Federalism and Climate Change*, 4 (citing David Hodas, "State Initiatives," in *Global Climate Change and U.S. Law*, edited by M. B. Gerrard [American Bar Association, 2007], 345).

23. Andreen et al., *Cooperative Federalism and Climate Change*. See also K. L. Doran, "U.S. Sub-federal Climate Change Initiatives: An Irrational Means to a Rational End?" 26 *Va. Envtl. L. J.* 181 (2008): 200; A. Kaswan, "The Domestic Response to Climate Change: What Role for Federal, State, and Litigation Initiatives?" 42 *U.S.F. L. Rev.* 39 (2007): 46–47

24. N. Lutsey and D. Sperling, "America's Bottom-Up Climate Change Mitigation Policy," 36 *Energy Pol'y* 673 (2008): 674, 675.

25. Lutsey and Sperling, "America's Bottom-Up Climate Change Mitigation Policy," 675.

26. R. B. McKinstry, Jr., and T. D. Peterson, "The Implications of the New 'Old' Federalism in Climate-Change Legislation: How to Function in a Global Marketplace When States Take the Lead," 20 *Pac. McGeorge Global Bus. & Dev. L. J.* 61 (2007): 72.

27. J. P. Dwyer, "The Practice of Federalism Under the Clean Air Act," 54 *Md. L. Rev.* 1183 (1995): 1190, 1216–19; P. R. Portney, K. N. Probst, and A. M. Finkel, "The EPA at 'Thirtysomething,'" 21 *Envtl. L.* 1461 (1991): 1472.

28. Dwyer, "The Practice of Federalism," 675.

29. M. A. Brown et al., *Shrinking the Carbon Footprint of Metropolitan America* (May 2008), 13, available at http://www.brookings.edu/~/media/Files/rc/reports/2008/05_carbon_footprint_ sarzynski/carbonfootprint_report.pdf.

30. Lutsey and Sperling, "America's Bottom-Up Climate Change Mitigation Policy," 680, 683.

31. See Energy Information Administration, "2004 State Emissions by Sector (Million Metric Tons of Carbon Dioxide)," available at http://www.eia.doe.gov/oiaf/1605/ggrpt/excel/tbl_statesector.xls (last accessed July 31, 2008); A. E. Carlson, "Federalism, Preemption, and Greenhouse Gas Emissions," 37 *U.C. Davis L. Rev.* 281 (2003): 290, 291.

32. M. Krebs, California Energy Commission, "Water-Related Energy Use in California," *Testimony Presented to the Assembly Committee on Water, Parks, and Wildlife* (February 20, 2007), 3; Navigant Consulting, Inc., "Refining Estimates of Water-Related Energy Use in California," *Report to the California Energy Commission* (December 2006), 5.

33. Navigant Consulting, Inc., "Refining Estimates," 2.

34. M. B. Gerrard, ed., *Global Climate Change and U.S. Law* (American Bar Association, 2007), 343, 363; S. Nadel et al., *Leading the Way: Continued Opportunities for New State Appliance and Equipment Efficiency Standards* (American Council for an Energy-Efficient Economy, March 2006); Kaswan, "The Domestic Response to Climate Change," 825, 835–36.

35. See generally B. S. Kingsley, "Making It Easy to Be Green: Using Impact Fees to Encourage Green Building," 83 *N.Y.U. L. Rev.* 532 (2008).

36. A. W. Reitze, Jr., "Air Quality Protection Using State Implementation Plans—Thirty-Seven Years of Increasing Complexity," 15 *Vill. Envtl. L. J.* 209 (2004): 357–58.

37. 127 S. Ct. 1438 (2007).

38. US EPA, "Control of Emissions from New Highway Vehicles and Engines," 68 *Fed. Reg.* 52922 (September 8, 2003).

39. US EPA, "Control of Emissions," 52929.

40. US EPA, "Notice of Decision Granting a Waiver of Clean Air Act Preemption for California's 2009 and Subsequent Model Year Greenhouse Gas Emission Standards for New Motor Vehicles," 74 *Fed. Reg.* 32744 (July 8, 2009).

41. US EPA, "Endangerment and Cause or Contribute Findings for Greenhouse Gases Under Section 202(a) of the Clean Air Act," 74 *Fed. Reg.* 66496 (December 15, 2009).

42. US EPA and Department of Transportation, "Light-Duty Vehicle Greenhouse Gas Emission Standards and Corporate Average Fuel Economy Standards," 75 *Fed. Reg.* 25324 (May 7, 2010).

43. L. Heinzerling, "Climate Change and the Clean Air Act," 42 *U.S.F. L. Rev.* 111 (2007): 133.

44. Carlson, "Federalism," 285.

45. National Research Council, Committee on State Practices in Setting Mobile Source Emissions Standards, *State and Federal Standards for Mobile-Source Emissions* (Washington, DC, 2006), 3–4; D. E. Adelman and K. Engel, "Adaptive Federalism: The Case Against Reallocating Environmental Regulatory Authority," 92 *Minn. L. Rev.* 1796 (2008).

46. US EPA, "Prevention of Significant Deterioration and Title V Greenhouse Gas Tailoring Rule," 75 *Fed. Reg.* 31514 (June 3, 2010); Letter from Lisa Jackson, US EPA Administrator, to Senator Jay D. Rockefeller IV (February 22, 2010).

47. 42 U.S.C. § 7651b(f).

The Limits of Cap-and-Trade Systems in Addressing Global Warming

Holly Doremus and W. Michael Hanemann

The successes of earlier emission trading programs such as the US acid rain program, implemented in 1990 to cap sulfur dioxide (SO_2) emissions, helped to establish the current enthusiasm for emission trading. Today, as David Driesen puts it, US Environmental Protection Agency (EPA) "rarely develops any pollution control program without including some form of environmental trading within it."[1] To combat global warming, the G8+5 nations recently issued a joint statement urging government commitments to reducing global greenhouse-gas (GHG) emissions to half their current levels by 2050.[2] Carbon trading is already the dominant global strategy for addressing climate change, and looks as though it may push everything else out of the picture at the US federal level. However, due to important physical and economic differences, emission trading is not likely to succeed as comprehensively for GHGs as it has for other pollutants. Given the enormity of the challenge, we will surely need both drastic behavioral shifts and radical technological innovation. Neither is likely to be supplied by a carbon market alone.

The Basics of Emission Trading

An emission trading system contains two components: caps on emissions by specified sources and the freedom for these entities to trade unused emission allowances. Both components influence the extent of aggregate emission reduction and the aggregate costs of that reduction. Past market strategies have focused specifically on capping emissions, for example, of leaded gasoline, SO_2, or nitrogen oxides (NO_x). In practice, these programs set emission targets and left it to producers to figure out for themselves how best to meet them. The other component of emission trading is the granting of permission for regulated entities to exceed their caps by obtaining permits to cover their excess emissions. From an economic perspective, this has two aspects: (1) the possibility of buying permits to cover excess emissions provides flexibility and allows polluters to substitute cheaper emission reductions elsewhere for more expensive reductions in their own regulated facility, reducing the overall cost of reaching the reduction goal, and (2) trading creates a price signal that reverberates through the economy and provides an incentive for firms to identify cheaper ways to control pollution.

Key Factors in the Ability to Address Global Warming

Point of Regulation

With respect to the point of regulation, there is an important distinction between leaded gasoline, SO_2, or NO_x and GHGs. With leaded gasoline, there was a single source, namely, refineries; therefore, the caps were set on individual refineries. With SO_2 and NO_x, there were many different sources, but electricity generation was the single dominant source, accounting for about two-thirds of all emissions. Hence, it was natural to focus regulation on electricity generation and to cap individual generating units.

GHGs, by contrast, lack a single dominant target. Carbon dioxide (CO_2) accounted for nearly 85 percent of the 7 billion metric tons of GHG emissions (calculated on the basis of global warming potential) in the United States in 2006, but methane, nitrous oxides, and other gases also contributed.[3] About 96 percent of the CO_2 came from the combustion of fossil fuels, with the rest from changes in land use (deforestation, etc.). The methane came mainly from landfills and cows.[4] Electricity generation accounted for about one-third of all CO_2-equivalent emissions; the next largest source was transportation, which accounted for 27 percent. Therefore, a regulatory strategy that just caps emissions from electricity-generating units—such as the Regional Greenhouse Gas Initiative emission trading system in the northeastern states—is unlikely to provide the scale of GHG reduction required to address the problem of global warming.

Another consideration is that emission caps for CO_2 can be implemented in two distinct ways. One approach involves *upstream* allocations, allowance requirements placed on CO_2 emissions at each point of entry of fossil fuels into the economy: coal, oil, and natural gas production and import and, where appropriate, import of major products derived from the combustion of fossil fuels, such as electricity. The other approach involves *downstream* allocations for major facilities that use fossil fuels throughout the economy: refineries, cement producers, aluminum producers, electricity generating units, and so forth. The downstream approach is similar to what was done with leaded gasoline, SO_2, and NO_x but, for CO_2, involves a much larger and more heterogeneous set of regulated entities spanning multiple sectors of the economy and therefore requires more complex and costly monitoring. Nevertheless, the downstream approach may be more effective in practice at inducing a significant reduction in CO_2 emissions. W. Michael Hanemann presents evidence from the SO_2 trading program that suggests that its success was mainly due not to the price signal that it created but rather to the emission caps that provided a direct, and salient, motivation for firms to take action.[5]

Technology Alternatives and Innovation

Two groups of strategies brought about the reduction in acid rain/SO_2 emissions. With respect to existing power plants, utilities were able to favor lower-emission plants (natural gas and nuclear instead of coal), modify combustion by switching from high-sulfur to low-sulfur coal, and install scrubbers to remove emissions postcombustion in some existing plants. With regard to new power plants, the action taken was to choose natural gas as the fuel source, especially combined-cycle natural gas, rather than oil or coal. These strategies are noteworthy for what was *not* done. Conservation and demand management played no role in attaining the emission reduction. Switching from fossil fuel to renewables (wind, solar, geothermal, etc.) also played no role. Furthermore, technological innovation played no role.

The experience of the acid rain market shows that markets do not necessarily spur innovation.[6] There was no boost to innovative low-emission technologies for coal combustion such as integrated gasification combined cycle, which lowers the emissions of SO_2, particulates, and mercury and improves combustion efficiency. To the extent that the reductions in acid-rain–causing emissions came from postcombustion removal of pollutants from emission streams, they relied on well-understood and mature technologies (flue gas scrubbers, etc.) that had been in use for more than twenty years. Using natural gas instead of coal or oil was an even more mature technology. Indeed, the cap-and-trade system worked extremely well because of the simplicity of the response it required of plant owners and operators, and because it required no basic technological innovation, with attendant cost and performance uncertainties.

This experience does not bode well for the prospects of carbon markets. Fuel switching is not an attractive option for existing coal-fired power plants because low-CO_2 coal does not exist. Moreover, there is no such thing as an add-on, postcombustion scrubber for CO_2. Carbon capture and sequestration may be possible for new plants but cannot practically be added on to existing plants. Consequently, unlike the SO_2 and NO_x responsible for acid rain, the only way to significantly reduce CO_2 emissions from existing coal-fired plants is to operate them less. Compared to SO_2, dealing with CO_2 emissions calls for an entirely different strategy for electricity generation. The generating technologies that matter for addressing global warming—high-thermal-efficiency coal combustion, carbon capture and sequestration, and renewable energy technologies such as solar, wind, wave, and geothermal—are not mature.

Technological innovation is needed but did not occur with past emission trading systems. Joseph Schumpeter famously identified three stages in the process of technological innovation: *invention*, the technical discovery of something new, which may involve both basic and applied research; *innovation*, the successful commercialization of a new product or process; and *diffusion*, when the product or process comes to be widely used through adoption by many firms or individuals.[7] Prior emission trading systems have produced only the third, diffusion of existing commercialized technologies. But in the case of climate change, that will not be enough. Invention and innovation are needed—the development and commercialization of technologies that do not exist yet or, at best, are still experimental (e.g., carbon capture and storage).

Consumer Behavior

In the United States, a high proportion of GHG emissions are directly attributable to individual decisions about consumption. In 1997, the US EPA wrote on its global warming Web site that individuals can affect nearly one-third of domestic emissions through choices about electricity use, waste production, and personal transportation.[8] Michael Vandenbergh and Anne Steinemann likewise assert that individuals in the United States directly accounted for the emission of nearly 13 trillion pounds of CO_2 in 2000, or roughly one-third of the nation's total.[9]

A cap-and-trade program targeted at utilities, consumer fuel producers, and large industrial emitters will not directly reach these behavioral emissions. In theory, such a cap-and-trade program should indirectly affect individual decisions that increase GHG emissions by increasing the price of electricity and fuel. Behavioral change is not always so simple, however:

- Many people are not aware of how much electricity the "vampires"—devices that consume electricity even when not in use—in their homes consume. Alternatives may be limited or unattractive; our homes are not conveniently wired with switches that turn electronics completely off at night, and power strips usually require awkward groping at floor level. Under these circumstances, sending a price signal by requiring that utilities buy allowances to cover their carbon emissions, thereby raising the price of electricity for consumers, is not likely to change consumption behavior by itself.

- In decisions about heating or air-conditioning use in existing buildings, price signals can motivate small, but not dramatic, changes. The occupant of a drafty home in New England may turn the thermostat down a bit as the cost of fuel oil rises but will not stop heating, nor will Arizona residents stop air-conditioning just because the price of electricity rises.

- Some choices about how many miles to drive are purely discretionary, but many others are not. A couple who work in different towns without convenient access to public transportation cannot easily adjust their driving habits when the price of gas goes up.

Appliance efficiency measures, building codes, and land use planning decisions can all strongly influence the GHG impacts of individual behavior. How these sorts of behavioral emission sources could be folded into a conventional carbon market is unclear; they would not be covered by any of the recent climate bills. The manufacturers of appliances undoubtedly produce emissions in the manufacturing process; perhaps crediting manufacturers based on the expected reduction in energy use over the life of the appliance could create an incentive to produce more efficient products. But consumers would still have to be persuaded to buy the more efficient appliances. New-home builders and buyers are responsible at some level for the global-warming effects of home design and subdivision layout, but buyers may have few choices, and builders are unlikely to be large direct emitters, may be constrained by local zoning, and may not be held accountable for the long-term outcomes of their decisions.

Conclusions

Despite many economists' preference for an approach to the regulation of CO_2 based on a national carbon tax or an upstream national cap-and-trade system, the actual experience with emission trading for SO_2, NO_x, and lead suggests that those measures, by themselves, would not suffice to attain the desired reduction in CO_2 emissions. Thus, emission trading will need to be accompanied by complementary measures such as building efficiency standards, appliance efficiency standards, vehicle emission standards, and other such regulatory measures. Some of those measures can and should be imposed by the federal government—for example, vehicle emission standards. But other measures are better suited to state and local action, such as building efficiency standards, financing programs for building retrofits, congestion pricing, smart growth programs, and other actions aimed at reducing CO_2 emissions from buildings and transportation. Given the fragmentation of decision making in those sectors, the prevalence of principal-agent problems, bounded rationality, and behavioral impediments to individual action, the stimulus provided by the price signal from an emission trading system alone is unlikely to be adequate.

Notes

1. David M. Driesen, "Trading and Its Limits," 14 *Penn. St. Envtl. L. Rev.* 14 (2006): 169.

2. *Joint Science Academies' Statement: Climate Change Adaptation and the Transition to a Low Carbon Society* (June 2008), available at http://www.insaindia.org/pdf/Climate_05.08_W.pdf; Narelle Towie, "Scientists Issue Declaration at Bali," *Nature News* (December 6, 2007); Sheryl Gay Stolberg, "Richest Nations Pledge to Halve Greenhouse Gas," *New York Times* (July 9, 2008): at A1.

3. US Environmental Protection Agency (EPA), *Inventory of U.S. Greenhouse Gas Emissions and Sinks: 1990–2006* (April 15, 2008), 2–4.

4. US EPA, *Inventory of U.S. Greenhouse Gas Emissions and Sinks.*

5. M. Hanemann, "Cap-and-Trade: A Sufficient or Necessary Condition for Emission Reduction?" 26 *Oxford Rev. Econ. Pol'y* 225 (2010).

6. For further discussion of the limits of markets in spurring innovation, see Adelman and Engel, chapter 8 in this volume.

7. J. A. Schumpeter, *Theorie der wirtschaftlichen Entwicklung* (1911; transl. 1934, *The Theory of Economic Development: An Inquiry into Profits, Capital, Credit, Interest and the Business Cycle*); for further discussion, see Hanemann, "Cap-and-Trade."

8. US EPA, "Global Warming—Emissions," available at http://yosemite.epa.gov/oar/globalwarming.nsf/content/EmissionsIndividual.html (last accessed July 2008).

9. M. P. Vandenbergh and A. C. Steinemann, "The Carbon-Neutral Individual," 82 *N.Y.U. L. Rev.* 1673 (2007): 1690–94.

Chapter 10

State Climate-Change Regulation

Will It Survive the Federal Challenge?

Daniel A. Farber

In Brief

- The US judicial system will play an essential role in coordinating state and federal actions taken to address the growing problems associated with global climate change.

- In the absence of a federal climate-change policy, judicial overview of state climate-change regulations primarily addresses impediments to the flow of commerce between states and will require the courts to weigh the legitimate benefits of proposed regulations against possible burdens on interstate commerce.

- If federal climate-change legislation is adopted that preempts state activity, then state statutes must give way to federal laws that are in direct conflict.

- In the absence of express federal preemption, the courts consider whether Congress left enough room for states to supplement federal climate-change legislation or foreclosed state regulation altogether.

- It is likely that the purpose of any future congressional climate-change policy, including a national cap-and-trade system, will be to decrease overall emissions and not to supersede the historic police powers of the states, although Congress is always free to say otherwise.

Climate change is a global problem, and there is little doubt about its seriousness and the challenges it poses for our society. Yet, despite these nearly undeniable facts, the federal government showed little initiative in addressing this serious issue for eight long years during the G. W. Bush administration. Perhaps surprisingly, state governments moved much more aggressively. By 2006, every state had taken steps of some kind to address climate change. California is in the lead with legislation aimed at reducing greenhouse emissions from automobiles and electrical generators, as well as an ambitious mandate to reduce emissions to 1990 levels by the end of this decade. Passage of federal climate-change legislation seems unlikely in the near future, but some states might continue to pursue independent climate-change measures even once federal regulations are in place. Though Congress has the final word on whether states can legislate on all matters within its legislative authority, it often remains silent or speaks ambiguously. This may well be true of any future federal climate legislation: either the statute will not address preemption, or, more likely, it would fail to do so explicitly. Courts, state governments, and the US Environmental Protection Agency (EPA) would then face the question of how much room remains for state climate regulation.

This chapter advocates for a bifurcated approach to determining the constitutional authority of states to pursue climate-change mitigation measures. Courts should reject regulations that discriminate against interstate or foreign commerce or ban otherwise lawful transactions under federal trading schemes. Apart from these clear-cut types of invalidity, the chapter advocates adoption of a strong presumption of validity for state climate-change regulation. That presumption would be overcome if a state law is in direct conflict with a statute or international agreement, or if it is clearly covered by a statutory preemption clause.

In practice, a state regulation has a good chance of surviving a preemption challenge if it avoids the most obvious constitutional pitfalls, including discriminating against interstate commerce, banning or burdening behavior explicitly authorized by federal law, taking steps with foreign countries that directly contradict presidential or congressional initiatives, or attaching penalties to transactions that occur wholly outside state borders. The Supreme Court has failed to provide clear guidance to states about the extent of their regulatory authority, so the outcome of litigation cannot be predicted with certainty. There are strong arguments, however, for giving state climate-change regulations the benefit of the doubt when applying these standards.

Indeed, climate change might affect our thinking about the constitutional dimension of federalism, including our understanding of federal legislative authority. The creation of new markets under the guise of cap-and-trade schemes (whether through new federal legislation or US EPA action) will make it even more difficult to draw lines around federal jurisdiction over interstate commerce. These markets, as well as the global web of interactions that result in climate change, will also make problematic the distinctions between local, national, and global concerns.

Given the difficulty of pigeonholing climate issues within conventional categories, courts should not be quick to invalidate state climate regulations, regardless of whether Congress has legislated. Society is more likely to respond too timidly to climate change; any fear of overregulation by states would be largely misplaced. The courts should content themselves with policing against the most obvious potential flaws in state legislation, and if there are more subtle flaws, Congress can address them in subsequent legislation.

The Role of the Dormant Commerce Clause in Evaluating State Legislation

In a unified national economy, the existence of a multitude of differing state environmental laws can impede the flow of commerce, imposing costs not only on consumers in the regulating jurisdiction but also on consumers and firms elsewhere. Yet, states have often been in the lead in the environmental arena, including through state climate legislation, because of the need to address pressing local problems. The tension between the local interest in regulation and the economic interests of other states cannot be resolved effectively by the courts of any of the states involved. Obviously, both the state that is engaging in regulation and the states that are affected by the regulation have interests that disable them from providing a completely neutral forum.

The federal courts have emerged as the tribunal for assessing these conflicting interests, applying what is called the dormant Commerce Clause doctrine. This section describes the current doctrine generally and then considers its application to state climate-change regulations.

At present, courts apply three tests for determining if state legislation conflicts with the dormant Commerce Clause. One test governs state legislation that discriminates against interstate commerce. Such laws are almost always held unconstitutional. For instance, the courts struck down a law that allowed private landfills to accept solid waste from in-state but not from out-of-state sources. States are simply not allowed to shut their borders to incoming or outgoing trade or transportation.

A second test applies to the state's proprietary activities. Such activities are virtually immune from restriction under the dormant Commerce Clause. An example of this would be a law that prohibited state-owned landfills from accepting waste from out-of-state sources. The government ownership of the landfill makes all the difference. Although the state cannot require private landfills to discriminate against out-of-state firms, state-owned landfills are entitled to do so. Thus, the state cannot block the private interstate market, but it has much more leeway in terms of its own financial or business transactions.

The third test applies to the remaining forms of state legislation, which are covered by a balancing test, the outcomes of which can be difficult to predict. The test is whether the legitimate purposes of the law are clearly outweighed by the burden on interstate commerce. The courts have used this test, for example, to uphold bans on environmentally harmful goods that apply equally to goods manufactured inside the state and those manufactured elsewhere.

State climate-change regulations will probably face dormant Commerce Clause claims. For example, efforts to reduce emissions by electrical generators may face claims that the regulations burden commerce, discriminate between in-state and out-of-state firms, or are guilty of extraterritorial regulation. In the absence of a comprehensive federal statute addressing climate change, the dormant Commerce Clause is the most significant legal hurdle for state climate-change regulation. Most difficulties, however, can be avoided simply by steering clear of some specific mistakes such as placing higher burdens on out-of-state firms and by carefully documenting the rationale for regulation and the supporting evidence. Assuming that states do not make the mistake of discriminating against out-of-state firms and that the proprietary exemption does not apply, courts will review their regulations under the balancing test. These cases often turn on the facts, making it important to create a record of careful policy analysis.

In applying the balancing test, one key factor is the strength of the state's regulatory interest. States should find it easy to demonstrate the strength of their interest, given what we now know about climate change. One of the most predictable impacts is sea-level rise, which will affect every coastal state. The Supreme Court has already found this harm to be serious enough and foreseeable enough to constitute a basis for standing by state governments. In *Massachusetts v. EPA*, the Court emphasized the existence of a semisovereign state interest in responding to climate change because of the threat posed to the state's citizens and even to its territory (as a result of sea-level rise).[2]

One possible counterargument is that, although the states' interests are weighty, state legislation can have only a minimal effect in attaining those goals. This argument might be made against California's automobile standards for greenhouse gases, but it should fail. The Court rejected a similar argument in *Massachusetts v. EPA*[3] in considering whether a federal action was too minor to have any effect on climate change by itself: "Agencies, like legislatures, do not generally resolve massive problems in one fell regulatory swoop. They instead whittle away at them over time, refining their preferred approach as circumstances change and as they develop a more-nuanced understanding of how best to proceed."[4]

States, like federal agencies, should not be faulted for their inability to solve a large problem in one fell swoop. Even small steps to address such a major problem may have value that easily outweighs any incidental effect on interstate commerce. Thus, as long as they avoid discriminatory bans on interstate commerce, states should have free rein to engage in climate regulation notwithstanding the dormant Commerce Clause.

Preemption: When Federal Action Overrides State Law

The dormant Commerce Clause is an implicit constitutional limitation on state authority. It applies regardless of whether Congress has legislated in the same areas as the state (unless Congress authorizes the state regulation) or whether the president has taken a position on a subject. State authority is also subject to additional restrictions, however, when the federal government has acted.

Typically, these restrictions arise when Congress has enacted relevant legislation that in some way conflicts with state law. More rarely, a presidential or congressional action relating to foreign affairs may also preempt a state. In any event, if and when Congress passes climate-change legislation, we can expect a spate of preemption claims. Until that time, the primary preemption threats will be from existing federal regulations of specific industries such as the wholesale electricity market. In the long run, however, it is hard to see how Congress can indefinitely avoid confronting the challenges of climate change. When it does so, key questions will be how Congress itself and then the federal courts view the preemption issue.

Contradictions Between Federal Mandates and State Law

This section addresses the validity of state regulations in areas where Congress has acted, unlike the dormant Commerce Clause, which operates regardless of federal legislation. It is clear, of course, that in cases of direct conflict with federal law, the state statute must give way.[5] Congress has the power to preempt state laws simply by enacting an express statutory provision to that effect.[6] The presence of a contradiction between federal mandates and state law, however, is often less than obvious, leading some to question whether the Court has taken statutory preemption too far.[7]

The absence of express preemption may not be enough to save a state law. The Supreme Court has set forth various factors for courts to consider in preemption cases where the statute does not directly address preemption.[8] The federal regulatory scheme may be so pervasive and detailed as to suggest that Congress left no room for the state to supplement it. The statute enacted by Congress may involve a field in which the federal interest is so dominant that enforcement of state laws is precluded. Other aspects of the regulatory scheme imposed by Congress may also support the inference that Congress has completely foreclosed state legislation in a particular area. This is often called "field" preemption.[9]

Even where Congress has not completely foreclosed state regulation, a state statute is void to the extent that it actually conflicts with a valid federal statute. Such a conflict can be found where compliance with both the federal and state regulations is impossible or, more often, where the state law interferes with the accomplishment of the full objectives of Congress.[10] These factors are obviously vague and can be difficult to apply.

The Supreme Court has done little to create a more rigorous framework for analysis. Indeed, even when a statute contains an express preemption or savings clause,[11] application of the statutory language may involve difficult problems of interpretation. Therefore, the only way to achieve a full understanding of the preemption issue is to examine particular cases in order to see what situations have been deemed appropriate for application of the preemption doctrine.

Perhaps in response to the difficulty of applying the standard preemption tests, the Supreme Court has enunciated a presumption against preemption. For example, in a decision dealing with state tort remedies against cigarette companies, the Court said that it "'start[s] with the assumption that the historic police powers of the States [are] not to be superseded by ... Federal Act unless that [is] the clear and manifest purpose of Congress.'"[12] It is not clear, however, how significant this presumption is in practice. The Court often finds that state laws are preempted by federal statutes even where reasonable minds (sometimes including four of the nine justices) might disagree with that conclusion.[13] States will undoubtedly rely on this generalized presumption in their defense of climate-change regulation, but how much actual ground they will gain is unclear. Furthermore, depending on whether the US EPA is supportive of state regulation, its views on preemption issues may either assist states or create an additional obstacle to state climate regulation.

As Congress becomes more involved with the issue, climate change is bound to present cases in which there is no clear basis for resolving the preemption issue and results are therefore likely to be unpredictable. A later section of this chapter examines how to resolve these issues, with particular attention to the possible preemptive effect of a federal cap-and-trade scheme. First, however, we need to consider another type of preemption.

Conflicts Between State Law and Federal Foreign Affairs

Apart from ordinary statutory preemption, state laws may also be subject to challenge because they trammel on federal prerogatives over foreign affairs. Unfortunately, constitutional doctrine seems to be in flux on this issue.[14] Climate change is obviously a global problem that will ultimately require concerted international action, but this does not necessarily mean that it is part of that realm of "foreign affairs" reserved to the federal government. The Supreme Court's decisions on this issue are confusing, and it is difficult to be sure where to draw the line.

It is not clear how seriously we should take foreign affairs preemption in the arena of climate change. To the extent that any international understanding has involved state governments, it does not seem to involve any direct exercise of governmental power by a joint entity or any binding obligation on the state to enact legislation. Without at least a presidential assertion that state climate regulations are interfering with an existing international agreement or with ongoing international negotiations, there seems little basis for finding foreign affairs preemption.

Moreover, the Supreme Court's only ruling on climate change to date, *Massachusetts v. EPA*,[15] contains some signals that might undermine a preemption claim. As we have seen, *Massachusetts v. EPA* speaks strongly to the legitimacy and strength of the states' interests in addressing climate change.[16] This assessment of the seriousness of a state's interest should weigh in its favor in considering foreign affairs preemption. In addition, although not directly addressing foreign affairs preemption, the Court made it clear that foreign affairs consideration could not override the otherwise plain language of federal pollution legislation. The Court in its ruling seemed skeptical of claims that domestic climate-change actions should be invalidated because of interference with presidential foreign policy efforts.[17]

Assuming that the Court does not retreat from *Massachusetts v. EPA*, the implication seems to be favorable for state legislation on the subject—though the sparse Supreme Court case law on foreign affairs preemption and its somewhat ambiguous pronouncements definitely leave uncertainty about the ultimate outcome.[18] As noted above, the initial decisions in the litigation over California's proposed greenhouse-gas limitations for vehicles rejected claims of foreign affairs preemption. For now, at least, foreign affairs preemption does not seem to be a serious threat to the validity of state climate regulation. Nor should it be, because states have a legitimate interest in helping to address the climate issue.

The Future of Climate-Change Federalism

Federal action on climate change is clearly not imminent, but the looming threat of climate change may eventually prompt a congressional response. Federal legislation will potentially raise two federalism issues. First, does Congress have the power to legislate over all aspects of the problem? Issues of federal power regarding climate change have not yet arisen, but sooner or later they will if Congress becomes serious about addressing the full spectrum of climate issues. Second, once Congress has acted, what remaining role may the states play? This is partly a matter of preemption (statutory and otherwise) and partly involves the dormant Commerce Clause.

In terms of understanding the scope of federal power, climate change provides a powerful example of the folly of drawing artificial distinctions between activity and failure to act, between the local and the interstate, or between economic and noneconomic activities, when Congress addresses complex systemic issues. All carbon dioxide sources and sinks are relevant to addressing climate change, making distinctions between types of sources irrelevant in terms of policy.

Artificial restrictions on jurisdiction make particularly little sense in terms of establishing a cap-and-trade scheme. For example, suppose that the federal government were to allow banking of isolated wetlands (over which it does not have jurisdiction) to be used for mitigation by developers of other wetlands over which it does have jurisdiction. Such use of isolated wetlands for mitigation would not exceed the commerce power, because only non-isolated wetlands, over which the government does have jurisdiction, are actually regulated. That the owners of such covered wetlands choose to meet their mitigation obligations through restoration or preservation of isolated wetlands is not the government's regulatory mandate.

Traditionally, state and local governments have been the major regulators of land use and urban development. Responding to climate change may result in changes to this tradition. Given the national and international scope of climate change, the need for an integrated national strategy for controlling emissions and planning adaptation is strong. The Supreme Court should not create constitutional barriers to meeting this national need.

Assuming that Congress someday enacts fairly comprehensive climate-change regulations, the continuing role of the states will be an open question. That question may be settled without any need for considering constitutional issues. Perhaps states and localities will lose interest in climate change or will be content to assume whatever responsibilities Congress delegates to them without going further. Or perhaps Congress will settle the matter with either clear preemption language or strong savings clauses. Assuming that states remain active and that Congress does not speak clearly to the question, however, dormant Commerce Clause and preemption issues are likely to arise. How should courts approach them?

The extent to which preemption poses a threat to state regulators depends in part on the type of regulation. Assume that the federal government has adopted a trading scheme, augmented by new product efficiency standards. In terms of the new product standards, Congress is likely to address preemption directly, either by continuing existing standards as discussed earlier or by providing alternative language addressing preemption. Similarly, if Congress establishes a trading system, states may also regulate activities that are outside of the trading system completely—for example, by imposing green building standards or requiring new development to be accessible to public transportation. These kinds of traditionally local regulations should pose no constitutional problems and are unlikely to be overturned by the federal courts.

State Regulations in Relation to Federal Cap-and-Trade Scheme

In considering the preemptive effect of a possible future federal cap-and-trade scheme, we can divide state regulations into four categories (see table 10.1). Category 1 consists of regulations that have no connection whatsoever to the scheme. As we have just seen, these should be immune from preemption absent clear express preemption by Congress. Category 2 involves state regulation of activities that could otherwise be used as offsets by firms that are within the cap-and-trade scheme. Category 3 involves state regulation of activities that are themselves subject to the trading scheme but where the state does not attempt to regulate the trade themselves. Category 4 consists of state efforts to limit trading by in-state entities. In general, the preemption claim becomes stronger as we move through the list, with the fourth category the most vulnerable to challenge.

Table 10.1. Preemptive Effects of Future Federal Cap-and-Trade Schemes on State Regulations

Type of state regulation	Definition	Example	Preemption outcome
Category 1	State regulation of activities that do not require allowances and do not qualify as offsets	State zoning to encourage public transportation or reduce automobile use	Not preempted absent clear express statutory language
Category 2	State regulation of activities that qualify as offsets	State mandates to plant trees	Not preempted absent clear express statutory language
Category 3	State regulation of activities that require federal allowance, but no state effort to regulate allowance transactions	Renewable energy portfolios	Not preempted absent express statutory language or direct effect on federal trading scheme
Category 4	State restrictions on allowance transactions by in-state firms as an adjunct to state regulation of the emissions of those firms	Ban on sale of allowances freed up by compliance with state rules	Preempted in the absence of clear savings clause

Category 2: Likely to Avoid Preemption Challenge

We can begin analysis of cap-and-trade preemption by considering the second category—state regulation of activities that (1) are not themselves covered by the trading scheme but (2) are available as potential offsets by entities covered by the scheme. For example, a trading scheme for power companies might allow the companies to offset their emissions by planting trees, which absorb carbon from the atmosphere. States might create other kinds of regulations to mandate planting trees or to preserve existing forests. A company might claim that a state law mandating tree planting would interfere with the free market in such offsets, because once an area is planted with trees it is no longer part of the supply of potential unused offset sites.

These category 2 regulations should withstand preemption challenge. For one thing, the offset scheme is likely to allow the use of offsets only for activities that are not otherwise legally mandated, because otherwise the offsets would not be procuring real reductions. In effect, the federal offset rules are likely to defer to state regulation. Moreover, it would be difficult to apply preemption to all state regulations that might decrease the level of every activity that might generate an offset, so considerations of workability argue against finding preemption. For example, if planting trees would qualify as an offset, every municipal decision to permit a parking lot would be in effect reducing the amount of land available for offsets, and it would be bizarre to think that Congress meant to preempt all such actions.

More general considerations support the validity of category 2 state regulations of potential offset activities. Even if the offset rules fail to explicitly require that the offset activity be additive rather than otherwise mandated by law, the general purpose of offsets is consistent with state regulation—the point of the offset activity is to obtain new reductions in emissions from other sources, rather than give the industry credit for reductions that would have happened otherwise.

Thus, state laws restricting activities that might otherwise be the subjects of offsets should not interfere with the goals of the trading scheme in a significant way. Assuming that the state restrictions are nondiscriminatory, the restrictions should also survive a balancing analysis under the dormant Commerce Clause, given the state's substantial interest in reducing emissions and the modest impact on the availability of offsets to interstate purchasers.

Category 3: Might Avoid Preemption Challenge

A more difficult question is posed by the third type of regulation, where the states regulate the very activity that is the subject of trading. For example, suppose that Congress establishes a national carbon dioxide trading system for electrical generators but that a state prohibits its utilities from entering into long-term supply contracts with high emitters, perhaps coupled with direct emission limitations on in-state generators. It might seem pointless for a state to mandate reductions without also banning sale of the allowances that are freed up. To the extent that state regulation merely results in shifting allowances between generators, it does not affect the total amount of emissions nationally.

A state might nevertheless want to mandate the lower emission levels in order to achieve long-term goals. As with the current California utility regulations, one goal might include pressing sources used by local customers to accelerate their achievement of lower emissions in order to avoid price uncertainty later. The state might also want to encourage the development of new technology.

Regulations of this kind should not pose a preemption problem. The regulations do shift the pattern of allowance purchases and sales, but do not affect the achievement of the national cap. Inevitably, when a state reduces some form of consumption, it lowers demand in the national market (even if only slightly), thereby decreasing production levels but shifting consumption to other states. This is a normal and innocuous effect of state regulation. The best argument against the validity of the scheme would be that the trading scheme was supposed to not only create incentives but also free industry to attain the national goals however it chose. But this argument sweeps too widely. States might regulate sources in many ways that would result in lower greenhouse emissions. For example, particulate regulations might push electrical generators into switching from coal to natural gas, resulting in lower emissions. It seems unlikely that Congress would want to prohibit all such state regulations given its clear desire to allow states to go beyond national standards in limiting conventional pollutants.

The real problem, however, is that state regulations of this kind will do little to address climate change. A state's actions by themselves will not affect national carbon dioxide emissions because reducing sources of emissions in that state simply frees up allowances that other generators can use. Thus, a state's restrictions will be effective in reducing national emissions only if the state can prohibit sources from trading the resulting allowances.

Category 4: May Not Survive Preemption Challenge

For this reason, states will be tempted to move into the fourth category of regulations, not only regulating covered activities but banning the sale of the resulting unused allowances. Congress might in fact want to prohibit generators from trading allowances that have been freed up because of legal restrictions imposed by state law. If Congress does not do so, however, there seems to be a strong argument for preemption in the absence of an applicable savings clause.[19] A preemption argument would be fairly strong, and even without preemption, there would be some chance that a court would rule that the state restriction creates a barrier to the interstate trade in allowances. Thus, states may wish to restrict themselves to activities in the second category by adopting restrictions on in-state utilities, even without the ability to block trades, either because of concerns about future regulatory changes (e.g., a lowering of the federal cap) that might affect prices and supplies for its consumers, or simply in the hope of forcing improvements in technology.

Regardless of which of the four classes of regulation is involved, emitters may well argue that any congressional cap-and-trade scheme is meant to be comprehensive and hence to preempt the field of climate-change regulation. This argument may be superficially appealing but should be rejected. There are other plausible explanations for why congressional regulations stop where they do, without necessarily indicating a desire to eliminate all regulation beyond those limits by states.

First, the limits of a trading system may involve other kinds of policy determinations. The limited scope or requirements of a federal trading scheme may involve practical determinations that other activities are not suitable for inclusion because of difficulties of monitoring or enforcement. Similarly, Congress might have feared that a lower cap would have undue national economic consequences, but state activities that do not in effect lower the national cap do not pose this concern even if they lower emissions in a particular state.

Second, the limitations of the scheme may reflect a compromise, and this compromise may well be that the federal scheme should cover only certain matters but leave others open to state regulation. Without some clear indication that Congress intended to resolve all possible claims between stakeholders in climate-change regulation by setting the limits of regulation by all levels of government, there is no reason to infer such a global settlement of all climate regulation issues. Indeed, Congress may have chosen not to regulate some activities precisely because it considers them more suitable for state regulation.

Furthermore, attempting to preempt all state regulation relating to climate change is likely to be futile. It seems inevitable that states will play a role in climate mitigation, either because they can regulate activities that are outside of whatever scheme Congress employs or because Congress will enlist them in implementation of federal goals, as it has under the Clean Air Act already. There are strong arguments for adopting a rule that state regulations are valid except where states attempt to prohibit participation in federally sanctioned markets or discriminate against out-of-state emitters.

Arguing for a Special Presumption Against Climate Preemption

There is considerable controversy over whether, in general, there should be a presumption against preemption.[20] In the case of climate change, at least, there are strong pragmatic arguments that reinforce the usual federalism-based contentions. These arguments may sway courts and are also relevant to congressional consideration of the preemption issue.

One argument against preemption is simply that federal regulation is very likely to need augmentation by state regulation. Thus, strong state regulation is likely to be a plus rather than a minus in terms of social welfare. Climate change involves an enormous collective action problem, since solving it will involve the combined activities of every major economy in the world. It is a truism that public goods tend to be undersupplied, and climate is the most public of all public goods. Thus, we should embrace climate actions by whoever undertakes them, for it is more likely that the actions will be too little than that they will be too much.

Moreover, climate change also involves another major externality, with the activities of the current generation potentially imposing massive costs on future generations. Again, the odds are that regulation will be too timid because it will reflect the interests of current generations rather than the later generations that today's society may be harming. Perhaps more significant, this also means that many of those who will be most affected have no voice in today's political process. They are the most underrepresented of all underrepresented groups—not only do they have no vote, but they have no capacity to speak for themselves. Courts have often acted to protect underrepresented groups,[21] and some canons of interpretation seem designed for this purpose. A presumption against preemption of state climate regulation would fit within this tradition.

Of course, there may be good reasons to limit state regulation of some particular aspects of climate change, such as the costs of nonuniform regulation or the exigencies of international negotiations. But courts are likely to be in a poor position to identify these problems or to balance them against the benefits of state regulation. Congress should be left with the primary responsibility for carving out exceptions from the otherwise broad sweep of state regulatory authority. It is likely that the first round of federal legislation on climate change will not be the last, for this is a problem that will be with us for decades if not generations, and the first round of regulatory efforts are unlikely to be the perfect solution. It is not unreasonable to expect Congress to address any overreaching by states in the course of this ongoing legislative process.

Given that the political system is likely to undersupply climate regulation, courts should be inclined to provide a friendly reception to any and all climate regulation, rather than subjecting it to skeptical scrutiny. Moreover, courts are likely to find it difficult to apply undue burden tests or implied preemption doctrines in this area. Courts can fairly easily weed out the most dubious forms of state regulation, involving discrimination against out-of-state firms or direct contradiction of federal law. But they are poorly situated to deal with the remaining, more debatable instances of state regulation, and they should leave it to Congress to balance the virtues of state regulation against any indirect interference with national interests.

Conclusion

Science has shown us just how tightly small-scale happenings are coupled with large-scale happenings. Climate is affected by millions of small-scale decisions about what appliances to use, what car to drive, how often to drive, and where to live, as well as by the decisions of major corporations about energy investments. In turn, climate will have effects on all of these decisions. Thus, we cannot properly say that climate change is either a purely local or a global affair—it involves the very local as well as the completely global.

Current legal doctrine interdicts certain kinds of state regulations but leaves the bulk of state regulation subject to judicial overview under vague standards of "undue burden" or posing an "obstacle" to federal law. *Massachusetts v. EPA* does not speak directly to this issue but contains some cautions against unduly minimizing the interests of the states in the area of climate change. If nothing else, *Massachusetts v. EPA* makes it clear that climate change is very much the legitimate concern of state governments, rather than being exclusively in the national or international domain.

There are other cogent arguments in favor of giving state climate regulations a clear presumption of validity. Underregulation is a greater risk than overregulation in the climate area, given the huge collective action problem in addressing the climate issue and the fact that some of the primary stakeholders are future generations that have no political voice. Moreover, the federal government's general environmental policy, as enunciated in sometimes forgotten but still-valid provisions of the National Environmental Policy Act, clearly favors federal–state cooperation and respect for the interests of later generations. Congress will probably be engaged in an ongoing process of legislation regarding climate, and any overreaching by states can best be addressed legislatively.

Given this presumption of validity, in the absence of clear preemptive language, any future federal cap-and-trade scheme should have only limited preemptive effect. It should not affect state regulation of activities that are not related to the trading system or of activities that might be potential offsets. As to state regulations of activities that generate or require allowances, preemption should be triggered only if the state attempts to ban or otherwise limit the purchase or sale of allowances. Congress can provide a broader scope of preemption if it so desires, but there is little reason for courts to impose preemption when Congress has failed to make clear its intention to do so.

Climate change poses formidable challenges to our governance system. American governance assigns, informally if not constitutionally, some matters to local authorities and others to the federal government. Responses to climate change, in terms of both mitigation and adaptation, will cut across these lines. Our society will have to be creative in responding to and remolding familiar doctrines where necessary to allow us to respond to the realities of the situation. It may seem unfamiliar and strange for states to regulate an issue that has such global repercussions as climate change. Yet, as Justice Louis Brandeis said in his famous dissent in *New State Ice Co. v. Liebmann*,[22] a decision involving the permissible scope of state regulation: "If we would guide by the light of reason, we must let our minds be bold."[23] Never has this advice been more relevant than to the unprecedented challenge posed by climate change.

Notes

1. For descriptions of state efforts, see R. B. McKinstry, Jr., "Laboratories for Local Solutions for Global Problems: State, Local, and Private Leadership in Developing Strategies to Mitigate the Causes and Effects of Climate Change," 12 *Penn St. Envtl. L. Rev.* (2004): 15, 15–16; B. Rabe, "Race to the Top: The Expanding Role of U.S. State Renewable Portfolio Standards," 7 *Sustainable Dev. L. & Pol'y* (2007): 10; for speculations about the causes of this state-level response, see J. R. DeShazo and J. Freeman, "Timing and Form of Federal Regulation: The Case of Climate Change," 155 *U. Pa. L. Rev.* (2007): 1499, 1516–38; K. Engel, "State and Local Climate Change Initiatives: What Is Motivating State and Local Governments to Address a Global Problem and What Does This Say About Federalism and Environmental Law?" 38 *Urb. Law.* (2006): 1015.

2. 127 S. Ct. 1438, 1456 (2007).

3. 127 S. Ct., 1457.

4. 127 S. Ct., 1457.

5. U.S. Const., art. VI, § 1, cl. 2. For a survey of cases in which state environmental regulation has been held preempted, see R. L. Glicksman, "From Cooperative to Inoperative Federalism: The Perverse Mutation of Environmental Law and Policy," 41 *Wake Forest L. Rev.* (2006): 719, 787–91.

6. See *Shaw v. Delta Air Lines, Inc.*, 463 U.S. 85, (1983): 95–96 (quoting *Jones v. Rath Packing Co.*, 430 U.S. 519, 525 [1977]).

7. E. A. Young, "The Rehnquist Court's Two Federalisms," 83 *Tex. L. Rev.* (2004): 1, 130–34.

8. K. H. Engel, "Harnessing the Benefits of Dynamic Federalism in Environmental Law," 56 *Emory L. J.* (2006): 159, 184.

9. *Rice v. Santa Fe Elevator Corp.*, 331 U.S. 218, 230 (1947).

10. See, for example, *McDermott v. Wisconsin*, 228 U.S. 115 (1913).

11. R. L. Fischman and A. M. King, "Savings Clauses and Trends in Natural Resources Federalism," 32 *Wm. & Mary Envtl. L. & Pol'y Rev.* (2007): 129.

12. *Cipollone v. Liggett Group, Inc.*, 505 U.S. 504, 516 (1992) (quoting *Rice v. Santa Fe Elevator Corp.*, 331 U.S. 218, 230 [1947]).

13. C. Massey, "'Joltin' Joe Has Left and Gone Away': The Vanishing Presumption Against Preemption," 66 *Alb. L. Rev.* (2003): 759.

14. J. Resnik, "Foreign as Domestic Affairs: Rethinking Horizontal Federalism and Foreign Affairs Preemption in Light of Translocal Internationalism," 57 *Emory L. J.* (2007): 31.

15. 127 S. Ct.

16. 127 S. Ct., 1455.

17. 127 S. Ct., 1455.

18. G. C. Hazard, Jr., "Quasi-Preemption: Nervous Breakdown in Our Constitutional System," 84 *Tul. L. Rev.* (2010): 1143.

19. *Clean Air Markets Group v. Pataki*, 338 F.3d 82 (2d Cir. 2003); R. L. Glicksman and R. E. Levy, "A Collective Action Perspective on Ceiling Preemption by Federal Environmental Regulation: The Case of Global Climate Change," 102 *Nw. U. L. Rev.* (2008): 579, 644–45.

20. For a review of the contending arguments, see Note, "New Evidence on the Presumption Against Preemption: An Empirical Study of Congressional Responses to Supreme Court Preemption Decisions," 120 *Harv. L. Rev.* (2007): 1604, 1607–11; for a more recent discussion of the presumption against preemption, see R. S. Peck, "A Separation-of-Powers Defense of the 'Presumption Against Preemption,'" 84 *Tul. L. Rev.* (2010): 1185.

21. See generally J. H. Ely, *Democracy and Distrust: A Theory of Judicial Review* (1980).

22. 285 U.S. 262, 280 (1932) (Brandeis, J., dissenting).

23. 285 U.S. 262, at 311.

Chapter 11

American Federalism in Practice

Barry G. Rabe

In Brief

- Federal inaction on climate-change policies leaves substantial opportunity for state engagement and innovation; more than half of the states have adopted two or more policies to reduce greenhouse-gas emissions.

- Reasons for state activity include fostering a state identity of being in the vanguard of national leadership regarding the climate-change issue, being instrumental players in federal climate-change policy debates, and reaping economic advantages from early investment and adoption of green technologies.

- Political feasibility, more so than economic viability, determines the types of policies adopted among states and, likely, the types of policies that may be adopted by the federal government in the future.

- In the short term, states will continue to be leaders in climate-change policy; in the longer term, one distinct option is a two-tiered system where the federal government establishes national greenhouse-gas emission standards while the states are encouraged to capitalize on low-cost emission reductions unique to their states, rewarded for previous reductions, and free to retain or develop more ambitious policies.

Most scholarly and journalistic analysis presents the odyssey of climate-change policy in the United States as if America were a unitary system of government. This leads to a familiar tale, whereby the federal government signed the Kyoto Protocol in 1997, spurned ratification four years later, and neither the Clinton nor G. W. Bush administration or respective congresses could agree to anything beyond climate research funding, subsidies for virtually all forms of energy, and voluntary reduction programs.

But as climate policy continues to evolve in the American case and many others, it is becoming increasingly evident that climate policy constitutes an issue of federalism or multilevel governance. As the emergence of California governor Arnold Schwarzenegger as a claimant to the title of "world leader" in the development of far-reaching climate policy attests, individual units across different federal or multilevel governance systems may have more in common with one another in climate policy than they have with the neighboring units of their own federation. Indeed, one can see stronger parallels between such jurisdictions as Connecticut and Sweden and North Carolina and Nova Scotia than exists across many members of the same federation. For President Barack Obama and his counterparts in Congress, any consideration of an expanded federal role must contend with a significant subfederal legacy of policies.

This chapter focuses primarily on the American case, considering more than a decade of state and federal policy experience and attempting to distill lessons that could guide future policy development. First, American subfederal policy development is summarized, including introduction to policies that have been enacted over the past decade and key factors that have led to such a robust state response in the absence of federal mandates or incentives. Second, the divergent paths taken by the fifty states are considered, as reflected in their greenhouse-gas emission trends since 1990 and varied levels of climate policy development. Third, the collective state experience provides possible lessons for future policy development at either subfederal or federal levels. Finally, alternative scenarios for future development of American climate policy are considered, mindful of the possibility of new federal policy initiatives in future years.

Toward a State-Centric American Climate Policy

The recent trend toward state-driven policy is hardly unprecedented in American federalism. In many instances, early state policy engagement has provided models that were ultimately embraced as national policy by the federal government. This has been evident in a range of social policy domains, including health care and education, and can result in either federal preemption that obliterates earlier state roles or a more collaborative system of shared governance.[1] In some cases, states have taken the lead and essentially sustained policy leadership through multistate collaboration and the absence of federal engagement. Through 2010, American climate policy followed this pattern, with prolonged federal inability to construct policy leaving substantial opportunity for state engagement and innovation.

Several factors have converged over the past two decades to place states in increasingly central roles. First, many states framed early policy steps that would have the effect of reducing greenhouse gases as being in their economic self-interest. This helps explain the ever-expanding state government interest in developing a set of technologies and skills to promote renewable energy, energy conservation, and expertise to foster a low-carbon economy and, frequently, to develop "homegrown" energy sources to foster long-term economic development.

Second, a growing number of states are beginning to experience significant impacts that may be attributable to climate change, whether through violent storms, forest fires, species migration, prolonged droughts, or changing vectors of disease transmission.

Third, some states have consciously chosen to be "first movers," often taking bold steps with the explicit intent of trying to take national leadership roles on climate policy. In some instances, such as California's legislation to restrict carbon emissions from vehicles and New York's efforts to establish a regional carbon emission trading zone in the northeastern United States, states are also trying to establish models that will influence their neighbors to join them and possibly position themselves to influence any future federal policy.

Fourth, state capitals have proven very fertile areas for the development of climate policy advocacy. In many instances, earlier state efforts reflected leadership from higher levels of state agencies working in environmental protection, energy, or other areas relevant to climate.[2] These policy entrepreneurs continue to operate but increasingly partner with other forces, such as legislators and advocacy groups, to form policy networks that build support for policy strategies that are particularly appealing to an individual state.[3]

Fifth, states also provide venues for alternative approaches to policy formation, including direct democracy and litigation that confronts federal institutions. Ballot propositions are proving an increasingly popular way to advance climate initiatives in cases where representative institutions stall. At the same time, the 2007 US Supreme Court verdict in *Massachusetts v. EPA* indicates that a collective of states can wage and ultimately win an intergovernmental court battle designed to force a reluctant federal agency to designate carbon dioxide as an air pollutant. The Obama administration moved rapidly to reverse its predecessor's rejection of this designation and then negotiated an intergovernmental pact in May 2009 that essentially used the California standard for vehicular carbon emissions as the bar for federal fuel efficiency standards.

Variation in State Policy Adoption and Emission Trends

None of these factors converge identically from state to state. Indeed, no two states have uniform profiles in terms of actual rates of greenhouse-gas emission growth or climate policy adoption. In turn, the combination of emission growth and policy development to date varies greatly among states, prompting them to consider different strategic positions. This may apply to either further state policy adoption or any bargaining position that states might assume in future negotiations over federal policy.

The ways in which governments can enact policies that purportedly stabilize or reduce greenhouse-gas emissions are virtually limitless. Since greenhouse-gas emissions emanate from essentially every sector of the economy, a vast range of policies and sectors could come into play. Table 11.1 distinguishes high and low intensity of state climate policy development, based on twenty policy options that are prominently addressed in either current practice or the scholarly literature. State policy options include renewable electricity mandates or portfolio standards, carbon taxes, renewable fuel mandates or equivalent programs that mandate expanded use of biofuels, carbon cap-and-trade programs, statewide emission reduction targets, mandatory reporting of carbon emissions, development of energy efficiency standards, and adoption of the carbon emission standards for vehicles enacted by California.

Twenty-six states, representing more than half the American population, have enacted twelve or more of the twenty climate policies, indicating a considerable degree of political support for policy and formal engagement in climate policy adoption. A few of these states, such as California, Massachusetts, Connecticut, and New York, have adopted nearly all of them. In some cases, states have revisited early policies and made them stricter by elevating initial emission reduction targets or earlier commitments to renewable energy.

The remaining twenty-four states and the District of Columbia have eleven or fewer such policies in operation, indicating less political support for policy or formal engagement in climate policy adoption. Over the past three years, several states have increased their level of policy involvement,

Table 11.1. State Climate Policies and Greenhouse-Gas Emission Growth, 1990–2007

State policies	Greenhouse-gas emission growth		Low (<16 percent)
	High (>16 percent)		Low (<16 percent)
High (12–20 policies)	Arizona	New Hampshire	California
	Colorado	New Jersey	Connecticut
	Illinois	Oregon	Delaware
	Iowa	Rhode Island	Hawaii
	Maine	Utah	Maryland
	Minnesota	Vermont	Massachusetts
	Montana	Wisconsin	New Mexico
	Nevada		New York
			Pennsylvania
			Texas
			Washington
Low (0–11 policies)	Alabama	North Carolina	District of Columbia
	Alaska	North Dakota	Indiana
	Arkansas	Oklahoma	Louisiana
	Florida	South Carolina	Michigan
	Georgia	Tennessee	Ohio
	Idaho	Virginia	South Dakota
	Kansas		West Virginia
	Kentucky		Wyoming
	Mississippi		
	Missouri		
	Nebraska		

Sources: US Environmental Protection Agency, *Inventory of U.S. Greenhouse Gas Emissions and Sinks 1990–2007*, EPA 430-R-09-004 (Washington, DC: US Environmental Protection Agency, 2009); Barry G. Rabe, "Racing to the Top, the Bottom, or the Middle of the Pack? The Evolving State Government Role in Environmental Protection," in *Environmental Policy: New Directions for the Twenty-First Century,* edited by Norman J. Vig and Michael E. Kraft (Washington, DC: CQ Press, 2010), 32.

though that trend slowed in 2009 as states awaited possible federal intervention and faced severe fiscal challenges. In turn, a few states faltered on policy involvements, such as Arizona and Utah, which in 2010 backed off from earlier commitments to join California and other western states (and some Canadian provinces) in the Western Climate Initiative, a regional approach to emission reductions.

At the same time, states vary markedly in their rate of total greenhouse-gas emission growth over time. Using the most recent data available, published by the US Environmental Protection Agency (EPA) in late 2009, we can consider state-by-state emission trends between 1990 and 2007. As shown in table 11.1, using a mean of 16 percent national growth in emissions during this period, thirty-two states are above the mean, including Arizona and Nevada, with emission growth rates exceeding 40 percent. The remaining eighteen states and the District of Columbia are below the mean. Although it is unclear how much of the trend in emissions is due to policy as opposed to other factors such as population trends and economic growth rates, this analysis provides another way to compare state performance beyond policy adoption.

These rather fundamental differences between states may be instructive in considering their receptivity to future policy initiatives, whether undertaken unilaterally, in concert with regional neighbors, or in response to possible future federal government actions. Each of the four quadrants of table 11.1 reflects a different blend of emission and policy adoption trends. The convergence of these factors illustrates the diverse contexts facing individual states as they contemplate future initiatives or engagement in intergovernmental bargaining as Congress considers a wide range of possible options. They further suggest that individual states may have considerable reason to view various climate initiatives in very different ways, depending upon where they stand in relation to the 1990 baseline that is used widely in American and international climate policy deliberations and whether they have made any significant commitment to policy adoption and implementation. Just as private businesses and industries are increasingly thought to adjust their strategies based on emission levels and internal incentives for action or inaction,[4] states may face similar strategic choices and be influenced by their current context.

Low Emissions, High Policy

States that have sustained low rates of emission growth while pursuing significant policy adoption may be eager to exert their influence over neighboring states and federal policy debates. They will be adamant that 1990 remain the emission baseline and insist upon maximal credit for achieving early reductions and being "first movers." Pulling other states or the entire nation into their orbit is likely to maximize their leverage on overall emission reductions. This might also serve to provide them with economic advantages, having already invested in technology and expertise associated with policy adoption and thereby forcing recalcitrant states to catch up. Such states will be keen to ensure that any future federal policy follows their example, both to ease transition costs and to maximize credit-claiming opportunities for political leaders.

California perhaps epitomizes this quadrant, taking the long-standing term of "California effect" in American intergovernmental policy leadership to new lengths in climate change.[5] The state has long played a pioneering role in environmental protection and other areas of policy, often stimulating cross-state diffusion and ultimate embrace at the federal level. In climate, California has adopted virtually every kind of policy imaginable. All such states that combine high policy development with low emission growth are on record as being concerned about climate change but want their emission track record to be rewarded and their early steps toward policy adoption to have considerable leverage in any future federal policy.

High Emissions, High Policy

The adoption of multiple climate policies does not guarantee their effectiveness or ability to achieve significant emission reductions given other competing factors. Indeed, Arizona, Minnesota, and Oregon, among other states, have adopted multiple forms of climate policy, including particularly early initiatives in the latter two states that have moved into implementation. But their rate of emission growth is well above national averages. States with this blend of emissions and policy development will likely approach intergovernmental negotiations from a somewhat different position. They will be more enthusiastic about modification of the 1990 baseline and seek credit for early policy initiatives even if these had little effect on reducing emission growth. They may seek special treatment or status for policies that were enacted more recently and are moving only into preliminary stages of implementation. This might include allowance of a two-tiered system, whereby states would be free to exceed federal minimum standards or released from adherence to any federal requirements through a waiver process. All of these states tend to view themselves as "mini-Californias," supporting cutting-edge policy experimentation and in the vanguard of national leadership on the climate-change issue. But they will want to be protected against penalty for any substantial emission growth and be rewarded for early policy adoption in the event of future federal engagement.

High Emissions, Low Policy

Seventeen states fall into the quadrant with above-average rates of emission growth and low levels of policy development; they are represented by more than one-third of the membership of the US Senate, a fact that can go far to block discussion on any legislative proposal. Many of these states are located in the Southeast, including Alabama, Florida, and Tennessee. They have generally experienced steady rates of population and economic growth, tend to have expanding manufacturing industrial bases, and rely heavily on coal for electricity. In turn, they are generally thought to have some of the weakest potential capacity for renewable energy and have historically taken few if any steps to promote alternative sources or energy efficiency. Moreover, these states tend to receive low rankings for their levels of commitment or institutional capacity to pursue environmental protection.[6]

In these states, not only is emission growth high and policy adoption minimal, but the states may view virtually any federal climate policy as a threat to their economic well-being.[7] They are likely to oppose any policy that would impose significant costs on them and would be particularly mindful of possible redistributive effects that could result from any federal emission reduction policies that would ultimately force them to purchase carbon credits, offsets, or renewable energy credits from outside their state and region. Moreover, they would have significant incentive to adjust the emission baseline to a date well after 1990 and seek substantial federal subsidies to compensate against any possible adverse economic consequences from federal policy implementation. They are likely to be hostile to any effort to apply ambitious state policies, such as those emanating from California, on a national basis.

Ironically, many of these states may be among the most vulnerable to climate change, at least over the next few decades. Coastal states such as North and South Carolina, Alabama, Florida, and Mississippi have become particularly concerned about growing risk from severe weather and significant temperature increases. Several such states are enmeshed in discussions of the future of insurance coverage for developed property, particularly from coastal property owners who are facing steep rate hikes due to increased vulnerability. This issue has begun to move climate change onto the agenda in Gulf Coast capitals such as Tallahassee, illustrating the potential for states to undertake major policy shifts in relatively short order. Each year of the past decade has seen additional states take major policy adoption steps.

Low Emissions, Low Policy

The odyssey of state experience with greenhouse-gas trends reveals that it is indeed possible to attain stable levels of emissions in the absence of climate policy designed to achieve these goals. In seven states and the District of Columbia, there has been minimal adoption of any greenhouse-gas reduction policies, yet all have emission growth rates well below the national averages for 1990 to 2007. However, these states are not exactly models for effective transition to a less carbon-intensive society: much of their stability is due to economic stagnation. In Michigan, for example, an increase in emissions in most sectors was offset by significant declines in manufacturing-based emissions since 1999, reflecting the marked contraction in that sector. Louisiana has undergone its own transitions, and both states may have declined even further due to continuing economic contraction in more recent years for which data are not yet available.

In some respects, this parallels the East German model for emission reduction, drawing comparisons with those portions of Eastern Europe that easily met Kyoto goals through industrial collapse in the early 1990s. Any such states will approach climate policy with trepidation and will be particularly inclined to combat any policies that might further weaken vulnerable economic sectors.

States in this quadrant are likely to seek minimal interference with threatened industry and also insist on very favorable financial terms to compensate them for any possible costs that might be imposed by federal policy. States of all sorts are keen to maximize federal transfer payments, but the demand may be particularly great in these states given their relative economic position. At the same time, such states will want to make sure that any future policy accords them maximum credit for their low rates of emission growth. Hence, the 1990 baseline will remain sacrosanct, and states in this quadrant will welcome any opportunities for credit-trading programs that could deal them a favorable hand, similar to Eastern European nations and Russia, which have attempted to maximize the value of their "hot air" credits.

Consequently, the combination of emission trends and policy adoption could influence future state action, either unilateral state policy or efforts to shape the direction of future federal policy. This variability may deter consensus on future federal policy given dramatically different strategic considerations facing different states and possibly different regions of the nation. At the same time, recent state experience illustrates that different types of climate policies may generate very different political responses that transcend any particular jurisdictional context. Some policies may be anathemas, whereas others may have considerable appeal across a diverse range of states and regions; this aspect of state experience may serve as a guide to likely political viability of policy options at the federal level.

Climate Policy Selection: Economic Desirability Versus Political Feasibility

The expanding body of state experience in climate policy affords insight into the political prospects for future enactment of various policy instruments intended to reduce greenhouse-gas emissions, whether through expanded state adoption or eventual embrace in some form by the federal government. As discussed above, greenhouse gases emanate from every sector of economic and social activity, opening up an almost infinite number of possible policy interventions. These range from more conventional command-and-control policies that emphasize rigid regulations and standards to economics-based policies that allow flexibility as long as overall emission reduction goals are met. States clearly have substantial latitude to choose from this range of policy tools, offering an indicator of how they fare when placed into a political context. Many scholars have noted a general shift in various areas of environmental protection toward economics-based policies, particularly in the American context.[8] This trend is energetically embraced by much scholarship on climate policy, with widespread endorsement of policies that make use of market-based mechanisms to maximize the likelihood that any reductions will be produced in as cost-effective manner as possible.[9]

But the preferences of scholars, particularly economists, are not readily translated into new policy. In fact, those policies having the strongest base of support from policy analysts appear to be the most difficult for state legislators and governors to adopt. In contrast, policies containing many features of more traditional approaches, long criticized by policy analysts, are far more successful in securing significant support from elected officials. The same dynamic may extend to the federal level, given its initial engagement in climate policy.

The American state experience with climate policy to date raises important questions about the political viability of policies likely to deliver emission reductions in the most cost-effective manner possible. In particular, experience suggests that state governments are extremely reluctant to impose strategies that are explicit about any costs that will be imposed, particularly if they are likely to occur at the point of product purchase or utility bill payment. Instead, states may have considerable incentive to produce far more complex policies requiring greater overall costs but ones that are less visible, because they are either hidden or spread out over a longer time. These options are delineated in table 11.2, with each key cell discussed below.

Economic Attractiveness, Political Anathema: Pity the Carbon Tax

A review of diverse literature on climate policy indicates broad consensus among scholars regarding the desirability of using carbon taxes as a central approach to climate policy. In 2007, a *Wall Street Journal* survey of leading economists showed overwhelming support for carbon taxes as the preferred tool for addressing climate change. "A tax puts pressure on the market, rather than forcing an artificial solution on it," noted one of the survey participants in a representative comment.[10]

In practice, such taxes give consumers incentives to use less carbon-intensive energy but do so without imposing uniform constraints on citizens or industries. In turn, the establishment of such a tax is thought to be relatively straightforward through expansion of existing tax code provisions, and compliance would likely be high since the tax would be applied at a point of purchase of carbon-based energy sources. All fifty states clearly have constitutional authority to establish multiple forms of carbon taxes, as they have long used a combination of sales and excise taxes for gasoline and can use their considerable power over utility regulation to apply taxes to electricity usage. The federal government also holds vast authority to move in this direction; proposals for such a federal energy tax date to the Nixon era.

In spite of this potential, no evidence suggests that any state has made carbon taxes a central platform of its climate protection strategies. Indeed, California, the state synonymous with an aggressive, across-the-board

Table 11.2. Economic Desirability and Political Feasibility of State
Climate Policy Tools

Political feasibility*	Economic desirability**		
	High	Medium	Low
High			Renewable portfolio standard (29)
Medium		Cap-and-trade (23)	
Low	Carbon tax (0)***		

*Measured by number of states adopting the policy. Numbers in parentheses indicate numbers of states that have adopted the policy: twenty-nine states have statutory renewable portfolio standard programs; twenty-three states are involved in regional cap-and-trade programs, although at least seven of these have more informal commitments; none operate carbon taxes.

**Reflected in the climate policy literature.

***Excludes public benefits charges/social benefits funds due to modest scope.

approach to greenhouse-gas reduction, has put nearly every imaginable climate policy into play with the conspicuous exception of carbon taxation. In 2006, California voters decisively rejected Initiative 87, a ballot proposition that would have increased statewide energy taxation as a climate policy tool.

Gasoline represents one narrow form of a carbon tax, most commonly through state excise taxes that apply solely to this transportation fuel. All fifty states have maintained some form of taxation, using most of the revenue to support highway maintenance and expansion. These taxes have changed little in the past decade, with a few notable exceptions, and there does not appear to be much political appetite for addressing this area of possible carbon tax development.

Electricity taxation is another state policy option and could be particularly significant in those states that rely heavily on fossil fuel or natural gas for their electricity. Eighteen states have established some form of specialized electricity taxation beyond conventional sales taxes, and at least some of the collected revenues are earmarked for energy efficiency programs or renewable energy development. These programs generate revenue ranging from $8 million per year in Illinois to $440 million per year in California, and the average cost per residential household across these eighteen states is quite low. They are sufficiently modest as to have little likely impact on carbon consumption, serving instead as a funding source for new energy initiatives.

Perhaps the most revealing aspect of the electricity taxation policies is that universally they are not referred to as taxes in authorizing legislation or on customer bills. Instead, they are characterized by terms such as "social benefit charges" or "public benefit fees"; a number of states do not even itemize them on customer electricity bills. The programs are designed to sustain a low enough level of taxation and are given a sufficiently innocuous title so as not to trigger opposition to new energy taxes. This "stealth" quality raises a number of interesting questions about future prospects for carbon taxes at either state or federal levels, underscoring the political complexities involved in being explicit about their function or setting them at levels sufficiently high to have a realistic capacity to deter energy consumption and greenhouse-gas generation.

Both the executive and legislative branches have carbon tax supporters. Prominent Obama appointees, including economic advisers Lawrence Summers and Paul Volcker, Budget Director Peter Orszag, and Energy Secretary Steven Chu, have endorsed this option, though less vocally since ascending to federal office. In turn, a coalition of ideological opposites, ranging from Congressman Pete Stark (D-CA) to Senator Bob Corker (R-TN), have endorsed some version of a carbon tax in the 111th Congress. Yet carbon tax proposals continue to face strong opposition, as reflected in numerous public opinion surveys, even if framed as "revenue neutral" through some return of funding to the citizenry. Indeed, these proposals were quickly shoved to the sidelines in House debate that led to the passage of a complex climate bill in mid-2009.

Economic Shortcomings, Political Attractiveness: Renewable Energy Mandates

Renewable portfolio standards (RPS) are nearly the converse of carbon taxes in terms of economic desirability and political feasibility as a climate policy option. They require all electricity providers within a state to increase the amount of power derived from renewable sources over time. Most of these policies steadily increase the total percentage or volume of electricity that must come from renewable sources and establish financial penalties in the event of noncompliance. This approach is also being applied to transportation fuels through mandates for biofuels such as ethanol.

Many climate scholars view policies like RPSs with trepidation on economic grounds. Such policies are generally more expensive per unit of greenhouse-gas emission reduction, because they mandate use of technologies that may be considerably more expensive than traditional electricity sources. Discerning the actual carbon-reduction impact of RPSs remains difficult because it is not always clear which type of existing source is being supplemented and because the policy does not reduce demand for electricity. As one prominent study of competing climate policy tools concludes, "The RPS may be one of the less efficient means of achieving greenhouse gas emission reductions. Unlike a more flexible carbon cap, it does not reward generation from non-renewable sources of low carbon power, and rewards energy conservation only very weakly."[11]

Misgivings over RPSs from an economic standpoint have not curtailed their rapid adoption and diffusion. Indeed, among the many climate policy options available to states, RPSs have clearly been the most popular politically. They have been approved in twenty-nine states and the District of Columbia and operate in well over half of the nation's congressional districts. RPSs are prominent in every section of the nation except the Southeast, although North Carolina enacted such a policy in 2007. Moreover, they are under active consideration in many other states, and nearly half of the current RPS states have set more ambitious goals than their initial standards through legislative reauthorization. Some states are establishing very high targets, such as 25 percent in New York by 2013, 20 percent in Colorado and New Jersey by 2020, and 18 percent in Pennsylvania by 2020.

It is not clear whether states adopting RPSs have conducted systematic economic analyses or assessed their capacity to reach their targets. In fact, a number of states have faced early implementation problems, ranging from local resistance to the siting of renewable generation facilities or transmission capacity to pressures from supporters of particular renewable energy sources to receive increasingly favored treatment in RPS implementation.[12] All raise added questions over long-term economic impact of these policies and whether neighboring states can work collaboratively to establish common renewable energy markets or instead erect barriers to discourage cross-border movement and purchase.

None of these issues has dampened political enthusiasm for the RPS approach, possibly in part because it is commonly framed as delivering multiple benefits, only one of which is climate-change mitigation. Most states enacting RPSs characterize them as strategic investments in future technologies that could provide long-term economic benefits, including in-state job creation. Concurrently, states have emphasized other cobenefits, including diminished release of conventional air contaminants through transition to new electricity sources, reduced dependence on other jurisdictions to sustain a supply of fossil fuel or uranium, and the sending of early "market signals" that encourage technology development.

Perhaps most significant, RPSs are framed as essentially cost free in political debates; any added costs for using renewable supplies are passed on to electric utilities, and ultimately their consumers, whether they realize it or not. This may explain why RPSs continue to draw broad, bipartisan support in states with every pattern of partisan control, and why political support for a federal version of an RPS continues to appear far greater in Congress than for other policies such as carbon taxes and cap-and-trade.

Moderate Economic and Political Attractiveness: Carbon Cap-and-Trade

Emission trading through some version of a carbon cap-and-trade system has emerged as a reasonably attractive policy option from both an economic and political perspective. Economists and policy analysts tend not to be quite as effusive about cap-and-trade as carbon taxes, but this approach is a very desirable alternative. Such a policy could theoretically be applied either to specific sectors that generate carbon emissions, such as electric utilities, or to an entire economic and political system. Ironically, this approach was actively pushed by the American federal government as a model for international climate policy during the negotiations that led to the Kyoto Protocol.

Under cap-and-trade, an overall budget for carbon releases is established and gradually reduced over time. Once emission allowances are allocated to individual sources or jurisdictions, they are then free to negotiate transactions to allow for the most inexpensive reductions. These may be achieved, at least in part, through so-called offsets, such as carbon sequestration through tree planting or subterranean storage.

This approach has considerable political appeal, reflected initially in the adoption by the European Union of its Emissions Trading Scheme and comparable proposals in Congress. Twenty-three states have made some level of commitment to their own version of a cap-and-trade program, ten of which are working through the Regional Greenhouse Gas Initiative (RGGI) that is operating a regional emission trading zone for utility sector emissions in the Northeast. Governor Schwarzenegger has also interpreted his state's 2006 climate legislation to allow for development of a comprehensive cap-and-trade system. Both the RGGI and California have been keen to expand their coverage to include as many of their neighbors as possible, including Canadian provinces. Seven midwestern states entered into a regional agreement of their own in 2007, though it has not moved beyond a very general statement of intent. Despite this flurry of activity, emission trading does not appear to retain as strong political support as tools such as RPS and mandatory vehicular fuel efficiency.

The economic elegance of cap-and-trade quickly dissolves once one moves toward actual policy development and implementation, as evidenced by early experience in the United States and elsewhere. In Europe, the Emissions Trading Scheme failed to establish an institutional structure that might have allowed it to run effectively. Each member of the European Union was permitted to allocate and monitor its own emission allowances; no overarching authority was in place to ensure accuracy and integrity. Early North American experience with the same tool underscores these difficulties. With the RGGI, multistage negotiations continued for more than four years, building on a history of northeastern regional collaboration on a wide range of environmental and energy issues. What emerged is a complex set of provisions in a treaty-like agreement, endorsed by the ten signatory states. The RGGI began operation in September 2008 and features a dizzying array of provisions that address such issues as offsets, early reduction credits, triggers, and safety valves that will require considerable administrative sophistication and intergovernmental collaboration to sustain.

Perhaps predictably, individual states and interest groups bring very different agendas to the negotiations over cap-and-trade programs, thereby weakening its economic purity. States with smaller populations or projections for higher population growth seek favored status in the allocation of emission allowances and insist that larger neighbors pay a disproportionately large share of governance costs. States more reliant on electricity imported from outside the cap-and-trade region view import constraints differently from those with greater energy self-sufficiency.[13] Many of these same issues emerged in Washington as Congress expanded consideration of its own version of a cap-and-trade system on a national basis during the 111th Congress.

Perhaps the political and governance challenges for carbon cap-and-trade are most evident in California. The 2006 authorizing legislation was clear about the desirability of a statewide emission cap but intentionally evaded the issue of whether a trading mechanism would be established because it was so politically divisive.[14] In 2007, Governor Schwarzenegger used his executive authority to insist on a cap-and-trade system, but this has proven extremely controversial. On one hand, industry groups argue that such a system will be particularly disadvantageous to them. On the other hand, some environmental groups contend that emission trading for carbon allows for market manipulation and profiteering; they contend that the 2006 statute suggests early and aggressive mandated reductions rather than a more flexible cap-and-trade system. Environmental justice advocates have further claimed that any trading system will place particular disadvantages on low-income and predominantly minority communities. Many legislators joined this chorus in Sacramento, alleging that Governor Schwarzenegger had exceeded his powers and should instead focus on an immediate command-and-control approach. In turn, industry has registered strong opposition to the cap-and-trade provisions and most aspects of the 2006 legislation. Some major organizations supported a ballot proposition that would freeze all implementation until the state unemployment rate dropped markedly, though this was soundly defeated in November 2010.

As California struggles to implement a cap-and-trade system, it is also negotiating the Western Climate Initiative, a multistate pact that generally follows the regional approach taken by the RGGI. Thus far, the governors of six other western states have joined forces with California in developing a regional cap-and-trade program, also working cooperatively with four Canadian provinces. There was some uncertainty, however, about whether all states will remain in this coalition over time. Not all of these states joined California in adopting authorizing legislation; serious intergovernmental bargaining continues over the terms of a multistate pact still in very early stages. In fact, Arizona and Utah withdrew from the cap-and-trade program, though not the regional agreement, in 2009. Furthermore, California's capacity to underwrite much of the implementation costs has come into question as the state's fiscal condition worsens.

Nonetheless, cap-and-trade was endorsed by President Obama as a cornerstone in his climate strategy and was a prominent component in the American Clean Energy and Security Act that passed the House of Representatives by a narrow margin in June 2009. The House struggled with the issue of how to treat existing state programs such as the RGGI and ultimately settled on an unusual arrangement, essentially placing them into a deep-freeze between 2012 and 2016 in the event a new federal program was operational, but keeping the option for future state implementation open thereafter. The federal bill did reject one key innovation in state policy: it refused to endorse the RGGI's approach to allocating allowances via auction. This approach establishes a clear pricing mechanism and also produces substantial revenue that can be targeted to alternative energy programs, more general fiscal pursuits, or some reimbursement to the citizenry through tax credits or rebates. But political opposition to cap-and-trade legislation remained significant and expanded markedly in 2009–10. Public opinion surveys suggest Americans are generally divided on the issue and unclear as to what "cap-and-trade" actually entails. This suggests numerous opportunities for opponents to frame public perception in negative ways, and this contributed to Senate inability to match House action on this issue.

Looking Ahead: From a State-Centric to a Federal System?

The evolution of the state role in American climate policy suggests that it is indeed possible, at some times and in some jurisdictions, to secure a base of political support for policies that promise to make some dent in greenhouse-gas emissions. Indeed, the state experience over the last decade offers an important set of insights and could provide a building block for new developments in this arena. Past experience could lead to continued expansion and diversification of the state role, or it could influence the design of future federal policy, whether or not involving formal collaboration and sharing of authority with states that have taken early action.

State experience does not lend itself to easy prediction of the future, either of further state policy diffusion or of eventual federal engagement. But it does suggest the possibility of three broad alternative directions over the coming years, as state policy dominance begins to confront its fit into the larger American political, economic, and policy context and as a newly active federal government demonstrates a desire to take a far more active role on climate change than ever before. Prior experience in American federalism suggests at least three distinct intergovernmental paths for American climate policy that might be pursued in the near future and beyond: a shift toward top-down policy, continued bottom-up policy, or a move toward collaboration.

Shift Toward Top-Down Policy

Substantial precedent exists for federal government preemption of existing state policies, though with greater frequency for energy policy than environmental protection policy. In such instances, Congress often acts in response to industry concerns about interstate regulatory variation by replacing a patchwork quilt of policies with a uniform program.[15] The frequency with which Congress uses this tool in domestic policy has increased in recent years.[16] A number of congressional climate policy proposals have embraced a rigorous form of preemption, essentially wiping out existing state policies as part of any larger bargain to create a national policy. Such policies could also establish a baseline later than 1990 for reductions.

This would invariably raise concerns about equity among those states that have achieved low emission growth and might be denied credit. Moreover, states that adopted and actively implemented their own policies argue that preemption would be particularly unfair to them as it would invalidate their early investments. In turn, some concerns have arisen that a federal preemption policy of modest scope might actually achieve lower emission reductions than the existing compilation of state policies. Nonetheless, any serious discussion of a congressionally enacted cap-and-trade program or a more traditional regulatory program has frequently turned to the possibility of federal usurpation of a policy arena heretofore developed and dominated by states. The combined opposition to new federal policies by certain industries and states (and their congressional representatives) remains significant.

This may explain why the initial climate policy steps of the incoming Obama administration focused on administrative strategies, beginning with rapid reconsideration of the G. W. Bush administration's 2008 refusal to declare carbon dioxide an air pollutant. Such a reversal was signaled almost immediately by the incoming Obama climate team and suggested a willingness to push through administrative interpretation of the Clean Air Act Amendments of 1990 and begin to impose national restrictions on greenhouse-gas emissions. This step would not have required new legislation and pressured Congress to take significant steps, such as a federal cap-and-trade program, to thwart such administrative action. Instead, the US EPA would take administrative action through an established framework of clean air legislation that does not specifically address carbon dioxide or climate change. It is not entirely clear what such a step would mean for existing state policies. The agency has proposed giving considerable latitude to states, but some, such as Texas and Virginia, have registered strong opposition and threatened to refuse to cooperate with any implementation effort.

Continued Bottom-Up Policy

A climate policy system that retains a strong bottom-up emphasis remains plausible. Congress and the executive branch failed to reach closure on any significant climate policy in the 111th Congress and appear highly unlikely to do so in future years. Thus, federal action may be confined to a specific sector or policy tool, leaving much opportunity for state engagement. Indeed, numerous areas of policy exist in which nationalization has seemed inevitable but has not occurred.[17]

The recent patterns of diffusion, proliferation, and regionalization in state climate policy seem likely to continue, short of federal preemption. This will be reflected in expanded adoption of policies already operational in multiple states and the growing pattern of multistate negotiation once neighboring states establish similar or identical policies. It is increasingly possible to envision "climate policy regions" whereby two or more states join common cause, building on early movement in this direction and perhaps collaborating further with Canadian provinces or Mexican states. It is even conceivable that the United States could at some point set a national cap and simply allocate overall allowance or reduction requirements state by state, allowing interstate bargaining over the mechanics of reduction like the European Union model. No current policy proposals in Congress follow this format, although it was reflected in the 2009 economic stimulus plan, the first major legislation of the Obama era likely to influence American greenhouse-gas emissions. The initiative allocates billions of dollars to a wide range of renewable energy and energy efficiency projects, as well as other climate-friendly initiatives, but gives enormous latitude to states and localities to determine how to use these funds. However, large deficits suggest that a second federal stimulus is unlikely, and in turn, states facing their own fiscal woes may face difficulties in carrying through with existing policy commitments, much less taking added steps.

The continuing divides in Washington, DC, could thwart far-reaching federal climate legislation or even produce protracted delay in implementation in the event of enactment, thereby leaving considerable opportunities for states for some time. One early Obama initiative underscored some of the complex ways in which these differences might be addressed. In May 2009, he embraced California's vehicle emission standards as a model for increased federal standards for vehicle fuel economy. This gave California and states that supported its legislation substantial influence in the federal process while also preventing them from establishing even higher state standards until at least 2016. This bargain reduced opposition from states such as Michigan that have opposed fuel economy increases, although California and allied states began to explore higher standards beyond 2016.

Toward Collaborative Federalism

An American climate policy that builds on the respective strengths of both state and federal governments and engages in active policy learning across governmental levels can be envisioned. Many states have considerable climate policy expertise and are well equipped to target areas of "low-hanging fruit," namely, low-cost emission reductions unique to their state. At the same time, the federal government has the ability to develop consistent rules and incentives on a national scale and, of course, the constitutional authority to work collaboratively with other nations. Perhaps the United States could evolve into a multilevel climate governance system, consistent with practice in other areas of environmental protection such as clean air and waste management.[18] One such option is a two-tiered mechanism whereby, unlike preemption, the federal government would establish a national standard but states would be free to retain or develop policies that were more ambitious. Such a policy could be crafted so as not to penalize states for early reductions; rather, it could reward them.

Climate policy may well follow an iterative path for some time, with some states continuing to be policy innovators, potentially influencing future rounds of federal policy. Recent experience in American intergovernmental relations finds few examples of such collaborative federalism in environmental protection or energy, reflecting the general difficulty of moving new legislation of any sort through Congress.[19]

The resurgent interest in climate change reflected in the actions of both President Obama and the 111th Congress raised the serious possibility that a new direction in federal climate legislation could be established during the next few years. Proposals in both the House and the Senate covered all three of the policy types presented here, although most attention was devoted to renewable energy mandates (for electricity and fuel) and a cap-and-trade system. High initial expectations for early federal government action on a major climate bill were, of course, complicated by the dire state of the American economy, reluctance to introduce any cost-imposition strategies during severe recession, and well-organized opposition to climate legislation.

The flurry of hearings on climate change in the 110th and 111th congresses suggests little serious effort at policy learning, with most discussion of intergovernmental lessons involving brief presentations by high-profile governors or periodic congressional threats to overturn preexisting state policies as part of a larger bargain with organized interests. Moreover, it remains clear that Congress is badly fragmented and faces steep hurdles before producing viable legislation. Unified Democratic Party control was hardly a guarantor of significant policy outputs on climate or other domestic issues, as demonstrated by the 111th Congress.[20] This experience suggests that a continued period of bottom-up policy development amid some forms of federal policy expansion such as the US EPA administrative role may be the most likely near-term outcome. In turn, continuing intergovernmental conflict (whether state to state or state to federal) is likely to persist for many years regardless of whether significant federal legislation is forthcoming.

Ironically, the American case offers striking parallels with climate policy in other federal and multilevel governance systems, whether or not they have ratified the Kyoto Protocol.[21] Ratifying parties such as Canada and the European Union have struggled mightily not only to meet their reduction targets but also to strike an effective balance of authority between central governments and their constituent units. Canadian provinces and EU nations vary by emission trend and level of policy engagement in ways that are highly analogous to the range of American state responses discussed herein. Australia bears especially striking resemblance to the United States, given its rejection of Kyoto under Liberal Party rule, prolonged federal-level policy inertia, a flurry of policy development in some but not all of its states, and expanded federal attention to climate policy following the election of new leaders in November 2007. In all of these contexts, however, bottom-up policy development and implementation continued even in situations in which expansion in the central government role took place. All of this suggests that climate policy can no longer be framed as the exclusive province of international relations and instead must also be acknowledged as an enduring challenge for multilevel governance. Even a dramatic election result, as in the American case in 2008, is unlikely to change this factor of climate policy.

Acknowledgment

An earlier version of this chapter appeared as "States on Steroids: The Intergovernmental Odyssey of American Climate Policy," *Review of Policy Research*, vol. 25, no. 2 (March 2008), pp. 105–28. My thanks to Blackwell Publishing and the editors of the journal for approving release of this revised version.

Notes

1. P. Teske, *Regulation in the States* (Washington, DC: Brookings Institution Press, 2004); P. Manna, *School's In: Federalism and the National Education Agenda* (Washington, DC: Georgetown University Press, 2006).

2. B. G. Rabe, *Statehouse and Greenhouse: The Emerging Politics of American Climate Change Policy* (Washington, DC: Brookings Institution Press, 2004); E. Montpetit, *Misplaced Distrust: Policy Networks and the Environment in*

France, the United States, and Canada (Vancouver: University of British Columbia Press, 2003).

3. H. Selin and S. VanDeveer, "Political Science and Prediction: What's Next for U.S. Climate Change Policy?" *Review of Policy Research*, vol. 24, no. 1 (2007): 1–27.

4. J. A. Layzer, "Deep Freeze: How Business Has Shaped the Global Warming Debate in Congress," in *Business and Environmental Policy*, edited by M. E. Kraft and S. Kamieniecki (Cambridge, MA: MIT Press, 2007), 93–126.

5. D. Vogel, *Trading Up: Consumer and Environmental Regulation in a Global Economy* (Cambridge, MA: Harvard University Press, 1995).

6. Resource Renewal Institute, *State of the States* (San Francisco: Resource Renewal Institute, 2001).

7. B. G. Rabe and P. A. Mundo, "Business Influence in State-Level Environmental Policy," in *Business and Environmental Policy*, edited by M. E. Kraft and S. Kamieniecki, 265–97 (Cambridge, MA: MIT Press, 2007).

8. D. J. Fiorino, *The New Environmental Regulation* (Cambridge, MA: MIT Press, 2006); D. A. Mazmanian and M. E. Kraft, eds., *Toward Sustainable Communities*, rev. ed. (Cambridge, MA: MIT Press, 2009).

9. R. B. Stewart and J. B. Wiener, *Reconstructing Climate Policy* (Washington, DC: American Enterprise Institute, 2003); D. G. Victor, *The Collapse of the Kyoto Protocol and the Struggle to Stop Global Warming*, rev. ed. (Princeton, NJ: Princeton University Press, 2004); W. J. McKibbin and P. J. Wilcoxen, *Climate Change Policy After Kyoto: Blueprint for a Realistic Approach* (Washington, DC: Brookings Institution Press, 2002); M. Jaccard, J. Nyboer, and B. Sadownik, *The Cost of Climate Policy* (Vancouver: University of British Columbia Press, 2002); C. Fischer and R. G. Newell, *Environmental and Technology Policies for Climate Mitigation* (Washington, DC: Resources for the Future, 2007): 04–05; J. E. Aldy and R. N. Stavins, eds., *Architectures for Agreement: Addressing Global Climate Change in the Post-Kyoto World* (Washington, DC: Resources for the Future, 2007); Congressional Budget Office, *Trade-Offs in Allocating Allowances for CO2 Emissions* (Washington, DC: Congressional Budget Office, 2007).

10. P. Izzo, "Is It Time for a New Energy Tax?" *Wall Street Journal*, February 8, 2007.

11. J. Bushnell, C. Peterman, and C. Wolfram, *California's Greenhouse Gas Policies: Local Solutions to a Growing Problem?* (Berkeley: University of California Energy Institute, 2007), 2.

12. Rabe and Mundo, "Business Influence."

13. B. G. Rabe, "Regionalism and Global Climate Change Policy: Revisiting Multi-state Collaboration as an Intergovernmental Management Tool," in *Intergovernmental Management in the 21st Century*, edited by T. Conlan and P. Posner (Washington, DC: Brookings Institution Press, 2008), 176–205.

14. B. G. Rabe, "Governing the Climate from Sacramento," in *Unlocking the Power of Networks*, edited by D. F. Kettl and S. Goldsmith (Washington, DC: Brookings Institution Press, 2009), 34–61.

15. P. S. Nivola, *Tense Commandments: Federal Prescriptions and City Problems* (Washington, DC: Brookings Institution Press, 2002); P. L. Posner "The Politics of Preemption: Prospects for the States," *PS: Political Science and Politics*, vol. 38, no. 3 (2005): 371–74.

16. J. F. Zimmerman, "Congressional Preemption During the George W. Bush Administration," *Publius: The Journal of Federalism*, vol. 37, no. 3 (2007): 432–52.

17. Teske, *Regulation in the States*; World Resources Institute, *Climate Policy in the State Laboratory: How States Influence Federal Regulation and the Implications for Climate Change Policy in the U.S.* (Washington, DC: World Resources Institute, 2007).

18. D. Scheberle, *Federalism and Environmental Policy: Trust and the Politics of Implementation* (Washington, DC: Georgetown University Press, 2004); Stewart and Wiener, *Reconstructing Climate Policy*.

19. T. Conlan and J. Dinan, "Federalism, the Bush Administration, and the Transformation of American Conservatism," *Publius: The Journal of Federalism*, vol. 37, no. 3 (2007): 279–303.

20. T. E. Mann and N. J. Ornstein, *The Broken Branch: How Congress Is Failing America and How to Get It Back on Track* (New York: Cambridge University Press, 2006).

21. B. G. Rabe, "Beyond Kyoto: Climate Change Policy in Multilevel Governance Systems," *Governance: An International Journal of Policy, Administration, and Institutions*, vol. 20, no. 3 (2007): 423–44.

Celebrating and Protecting Diversity in Climate-Change Responses

This volume has shown that the complex and varied challenges presented by climate change have produced responses from many different actors at many different political, geographic and social scales. The public and politicians have for some time recognized that climate change is a complex phenomenon and that achieving national and global social or political consensus on solutions will be difficult. But the idea that local, state, and regional actors might be critical players in responding to climate change is less obvious, and in some ways even counterintuitive.

The reasons are simple. Climate change is a global challenge. Greenhouse gases produced anywhere feed into, and have a collective impact on, the global climate system. Therefore, the required scale of the response to climate change would seem to be inherently global. The failure of major greenhouse-gas–producing nations, especially China, to commit over the past decade to reducing the production of such gases has been one of the explicit justifications for the United States in holding back from major international climate-change commitments, including the Kyoto Protocol.

This book demonstrates that there are multiple justifications for climate-change responses by state and local governments, translocal organizations of government actors (the memorably acronymed TOGAs), tribes, non-government actors, businesses, and private individuals. Indeed, such local actions may be *necessary* for an effective national and global response.

Local actors can serve as laboratories of innovation. Local actors understand the natural, social, economic, and political conditions that make it possible to apply larger collective goals and requirements (e.g., reducing the "carbon footprint" of individuals, businesses, and governments) in an efficient and wise manner. Local actions may be essential in the absence of national and global responses to climate change—for preserving wealth and health, in preparing for changes already under way and others that appear to be "locked in" regardless of additional efforts at mitigation, and in creating both knowledge and a political foundation for more effective collective responses at larger scales.

One way to view the responses by state and local actors since the mid-1990s is that they are part of a distinct era—one of inadequate national and international responses to climate change. In this view, when (and if) the national government steps forward with a more coherent and aggressive response to climate change, the more local responses will be trumped and fade away. In this view, local responses have been compelled by national and global politics but are necessarily and perhaps radically incomplete.

This volume reflects a different view, demonstrating that, as a matter of earth science, political science, policy, and experience, great variation in responses to climate change at local levels should be expected, and that local responses are overwhelmingly a positive development. The logic and experience reflected in these chapters suggest that local responses to climate change will occur and should be encouraged, regardless of federal and international initiatives.

This is not just a descriptive point. It has implications for federal and state legislatures, the executive branch, and the courts. The chapters in this volume suggest that the following six principles should guide future climate policy across the branches of government.

1. Local and Regional Actions Create the Foundation for Robust Climate-Change Responses

Current and future responses to climate change are as much local and regional as they are national and international. A variety of responses to climate change at different scales by different kinds of actors—efforts at both mitigation and adaptation—may be essential to finding effective and efficient solutions.

The virtues of local responses to climate change do not arise solely from coordination among local actors or from gap-filling in the absence of national and international action on climate issues. This book reveals multiple justifications for responses by state, local, and tribal governments, as well as collaborations among them, in providing a robust response to climate change. This response includes efforts at both *mitigation*, reducing present and future production of greenhouse gases, and *adaptation*, adjusting political, social, and economic institutions to take account of climate change effects that have occurred and are likely to occur regardless of mitigation efforts.

Climate change defies the drawing of neat and simple boundaries: climate change, its sources, and impacts cannot be sorted and placed into mutually exclusive categories of local, state, regional, national, and international.

Likewise, federalism defies the drawing of simple boundaries. While national, state, and local governments are distinct entities with constitutionally defined powers, their interests, authorities, and powers overlap. In reality, few distinctly national or distinctly local issues or interests exist. Given the complexity of climate change, the overlapping and shared governing powers characteristic of US federalism may be suited for providing robust policy responses.

2. Congress and the Executive Branch Should Support State and Local Responses

Congressional and executive climate-change policies should recognize and reward states that have aggressively addressed climate change and should provide national standards and incentives for less active states to adopt and implement climate-change policies.

Emphasizing state and local action does not mean that there is no role for federal (or multinational or global) policy on climate change. However, this emphasis does have implications for federal action. In order to maintain the activity of states now engaged with climate change, federal climate-change policies should support the diversity of responses and climate-change–policy profiles of states. Federal policies could also encourage states that have yet to act.

3. Federal Courts Should Narrowly Construe Preemption Claims Against State and Tribal Climate-Change Policy

Federal courts should presume that state and tribal climate-change actions are *not* preempted unless state/tribal action explicitly violates the US Constitution or Congress has expressly prohibited it.

Given the complexity of climate change, a positive premium should be placed on encouraging more policy action and policy experiments by states and American Indian tribes. States and tribes should be encouraged to remain active and engaged with climate-change policies even if the federal government develops more extensive ones. Vibrant state/tribal action requires Congress to preempt such action only in the most limited circumstances, and with substantial justification. Federal courts should apply the presumption against preemption when considering claims that state/tribal climate-change actions are preempted. The executive branch should limit preemption claims to those cases where state or tribal action explicitly violates the US Constitution or Congress has expressly prohibited it.

4. Support Regional and Nongovernmental Alignments for Climate Change

Federal and state governments should encourage and support regional governance, and the federal government should support the active engagement of subnational actors in national policy making, administration, and implementation.

For decades, various state and local public officials (governors, legislators, county administrators, and mayors, to name a few) have been communicating, developing policy positions, educating, and engaging with officials at all levels of government through translocal organizations of government actors (TOGAs) and arrangements such as administrative agreements. Some TOGAs have recently been active around climate change, encouraging their members to adopt climate-change policies and issuing resolutions encouraging the federal government to act. Likewise, several groups of states have devised regional agreements over energy policy.

Bringing practical concerns of subnational actors into climate-change policy making may be accomplished in a variety of ways, from courts granting TOGAs standing to file lawsuits to challenge or enforce federal environmental laws, to federal rules requiring federal agencies to consult with TOGAs as they develop regulations and management plans to implement federal environmental laws, to supporting states' experimentation and efforts at regional energy and climate-change initiatives. Pursuing a variety of approaches may prove the optimal way to identify which are most workable and acceptable to subnational and federal officials.

5. Congress and State Legislatures Should Encourage Collaborative Policy Responses

Congress and state legislatures should encourage and strengthen collaborative management efforts in response to climate change among government agencies, interest groups, and citizens. Legislatures can do so by revising personnel and budget requirements to recognize and reward collaborative activities, by adopting accountability measures appropriate for collaborative efforts, and by providing distinct funding for collaborative efforts.

Climate-change sources and impacts span jurisdictional boundaries, placing an even greater premium on coordination and collaboration among governments, interest groups, and citizens. States and localities can support and enhance communication and coordination among governments and encourage and expand their policy experimentation in relation to climate change. However, collaborative work across traditional jurisdiction boundaries can raise questions of political accountability. If the national government, states, and localities are to encourage new multijurisdictional initiatives, they will also need to think about new ways to ensure accountability to the public that directs and funds the agents in each state.

6. Federal Policy: Carbon Pricing and Beyond

A national carbon tax or a cap-and-trade system may be essential to establishing a nontrivial price for carbon. The need for additional national policies to address sources and types of emissions that are beyond the reach of a cap-and-trade system merits exploring the possibilities of cooperative state–federal programs to address greenhouse-gas emissions, perhaps similar to those traditionally employed in environmental law.

Proposed federal legislation addressing climate change has largely been limited to a national cap-and-trade system. A number of authors note, however, that the federal government needs to pursue additional policies if substantial reductions in greenhouse-gas emissions are to be realized. One option might be a national climate-change law in which the federal government sets national emission reduction goals and works with states to craft regulations and plans well matched to each state's economic, political, and social interests.

Significant greenhouse-gas emission reductions are within the reach of current governance and administrative models, and existing technologies. The United States can face climate change head-on by taking full advantage of the strengths inherent in its federal system. It can move far down the path toward a low-carbon economy and society over the next two to three decades by building upon existing knowledge, experience, and technologies. To do so, the federal government and the courts should look favorably upon the wide variety of mitigation efforts by local, state, tribal, and regional actors. The energy that has so far been exhibited by these same actors in pursuing policy experimentation and the diffusion of ideas and new mitigating technologies should be supported and enabled at all levels and across all branches of government.

Acknowledgments

This book had its origins in a conference, "Federalism and Climate Change: The Role of the States in a Future Federal Regime," jointly sponsored by the James E. Rogers College of Law and the Rehnquist Center for the Constitutional Structures of Government in February 2008. The theme of this highly successful conference, attended by legal scholars, policymakers, judges, journalists, and activists, was the future role of state governments in the development and implementation of federal programs to address climate change. The keynote address was provided by Justice Stephen Breyer, who spoke on the Supreme Court's first climate-change opinion, *Massachusetts v. EPA*.

Papers from the conference were published in Volume 50, Issue 3, of the *Arizona Law Review* in 2008. In particular, we thank Grace Campbell, Kara Ellis, Jennifer Gibbons, and Meredith Marder for their permission to build book chapters modified from articles in that publication.

The papers published in the *Arizona Law Review* are written for lawyers and focus primarily on legal issues. This book includes substantially revised and rewritten chapters from that volume and adds several additional chapters, including ones by climate and political scientists. All of the material has also been set in a conceptual and practical framework to make the book focused, coherent, and highly readable. Working closely with authors, the editors of this volume worked hard to make the text accessible and useful to a wide range of readers, including policy makers and educated citizens interested in these issues.

Coordinating this volume has been a great pleasure from the start, thanks to the support provided by the authors. Their enthusiasm, creativity, hard work, and patience through multiple revisions made this effort a joy for us as editors. We particularly appreciate the authors' participation in the original 2008 conference on climate change and federalism, and their additional participation (with new authors) in an October 2009 workshop focused on the book. The workshop allowed for important conversations to occur among policy and legal scholars, resulting in a more integrated and focused volume.

We would like to recognize the University of Arizona Press, which has supported not only this book but also the EDGE Books series, of which this is the second publication. In particular, we thank Kathryn Conrad, interim director, and Allyson Carter, editor-in-chief, for their counsel, support, and recognition that EDGE Books is a new and different way to produce scholarly books aimed at a broad readership.

The volume editors are extremely grateful for the hard work, dedication, persistence, and patience of the development editors. Emily McGovern has seen this project through from beginning to end, spending countless hours editing chapters, wrestling with language, and encouraging authors to rise to the occasion. Her good humor, gentle but firm suggestions, and attention to detail made the process of constructing this volume a joy while producing a coherent, accessible, high-quality book. Betsy Woodhouse, who joined the project when Emily took maternity leave, provided a much needed spark to ensure the timely completion of the volume. Her careful reading of the chapters, her expertise with subheadings, and her insistence on timeliness ensured the success of this volume.

We are deeply grateful to the Udall Center for Studies in Public Policy for its staff and facilities' support, and to Barbara Lopez, Judy Parker, Bertha Skye, and Carol Ward at the James E. Rogers College of Law, who assisted in formatting the drafts. Graduate research assistant Janet McCaskill, then in the School of Government and Public Policy, helped develop the "In Brief" chapter summaries. Barbara Morehouse read multiple versions of the volume and provided very helpful comments and guidance. And anonymous reviewers provided many insights that made this book stronger.

We are indebted to many for their generous financial support. Funding from the University of Arizona's James E. Rogers College of Law, the Institute of the Environment (formerly the Institute for the Study of Planet Earth), and the School of Government and Public Policy made this effort possible.

Finally, the two secondary editors, Kirsten Engel and Sally Rider, would like to recognize the outstanding efforts of the lead editor, Edella Schlager, to bring this volume to fruition. Edella provided intellectual leadership, identifying themes and crosscurrents that render this collection a truly unique and important contribution to scholarly and public understanding of federalism and climate change. She was also a personal force, generating the interest, enthusiasm, and discipline to help the diverse interdisciplinary group of authors manifest their ideas in well-crafted prose. We are much indebted to Edella's dedication and hard work.

About the Contributors

David E. Adelman is Harry Reasoner Regents Chair in Law, University of Texas School of Law.

Bethany Albertson is an assistant professor in the Department of Government at the University of Texas at Austin.

S. James Anaya is the Regents' and James J. Lenoir Professor of Human Rights Law and Policy at the James E. Rogers College of Law, the University of Arizona, and is the United Nations Special Rapporteur on the Rights of Indigenous Peoples.

Joshua Civin is an attorney at the NAACP Legal Defense and Educational Fund, Inc. A graduate of Yale Law School, he served as a law clerk to US Supreme Court Justice Ruth Bader Ginsburg and from 1994 to 1997 represented the First Ward on New Haven, Connecticut's Board of Aldermen.

Holly Doremus is professor of law at the University of California, Berkeley, and a member scholar of the Center for Progressive Reform.

Kirk Emerson is a senior policy associate at the University of Arizona's School of Government and Public Policy, the Udall Center for Studies in Public Policy, and the Institute of the Environment. She served as the founding director of the US Institute for Environmental Conflict Resolution at the Morris K. and Stewart L. Udall Foundation.

Kirsten H. Engel is professor and director of the Environmental Law Program in the University of Arizona James E. Rogers College of Law. She has served as senior counsel for the Public Protection Bureau and acting chief of the Environmental Protection Division of the Massachusetts Office of the Attorney General.

Daniel A. Farber is Sho Sato Professor of Law; faculty co-director of the Center for Law, Energy, and Environment; and chair of the Energy Resources Group, University of California.

Joseph Frueh is an attorney at Latham and Watkins LLP in Los Angeles. A graduate of Yale Law School, he served as a law clerk to Judge John T. Noonan, Jr., on the US Court of Appeals for the Ninth Circuit.

W. Michael Hanemann is Chancellor's Professor, Department of Agricultural and Resource Economics, University of California, Berkeley, and a visiting professor at the Department of Economics, W. P. Carey School of Business, Arizona State University.

James Hopkins is associate clinical professor to the Indigenous Peoples Law and Policy Program at the James E. Rogers College of Law, the University of Arizona, and is chief justice of the Pascua Yaqui Court of Appeals.

Andrew Karch is Arleen C. Carlson Associate Professor in the Department of Political Science at the University of Minnesota and the author of *Democratic Laboratories: Policy Diffusion Among the American States* (2007).

Diana Liverman is codirector of the Institute of the Environment and professor of geography and development at the University of Arizona, and visiting professor of environmental policy and development at Oxford University.

Marc Miller serves as vice dean and Ralph W. Bilby Professor of Law at the University of Arizona James E. Rogers College of Law. He serves as series editor for the Edge book series published at the University of Arizona Press.

Jonathan Overpeck is the codirector of the Institute of the Environment at the University of Arizona, where he is also a professor of geosciences, professor of atmospheric sciences, and an editor of the Edge book series published at the University of Arizona Press.

Fran Pavley is a California state senator who represents portions of Los Angeles and Ventura counties. While in the State Assembly she authored landmark climate change laws AB 32 and AB 1493. These laws have become models for other states and nations.

Barry G. Rabe is a professor of public policy at the Gerald Ford School of Public Policy at the University of Michigan. He is the author of four books, including *Statehouse and Greenhouse* (2004) and *Greenhouse Governance: Addressing Climate Change in the United States* (2010).

Judith Resnik is the Arthur Liman Professor of Law at Yale Law School. Her recent books include *Representing Justice: Invention, Controversy, and Rights in City-States and Democratic Courtrooms* (with Dennis Curtis, 2011), *Migrations and Mobilities: Citizenship, Borders, and Gender* (with Seyla Benhabib, 2009, and *Federal Court Stories* (with Vicki Jackson, 2010).

Sally Rider is director of the nonpartisan William H. Rehnquist Center on the Constitutional Structures of Government at the University of Arizona James E. Rogers College of Law.

Robert A. Schapiro is professor of law at Emory University School of Law, where he directs the Center on Federalism and Intersystemic Governance. His recent publications include *Polyphonic Federalism: Toward the Protection of Fundamental Rights* (2009).

Edella Schlager is a professor in the School of Government and Public Policy at the University of Arizona. She has coauthored *Common Waters, Diverging Streams: Linking Institutions and Water Management in Arizona, California, and Colorado* (with William Blomquist and Tanya Heikkila, 2004) and *Embracing Watershed Politics* (with William Blomquist, 2008).

Barton H. Thompson, Jr. is the Robert E. Paradise Professor in Natural Resources Law, Stanford Law School, and Perry L. McCarty Director, Woods Institute for the Environment, Stanford University.

Index